The Madness of
Art

The Madness of

Art

INTERVIEWS WITH
POETS AND WRITERS

Robert Phillips

Syracuse University Press

Copyright © 2003 by Syracuse University Press
Syracuse, New York 13244–5160

All Rights Reserved

First Edition 2003
03 04 05 06 07   6 5 4 3 2 1

The paper used in this publication meets the minimum requirements
of American National Standard for Information Sciences—Permanence
of Paper for Printed Library Materials, ANSI Z39.48–1984.∞™

Library of Congress Cataloging-in-Publication Data

Phillips, Robert S.
    The madness of art : interviews with poets and writers / Robert
Phillips.— 1st ed.
        p. cm.
    Includes bibliographical references and index.
    ISBN 0–8156–0783–0
1. Authors, American—20th century—Interviews. 2. American
literature—20th century—History and criticism—Theory, etc. 3.
English literature—20th century—History and criticism—Theory, etc.
4. Authors, English—20th century—Interviews. 5. Authorship. I.
Title.
PS221 .P48 2003
810.9'005—dc21   2002151304

Manufactured in the United States of America

For my son, Dr. Graham V. B. Phillips,
who knew half a dozen of them personally.

Robert Phillips is John and Rebecca Moores Professor of English at the University of Houston, where he has taught since 1991. He has written or edited some thirty books, including seven volumes of poetry, three of fiction, and twenty of criticism, belles-lettres, and anthologies. Three of his books have been named "Notable Books of the Year" by the *New York Times Book Review*. In 2001 he edited *New Selected Poems of Marya Zaturenska,* published by Syracuse University Press. His awards include the Enron Teaching Excellence Award, a Pushcart Prize, the Arents Pioneer Medal from Syracuse University, and an Award in Literature from the American Academy and Institute of Arts and Letters, MacDowell Colony and Yaddo Fellowships, and a National Public Radio Syndicated Fiction Project Award. He is a former councilor of the Texas Institute of Letters, as well as the poetry editor of the *Texas Review* and chairman of the Poets' Prize.

Contents

Illustrations

Introduction

ACCORDING TO LITERARY HISTORIAN Malcolm Cowley, the modern literary interview as we know it originated in the spring of 1953. That was when the first issue of the *Paris Review* appeared, with its interview of novelist E. M. Forster. Most previous interviews with writers had been of two types. The first were conducted by a disciple of the Great Man, as in Boswell's interviews with Dr. Johnson or Eckermann's with Goethe. In the second type, reporters—often quite ignorant about the interviewee or his work—tried to get the subject to say something sensational or controversial, something that would make "good copy." By contrast, interviews in the *Paris Review,* while not worshipful, were conducted by individuals who had done their homework, read all of the subject's work, and carefully compiled a list of relevant questions. In its first interview of Forster, interviewers P. N. Furbank and F. J. H. Haskells even submitted their questions in advance, so he could ponder them and come prepared with thoughtful replies. After completion, the interview was submitted to Forster for second and even third thoughts—a practice unheard of until that time.

Previously, most readers would have agreed with Henry James, who, in that highly disturbing tale, "The Death of the Lion," admonished, "The artist's life's his work, and this is the place to observe him. What he has to tell us is with *this* perfection. My dear sir, the best interviewer's the best reader." But George Plimpton and his fellow *Paris Review* editors and interviewers achieved another perfection, that of the carefully constructed, carefully edited interview: not speech as it often awkwardly erupts, with all its "er's" and "um's" and repetitions, but rather an ideal speech in an idealized interview. In short, a work of art. Sometimes an interview can rank among its subject's finer work, becoming a new essay by the subject. Wilfrid Sheed once stated, "I would trade half of *Childe Harold* for such an interview with Byron and all of *Adam Bede* for the same with George Eliot." The best interview is not only a portrait by the interviewer, but also a self-portrait by which the subject wishes to be remembered. If not the truth about the subject, the interview is a version of the truth to which that subject subscribes.

The following represent my contributions to this recent art form. An interview with fiction writer Shirley Ann Grau appeared too late for inclusion. More than half appeared in the famous *Paris Review* series, but several have not previously been collected in book form and are available only in back issues in libraries. All but two of the subjects were close personal friends, and one was an acquaintance, affording me a singular advantage: I knew not only the subjects' work, but also the subjects themselves. The one exception was Philip Larkin. He was England's most famous living poet, and I achieved a rare interview with him—but only through correspondence; he refused a meeting and insisted that we conduct the entire interview by post.

Even more rare was the interview with Marya Zaturenska. Zaturenska won the Pulitzer for poetry in 1937, when she was a young woman, and descended into increasing obscurity. She was dropped from anthologies and excluded from critical surveys. Part of the reason may have been her coauthorship of the outspoken *History of American Poetry 1900–1940,* which infuriated a generation of literary figures. Whatever the reason, at the time of our interview she was an all-but-forgotten writer.

The Larkin interview, at his insistence, was conducted entirely by post. ("You will get a much better interview that way.") The Oates and Spencer interviews consist of some material sent by post and some material recorded on tape. All the others were conducted one-on-one, recorded on tape, and then transcribed, edited, and often rearranged to enhance meaning and achieve balance and order. Each was submitted to the subject, who often made corrections and additions—rarely deletions.

I wish I had interviewed more of my friends and a few of my acquaintances. At times in my life, I could have placed a tape recorder between myself and James T. Farrell, Delmore Schwartz, Dwight Macdonald, Horace Gregory, E. E. Cummings, Isabella Gardner, Carson McCullers, Shirley Jackson, Stanley Edgar Hyman, Howard Moss, John Lehmann, and Robert Francis—all now gone. The *Paris Review* did not interview any of the above. Howard Moss died the very week he was to be interviewed by Dana Gioia. It is my impression that there is no extant interview with Delmore Schwartz—one of the great conversationalists of the century. For me, interviewing Delmore Schwartz in the early 1960s would have been an act akin to saddling a unicorn—unthinkable. Yet I reflect now on lost opportunities: the chance to ask Schwartz how he happened upon the device of projecting his parents' courtship on a movie-house screen in "In Dreams Begin Responsibilities," or to ask Shirley Jackson just what *did* she mean by "The Lottery"?

But rather than fret over missed chances, I am happy to gather these eight interviews as a book on the art of writing, or "the madness of art." (The phrase is from James, but Goyen and Spencer also address the issue.) Four of the subjects are poets; four are fiction writers. Spencer, Smith, Styron, and Oates have written plays, as well. Between the births of the oldest and the youngest of the writers interviewed, a span of some thirty-six years elapses, along with a lot of literary history. Zaturenska knew Willa Cather, Vachel Lindsay, and Kenneth Fearing. She met W. B. Yeats. William Jay Smith knew Sinclair Lewis, Louise Bogan, and Dylan Thomas. Other than their profound seriousness about writing, the group seems to have little in common. Surely their writing habits varied. Larkin seems to have had to live and write in a top-floor flat, writing in notebooks in pencil in the evenings after doing the dishes. Zaturenska, who devoted much of her adult life to looking after her invalid husband, fellow poet Horace Gregory, found that she wrote best when away from home, while on an extended stay at one of the writers' colonies such as Yaddo or MacDowell. Elizabeth Spencer writes in the mornings, for many years taking over the dining room table after her husband left for work. Seven of the eight do not use a computer, though Oates used one for a time after visiting John Updike and being shown his. "You should get one of these, Joyce," he chided. "Just think, it could triple your output." "I don't think output has been my problem, John," she replied.

Output definitely varies. Larkin produced but one book a decade, while my university library holds more than ninety books by Oates. And occupations vary. All but Zaturenska and Larkin taught at one time or another, but there were other attempts at wage earning. Spencer had a go as a newspaper reporter, Goyen and Styron as book editors, Shapiro as the editor of literary quarterlies, and Smith served as a member of the Vermont House of Representatives. Interestingly, Zaturenska, Shapiro, and Larkin were all trained as librarians, in contrast to today's writers, who almost unanimously seek careers as teachers of creative writing. Shapiro had a long career as a professor, and Oates still holds that position—although Shapiro claimed he was not really a professor, but a sort of "mad guest" of the university. Smith admits to having been a really poor teacher. Larkin found the notion of teaching unthinkable: "Quite sickens me with the whole business of literature." Goyen thought teaching the best job for a writer; Zaturenska thought it the worst. Styron earned enough from his best sellers and film rights that he taught only one semester at Yale.

Nor do the interviewees agree on the subject of travel and its relationship to writing. Smith did some of his best work while living in Europe, particularly Italy. "Living abroad made me feel more American than ever," he concludes. Spencer wrote some of her best novels and several of her finest stories about experiences observed or felt in Italy and while living in Canada. Styron set an entire novel in Italy. Oates travels extensively by car in the United States and lived in the United Kingdom for a year. Shapiro, on the other hand, found travel to be the one surefire way to stop him from writing. Larkin never traveled, or almost never. He once said he'd agree to go to China if he could go and return on the same day.

One thing most agree upon is that an unhappy childhood seems to be an excellent beginning for a writing career. Everything that comes after is compensation. And all eight have been richly rewarded for their creative work. Larkin received the Queen's Gold Medal for Poetry, and was offered, but declined, England's Poet Laureateship. Styron won the Pulitzer Prize and Shapiro both the Pulitzer and the Bollingen Prizes. He and Spencer and Smith and Styron and Oates were elected to membership in the American Academy of Arts and Letters. Oates and Styron each won the National Book Award for Fiction (Oates in 1970 and Styron in 1980), and Spencer was twice a finalist for it. In addition to winning a Pulitzer, Zaturenska was twice a finalist for the National Book Award in Poetry. Goyen was awarded two Guggenheim fellowships, and Spencer received one as well.

Together these interviews discuss questions of identity and creativity, and the accidents of consonance and serendipity in writing. As my esteemed colleague Daniel Stern wrote in his introduction to another book of interviews, "Perhaps, best of all, closing the book we will begin to see the connections between the telling of stories and the living of lives we have not seen before."

.   .   .

Five of these interviews appeared in the *Paris Review,* the others in *Gulf Coast, Modern Poetry Studies, New Letters,* and *New Virginia Review.* Thanks to the editors of each for permission to reprint. The Elizabeth Spencer interview as it appears here is a composite of two separate interviews originally published individually.

Thanks also to Greg Johnson, who assisted with the checklist of publications by Joyce Carol Oates, and to Shannon Borg and Mary Lou Penaz for word processing. Special thanks to Max Eberts for moral support, to Greg Fraser for his advice and punctilious copyediting, and to Adam Muhlig for the index.

Robert Phillips
University of Houston

Chronology

1902   Marya Zaturenska born

1913   Karl Shapiro born

1915   William Goyen born

1918   William Jay Smith born

1921   Philip Larkin born; Elizabeth Spencer born

1925   William Styron born

1938   Joyce Carol Oates born; Marya Zaturenska awarded Pulitzer Prize for *Cold Morning Sky*

1945   Karl Shapiro awarded Pulitzer Prize for *V-Letter and Other Poems*

1946–47   Shapiro appointed Consultant in Poetry, the Library of Congress

1950   Philip Larkin's first book, *The North Ship,* published; William Goyen's *The House of Breath* published and nominated for first National Book Award for Fiction

1952   Styron's *Lie Down in Darkness* finalist for National Book Award

1955   Zaturenska's *Selected Poems* finalist for National Book Award; Larkin's *The Less Deceived* published

1957   Elizabeth Spencer's *The Voice at the Back Door* finalist for National Book Award

1958   William Jay Smith's *Poems: 1947–1957* finalist for National Book Award

1959   Shapiro's *Poems of a Jew* finalist for National Book Award

1961   Spencer's *The Light in the Piazza* finalist for National Book Award

1964   Larkin's *The Whitson Weddings* published

1967   Smith's *The Tin Can and Other Poems* finalist for National Book Award

1968   Styron's *The Confessions of Nat Turner* awarded Pulitzer Prize and finalist for National Book Award; Oates's *A Garden of Earthly Delights* finalist for National Book Award

1969   Shapiro awarded Bollingen Prize in Poetry; Oates's *Expensive People* finalist for National Book Award

1970   Oates's *them* receives National Book Award in Fiction

1970–71   Smith appointed Consultant in Poetry, the Library of Congress

1972   Oates's *Wonderland* finalist for National Book Award

1974   Larkin's *High Windows* published

1976   Goyen's *Collected Stories* nominated for Pulitzer Prize

1980   Styron's *Sophie's Choice* finalist for National Book Award; Smith's *Army Brat: A Memoir* published

1981   *The Stories of Elizabeth Spencer* published

1982   Spencer receives Award of Merit Medal for the Short Story from the American Academy of Arts and Letters; Zaturenska dies

1983   Goyen dies; Larkin's *Required Writing* published

1985   Larkin dies

1988   Shapiro's *The Younger Son* (Volume 1 of his autobiography) published; Larkin's *Collected Poems* published

1990   Oates's *Because It Is Bitter and Because It Is My Heart* finalist for National Book Award; Shapiro's *Reports of My Death* (Volume 2 of his autobiography) published; Styron's *Darkness Visible* published

1993   Styron's *A Tidewater Morning* published

1995   *William Goyen: Selected Letters from a Writer's Life*, edited by Robert Phillips, published

1998   Smith's *The World Below the Window: Poems 1937–1997* published; Spencer's *Landscape of the Heart: A Memoir* published; Shapiro's *The Wild Card: Selected Poems, Early & Late* published

2001   *The Diaries of Marya Zaturenska, 1938–1944* edited by Mary Beth Hinton, published; Zaturenska's *New Selected Poems,* edited by Robert Phillips, published

2003   Shapiro's *Essay on Rime with Trial of a Poet*, edited by Robert Phillips, reprinted

The Madness of
Art

> We work in the dark—we do what we can—
> we give what we have. Our doubt is our
> passion and our passion our task.
> The rest is the madness of art.
>
> —Henry James, "The Middle Years"

Philip Larkin
Photograph by Christopher Barker

Philip Larkin

Number 32 Pearson Park, Hull, England, was Philip Larkin's address for most of his last eighteen years, the place that became his home more than any other. The three-story, red-brick house, in which he occupied the top flat, had once been an American consulate and stands on the southern corner of the park from which the street takes its name, to the north of the center of Hull. The house views a stand of chestnut trees. It was here that I expected to meet with Larkin—here, or at his office in the Brynmor Jones Library at the University of Hull, where he was university librarian. But it was not to be. Larkin stipulated that the interview be conducted entirely by post. In a reply—on letterhead that paraded the following degrees and honors: C.B.E., C. Litt., M.A., D. Lit., D. Litt., F.R.S.L., and F.L.A.—he wrote, "You will get much better answers that way."

I didn't care: that Larkin agreed to an interview at all was a wonder, given how temperamentally and geographically remote he was. The Times Literary Supplement *wrote of him, "He has refused almost all invitations to judge, recite, review, lecture, pontificate, or to be interviewed." Yet when approached to do an interview for the* Paris Review, *he warily consented. "Personally, I think I have been interviewed far too much already; I always say the same things, and it must be getting very boring by now. However, the* Paris Review *series is of course known to me, and I can see I should be in good company." That latter may be a reference to the interview with his close friend Kingsley Amis, which the* Paris Review *had published. Another reason Larkin granted the interview may have been that he felt he was near the end of his days. To my knowledge, it was the last interview he ever granted.*

Not only did we not begin the interview as friends, but we ended it as something less. At the conclusion of our collaboration, when I asked him to sign my Larkin first editions, he responded, "Every book that I sign for a stranger devalues those I've signed for friends!" He agreed to sign one. I submitted the Faber & Faber edition of High Windows, *which he chastely inscribed "Philip Larkin"—period. But I know he valued the interview. It is one of only two he included in his volume of selected prose,* Required Writing. *(He never asked my permission to include it, nor was I paid.)*

The interview was begun on November 28, 1981, when I sent Larkin the first batch of eighty-one questions. A long silence ensued. I did not receive a response until March 2 of the following year. But he returned sixteen closely typed pages, with corrections in bright pink ink. He had answered fifty-six of the original eighty-one queries. The covering letter stated, "Here at last is your interview. It has taken rather a long time because to my surprise I found writing it suffocatingly boring."

The result was far from boring. I submitted five additional questions to Larkin, and the final interview appeared in the Paris Review *in the summer of 1982. The poet would die three years later, at the age of sixty-three.*

.   .   .

PHILLIPS. Can you describe your life at Hull? Do you live in a flat or own a house?

LARKIN. I came to Hull in 1955. After eighteen months (during which I wrote "Mr. Bleaney"), I took a university flat and lived there for nearly eighteen years. It was the top flat in a house that was reputedly the American Consulate during the war, and though it might not have suited everybody, it suited me. I wrote most of *The Whitsun Weddings* and all of *High Windows* there. Probably I should never have moved if the university hadn't decided to sell the house, but as it was, I had to get out and find somewhere else. It was a dreadful experience, as at that time houses were hard to find. In the end, friends reported a small house near the university, and I bought that in 1974. I haven't decided yet whether or not I like it.

PHILLIPS. How many days a week do you work at the library, and for how many hours a day?

LARKIN. My job as university librarian is a full-time one, five days a week, forty-five weeks a year. When I came to Hull, I had eleven staff; now there are over a hundred of one sort and another. We built one new library in 1960 and another in 1970, so that my first fifteen years were busy. Of course, this was a period in university expansion in England, and Hull grew as much if not more than the rest. Luckily, the vice chancellor during most of this time was keen on the library, which is why it is called after him. Looking back, I think that if the Brynmor Jones Library *is* a good library—and I think it is—the credit should go to him and to the library staff. And to the university as a whole, of course. But you wouldn't be interested in all that.

PHILLIPS. What is your daily routine?

LARKIN. My life is as simple as I can make it. Work all day, cook, eat, wash up, telephone, hack writing, drink, television in the evenings. I almost never go out. I suppose everyone tries to ignore the passing of time: some people by doing a lot, being in California one year and Japan the next; or there's my way—making every day and every year exactly the same. Probably neither works.

PHILLIPS. You didn't mention a schedule for writing . . .

LARKIN. Yes, I was afraid you'd ask about writing. Anything I say about writing poems is bound to be retrospective, because in fact I've written very little since moving into this house, or since *High Windows,* or since 1974, whichever way you like to put it. But when I did write them, well, it was in the evenings, after work, after washing up (I'm sorry—you would call this "doing the dishes"). It was a routine like any other. And really it worked very well: I don't think you can write a poem for more than two hours. After that you're going round in circles, and it's much better to leave it for twenty-four hours, by which time your subconscious or whatever has solved the block and you're ready to go on.

The best writing conditions I ever had were in Belfast, when I was working at the university there. Another top-floor flat, by the way. I wrote between eight and ten in the evenings, then went to the university bar till eleven, then played cards or talked with friends till one or two. The first part of the evening had the second part to look forward to, and I could enjoy the second part with a clear conscience because I'd done my two hours. I can't seem to organize that now.

PHILLIPS. Does, or did, writing come easily for you? Does a poem get completed rapidly, or slowly?

LARKIN. I've no standards for comparison. I wrote short poems quite quickly. Longer ones would take weeks or even months. I used to find that I was never sure I was going to finish a poem until I had thought of the last line. Of course, the last line was sometimes the first one you thought of! But usually the last line would come when I'd done about two-thirds of the poem, and then it was just a matter of closing the gap.

PHILLIPS. Why do you write, and for whom?

LARKIN. You've been reading Auden: "To ask the hard question is simple." The short answer is that you write because you have to. If you rationalize it, it seems as if you've seen this sight, felt this feeling, had this vision, and have got to find a combination of words that will preserve it by setting it off in other people. The duty is to the original experience. It doesn't feel like self-expression, though it may look like it. As for *whom* you write, well, you write for everybody. Or anybody who will listen.

PHILLIPS. Do you share your manuscripts with anyone before publishing them? Are there any friends whose advice you would follow in revising a poem?

LARKIN. I shouldn't normally show what I'd written to anyone: What would be the point? You remember Tennyson reading an unpublished poem to Jowett; when he had finished, Jowett said, "I shouldn't publish that if I were you, Tennyson." Tennyson replied, "If it comes to that, Master, the sherry you gave us at lunch was downright filthy." That's about all that can happen.

But when we were young, Kingsley Amis and I used to exchange unpublished poems, largely because we never thought they could be published, I suppose. He encouraged me, I encouraged him. Encouragement is very necessary to a young writer. But it's hard to find anyone worth encouraging: there aren't many Kingsleys about.

PHILLIPS. In his *Paris Review* interview, Kingsley Amis states you helped him with the manuscript of *Lucky Jim*. What was the basic nature of that working relationship? Is part of that novel based upon your own experiences on staff at Leicester University?

LARKIN. Well, it's all so long ago, it's hard to remember. My general conviction was that Kingsley was quite the funniest writer I had ever met—in letters and so on—and I wanted everyone else to think so, too. I know he says he got the idea of *Lucky Jim* from visiting me when I was working at University College Leicester. This has always seemed rather tenuous to me: after all, he was working at University College Swansea when he was writing it, and the theme—boy meets apparently nasty girl, but turns her into a nice girl by getting her away from nasty environment—is one I think has always meant a lot to Kingsley. He used it again in *I Want it Now*. When I read the first draft I said, "Cut this, cut that, let's have more of the other." I remember I said, "Let's have more *faces*"—you know, his Edith Sitwell face, and so on. The wonderful thing was that Kingsley could "do" all those faces himself—"Sex Life in Ancient Rome," and so on. Someone once took photographs of them all. I wish I had a set.

PHILLIPS. How did you come to be a librarian? Had you no interest in teaching? What was your father's profession?

LARKIN. Oh, dear, this means a lot of autobiography. My father was a city treasurer, a finance officer. I never had the least desire to "be" anything when I was at school, and by the time I went to Oxford the war was on and there wasn't anything to "be" except a serviceman or a teacher or a civil servant. In 1943, when I graduated, I knew I couldn't be the first, because I'd been graded unfit (I suppose through eyesight), nor the second, because I stammered, and then the Civil Service turned me down twice, and I thought, "Well, that lets me out," and I sat at home writing *Jill*. But of course in those days the government had powers to send you into the mines or onto the land or into industry, and they wrote quite politely to ask what in fact I was doing. I looked at the daily paper (the *Birmingham Post*: we were living in Warwick then) and saw that a small town in Shropshire was advertising for a librarian, applied for it, and got it, and told the government so, which seemed to satisfy them.

Of course, I wasn't a real librarian, more a sort of caretaker—it was a one-man library—and I can't pretend I enjoyed it much. The previous librarian had been there about forty years, and I was afraid I should be there all my life, too. This made me start qualifying myself professionally, just in order to get away, which I did in 1946. By then I'd written *Jill,* and *The North Ship,* and *A Girl in Winter.* It was probably the "intensest" time of my life.

PHILLIPS. Is Jorge Luis Borges the only other contemporary poet of note who is also a librarian, by the way? Are you aware of any others?

LARKIN. Who is Jorge Luis Borges? The writer-librarian I like is Archibald MacLeish. You know, he was made Librarian of Congress in 1939, and on his first day they brought him some papers to sign, and he wouldn't sign them until he understood what they were all about. When he did understand, he started making objections and counter-suggestions. The upshot was that he reorganized the whole Library of Congress in five years simply by saying, "I don't understand and I don't agree," and in wartime, too. Splendid man.

PHILLIPS. What do you think of the academic world as a milieu for the working creative writer—teaching, specifically?

LARKIN. The academic world has worked all right for me, but then, I'm not a teacher. I couldn't be. I should think that chewing over other people's work, writing, I mean, must be terribly stultifying. Quite sickens you with the whole business of literature. But then, I haven't got that kind of mind, conceptual or ratiocinative or whatever it is. It would be death to me to have to think about literature as such, to say why one poem was "better" than another, and so on.

PHILLIPS. We've heard that you don't give readings from your own work. In America, this has become a business for poets. Do you enjoy attending the readings of others?

LARKIN. I don't give readings, no, although I have recorded three of my collections, just to show how *I* should read them. Hearing a poem, as opposed to reading it on the page, means you miss so much—the shape, the punctuation, the italics, even knowing how far you are from the end. Reading it on the page means you can go at your own pace, taking it in properly; hearing it means you're dragged along at the speaker's own rate, missing things, not taking it in, confusing "there" and "their" and things like that. And the speaker may interpose his own personality between you and the poem, for better or worse. For that matter, so may the audience. I don't like hearing things in public, even music. In fact I think poetry reading grew up on a false analogy with music: The text is the "score" that doesn't "come to life" until it's "performed." It's false because people can read words, whereas they can't read music. When you write a poem, you put everything into it that's needed: the reader should "hear" it just as clearly as if you were in the room saying it to him. And of course this fashion for poetry readings has led to a kind of poetry that you *can* understand first go: easy rhythms, easy emotions, easy syntax. I don't think it stands up on the page.

PHILLIPS. Do you think economic security an advantage to the writer?

LARKIN. The whole of British postwar society is based on the assumption that economic security is an advantage to everyone. Certainly *I* like to be economically secure. But aren't you, really, asking about *work?* This whole question of how a writer actually gets his money—especially a poet—is one to which there are probably as many answers as there are writers, and the next man's answer always seems better than your own.

On the one hand, you can't live today by being a "man of letters" as easily as a hundred or seventy-five years ago, when there were so many magazines and newspapers all having to be filled. Writers' incomes, as writers, have sunk almost below the subsistence line. On the other hand, you *can* live by "being a writer," or "being a poet," if you're prepared to join the cultural entertainment industry and take handouts from the Arts Council (not that there are as many of them as there used to be) and to be a "poet in residence" and all that. I supposed I could have said—it's a bit late now—I could have had an agent, and said, "Look, I will do anything for six months of the year, as long as I can be free to write for the other six months."

Some people do this, and I suppose it works for them. But I was brought up to think you had to have a job, and write in your spare time, like Trollope. Then, when you started earning enough money by writing, you phase the job out. But in fact I was over fifty before I could have "lived by my writing"—and then only because I had edited a big anthology—and by that time you think, "Well, I might as well get my pension, since I've gone so far."

PHILLIPS. Any regrets?

LARKIN. Sometimes I think, "Everything I've written has been done after a day's work, in the evening. What would it have been like if I'd written in the morning, after night's sleep? Was I wrong?" Some time ago a writer said to me—and he was a full-time writer, and a good one—"I wish I had your life. Dealing with people, having colleagues. Being a writer is so lonely." Everyone envies everyone else.

All I can say is, having a job hasn't been a hard price to pay for having economic security. Some people, I know, would sooner have the economic insecurity because they have to "feel free" before they can write. But it's worked for me. The only thing that does strike me as odd, looking back, is that what society has been willing to *pay* me for is being a librarian. You get medals and prizes and honorary this-and-thats—and flattering interviews—but if you turned round and said, "Right, if I'm so good, give me an index-linked permanent income equal to what I can get for being an undistinguished university administrator"—well, reason would remount its throne pretty quickly.

PHILLIPS. How did you come to write poems? Was time a factor in choosing poetry over the novel form?

LARKIN. What questions you ask. I wrote prose and poems equally from the age of, say, fifteen. I didn't choose poetry: poetry chose me.

PHILLIPS. Nicely put. Your last novel, *A Girl in Winter*—which is a small masterpiece—was published twenty-five years ago. Do you think you will ever write another?

LARKIN. I don't know: I shouldn't think so. I tried very hard to write a third novel for about five years. The ability to do so had just vanished. I can't say any more than that. . . .

PHILLIPS. *Jill* was written when you were about twenty-one, and your second novel only a year or so later. Was it your intention, then, to be a novelist only?

LARKIN. I wanted to "be a novelist" in a way I never wanted to "be a poet," yes. Novels seem to me to be richer, broader, deeper, more enjoyable than poems. When I was young, *Scrutiny* ran a series of articles under the general heading of "The Novel as Dramatic Poem." That was a stimulating and exciting conception. Something that was both a poem and a novel. Of course, thinking about my own two stories means going back nearly forty years, and at this distance I can't remember what their genesis was.

I seemed to recall that *Jill* was based on the idea that running away from life, John's fantasy about an imaginary sister, might lead you straight into it—meeting the real Jill, I mean. With disastrous results.

A Girl in Winter, which I always think of as *The Kingdom of Winter,* which was its first title, or *Winterreich,* as Bruce Montgomery used to call it—well, that was written when I was feeling pretty low, in this first library job I told you about. It's what Eliot would call an objective correlative. When I look at it today, I do think it's remarkably . . . I suppose the word is *knowing* . . . not really mature, or wise, just incredibly clever. By my standards, I mean. And considering I was only twenty-two. All the same, some people whose opinion I respect prefer *Jill* as being more natural, more sincere, more directly emotional.

PHILLIPS. In your preface to the reprint of *Jill,* you say it is "in essence an unambitious short story." What is your definition of a novel?

LARKIN. I think a novel should follow the fortunes of more than one character.

PHILLIPS. At least one critic has cited *Jill* as the forerunner of the new British postwar novel—the literature of the displaced working-class hero which spawned later works by Alan Sillitoe, John Wain, Keith Waterhouse, Amis, and others. Do you feel a part of any of this?

LARKIN. I don't think so, no. Because *Jill* has none of the political overtones of that genre. John's being working class was a kind of equivalent of my stammer, a built-in handicap to put him one down.

I'm glad you mention Keith Waterhouse. I think *Billy Liar* and *Jubb* are remarkably original novels, the first very funny, the second harrowing. Much better than my two.

PHILLIPS. You're extremely modest. Wouldn't you say that an open assumption of the British sense of class is important to your work—*Jill, A Girl in Winter,* a poem like "The Whitsun Weddings"?

LARKIN. Are you suggesting there's no sense of class in America? That's not the impression I get from the works of Mr. John O'Hara.

PHILLIPS. O'Hara overstated. Did you prefigure a shape to your two novels, or did they evolve? You've stated your mentors in poetry, especially Hardy. But who in fiction early on did you frequently read and admire?

LARKIN. Hard to say. Of course, I had read a great many novels, and knew the mannerism of most modern writers, but looking back I can't say I ever imitated anyone. Now don't think I mind imitation, in a young writer. It's just a way of learning the job. Really, my novels were more original than my poems, at the time. My favorite novelists were Lawrence, Isherwood, Maugham, Waugh—oh, and George Moore. I was on a great Moore kick at the time: probably he was at the bottom of my style, then.

PHILLIPS. *A Girl in Winter* reminds me stylistically of Elizabeth Bowen's fiction, particularly *The Death of the Heart* and *The House in Paris*. Is Bowen a writer you've also admired?

LARKIN. No, I hadn't read Elizabeth Bowen. In fact, someone lent me *The Death of the Heart* when *A Girl in Winter* came out—two years after it was finished. I quite liked it, but it was never one of my personal favorites.

PHILLIPS. Let's talk about the structure of *A Girl in Winter* for a moment. Did you write it chronologically? That is, did you write Part Two first, then shuffle the pack for effect and counterpoint? Or did you actually conceive the novel as present-to-past-to-present?

LARKIN. The second way.

PHILLIPS. Letters are an important and integral part of both novels, as plot and as texture. Are you a voluminous letter writer?

LARKIN. I suppose I used to write many more letters than I do now, but so did everyone. Nowadays I keep up with one or two people, in the sense of writing when there isn't anything special to say. I love *getting* letters, which means you have to answer them, and there isn't always time. I had a very amusing and undemanding correspondence with the novelist Barbara Pym, who died in 1980, that arose simply out of a fan letter I wrote her, and went on for over ten years before we actually met. I hope she liked getting my letters: I certainly liked hers. I talk about our correspondence in a foreword I provided for the U.K. edition of her posthumous novel, *An Unsuitable Attachment.*

PHILLIPS. Can you describe your relationship with the contemporary literary community?

LARKIN. I'm somewhat withdrawn from what you call "the contemporary literary community," for two reasons: in the first place, I don't write for a living, and so don't have to keep in touch with literary editors and publishers and television people in order to earn money; and in the second, I don't live in London. Given that, my relations with it are quite amicable.

PHILLIPS. Is Hull a place where you are likely to stay put? If so, have you as a person changed since the writing of the poem "Places, Loved Ones"—or is the speaker of that poem a persona?

LARKIN. Hull is a place where I *have* stayed. On my twenty-fifth anniversary, I held a little luncheon for the members of my staff who'd been there as long as I had, or almost as long, and they made me a presentation with a card bearing the very lines you mean. *Touché,* as the French say.

PHILLIPS. As a bachelor, have you sometimes felt like an outsider? Or, like the speaker of your poems, "Reasons for Attendance," "Dockery and Son," and "Self's the Man," have you enjoyed being single and remained so because you preferred living that way?

LARKIN. Hard to say. Yes, I've remained single by choice, and shouldn't have liked anything else, but of course most people do get married, and divorced, too, and so I suppose I am an outsider in the sense you mean. Of course, it worries me from time to time, but it would take too long to explain why. Samuel Butler said, "Life is an affair of being spoilt in one way or another."

PHILLIPS. Is the character John Kemp in any way based upon your own youth? Were you *that* shy?

LARKIN. I would say, yes. I was and am extremely shy. Anyone who has stammered will know what agony it is, especially at school—it means you never take the lead in anything or do anything but try to efface yourself. I often wonder if I was shy because I stammered, or vice versa.

PHILLIPS. Was your childhood happy?

LARKIN. My childhood was all right, comfortable and stable and loving, but I wasn't a happy child, or so they say. On the other hand, I've never been a recluse, contrary to reports: I've had friends and enjoyed their company. In comparison with some people I know, I'm extremely sociable.

PHILLIPS. Do you feel happiness is unlikely in this world?

LARKIN. Well, I think if you're in good health, and have enough money, and nothing is bothering you in the foreseeable future, that's as much as you can hope for. But "happiness," in the sense of a continuous emotional orgasm, no. If only because you know that you are going to die, and the people you love are going to die.

PHILLIPS. After "Trouble at Willow Gables," did you write any other short stories or tales?

LARKIN. No. I think a short story should be either a poem or a novel. Unless it's just an anecdote.

PHILLIPS. Have you ever attempted a truly long poem? I've never seen one in print. If not, why?

LARKIN. I've written none. A long poem for me would be a novel. In that sense, *A Girl in Winter* is a poem.

PHILLIPS. What about a play or a verse play?

LARKIN. I don't like plays. They happen in public, which, as I said, I don't like. And by now I have grown rather deaf, which means I can't hear what's going on. Then again, they are rather like poetry readings: they have to get an instant response, which tends to vulgarize. And of course, the intrusion of *personality*—the actor, the producer (or do you call him the director?)—is distracting.

All the same, I admire *Murder in the Cathedral* as much as anything Eliot ever wrote. I read it from time to time, for pleasure, which is the highest compliment I can pay.

PHILLIPS. Did you ever meet Eliot?

LARKIN. I didn't know him. Once I was in the Faber offices—the old ones, "24, Russell Square," that magic address!—talking to Charles Monteith, and he said, "Have you ever met Eliot?" I said no, and to my astonishment he stepped out and reappeared with Eliot, who must have been in the next room. We shook hands, and he explained that he was expecting someone to tea and couldn't stay. There was a pause, and he said, "I'm glad to see you in this office." The significance of that was that I wasn't a Faber author—it must have been before 1964, when they published *The Whitsun Weddings*—and I took it as a great compliment. But it was a shattering few minutes: I hardly remember what I thought.

PHILLIPS. And what about Auden? Were you acquainted?

LARKIN. I didn't know him either. I met Auden once at Stephen Spender's house, which was very kind of Spender, and in a sense he was more frightening than Eliot. I remember he said, "Do you like living in Hull?" and I said, "I don't suppose I'm unhappier there than I should be anywhere else." To which he replied, "Naughty, naughty." I thought that was very funny.

But this business about meeting famous writers is agonizing: I had a dreadful few minutes with Forster. My fault, not his. Dylan Thomas came to Oxford to speak to a club I belong to, and we had a drink the following morning. He wasn't frightening. In fact, and I know it sounds absurd to say so, but I should say I had more in common with Dylan Thomas than with any other "famous writer," in this sort of context.

PHILLIPS. You mention Auden, Thomas, Yeats, and Hardy as early influences in your introduction to the second edition of *The North Ship*. What in particular did you learn from your study of these four?

LARKIN. Oh, for Christ's sake, one doesn't *study* poets! You *read* them, and think, "That's marvelous, how is it done, could I do it?" and that's how you learn. At the end of it, you can't say, "That's Yeats, that's Auden," because they've gone, they're like scaffolding that's been taken down. Thomas was a dead end. What effects? Yeats and Auden, the management of lines, the formal distancing of emotion. Hardy, well . . . not to be afraid of the obvious. All those wonderful dicta about poetry: "The poet should touch our hearts by showing his own;" "The poet takes note of nothing that he cannot feel;" "The emotion of all the ages and the thought of his own"—Hardy knew what it was all about.

PHILLIPS. When your first book, *The North Ship,* appeared, did you feel you were going to be an important poet?

LARKIN. No, certainly not. I've never felt that anyway. You must remember, *The North Ship* was published by an obscure press—The Fortune Press—that didn't even send out review copies; it was next door to a vanity press. One had none of the rewards of authorship, neither money (no agreement) nor publicity. You felt you'd cooked your goose.

PHILLIPS. How can a young poet know if his work is any good?

LARKIN. I think a young poet, or an old poet, for that matter, should try to produce something that pleases himself personally, not only when he's written it but a couple of weeks later. Then he should see if it pleases anyone else, by sending it to the kind of magazine he likes reading. But if it doesn't, he shouldn't be discouraged. I mean, in the seventeenth century every educated man could turn a verse and play the lute. Supposing no one played tennis because they wouldn't make Wimbledon? First and foremost, writing poems should be a pleasure. So should reading them, by God.

PHILLIPS. How do you account for the great maturity and originality which developed between your first poetry collection, *The North Ship,* and your second, *The Less Deceived*?

LARKIN. You know, I really don't know. After finishing my first books, say by 1945, I thought I had come to an end. I couldn't write another novel, I published nothing. My personal life was rather harassing. Then in 1950 I went to Belfast, and things reawoke somehow. I wrote some poems, and thought, "These aren't bad," and had that little pamphlet, *XX Poems,* printed privately. I felt for the first time I was speaking for myself. Thoughts, feelings, language cohered and jumped. They have to do that. Of course, they are always lying around in you, but they have to get together.

PHILLIPS. You once wrote that "The impulse to preserve lies at the bottom of all art." In your case, what is it you are preserving in your poems?

LARKIN. Well, as I said, the experience. The beauty.

PHILLIPS. Auden admired your forms. But you've stated that form holds little interest for you—content is everything. Could you comment on that?

LARKIN. I'm afraid that was a rather silly remark, especially now when form is so rare. I read poems, and I think, "Yes, that's quite a nice idea, but why can't he make a *poem* of it? Make it memorable? It's no good just writing it down!" At any level that matters, form and content are indivisible. What I meant by content is the experience the poem preserves, what passes it on. I must have been seeing too many poems that were simply agglomerations of words when I said that.

PHILLIPS. In one early interview you stated that you were not interested in any period but the present, or in any poetry but that written in English. Did you mean that quite literally? Has your view changed?

LARKIN. It has not. I don't see how one can ever know a foreign language well enough to make reading poems in it worthwhile. Foreigners' ideas of good English poems are dreadfully crude: Byron and Poe and so on. The Russians liking Burns. But deep down, I think foreign languages irrelevant. If that glass thing over there is a window, then it isn't a fenster, or a *fenêtre,* or whatever. *Hautes Fenêtres,* my God! A writer can have only one language, if language is going to mean anything to him.

PHILLIPS. In D. J. Enright's *Poets of the Nineteen-Fifties,* published in 1955, you made several provocative statements about archetypes and myth which have become well known. Specifically: "As a guiding principle I believe that every poem must be its own sole freshly created universe, and therefore have no belief in 'tradition' or a common myth-kitty. . . . To me the whole of the ancient world, the whole of classical and biblical mythology means very little, and I think that using them today not only fills poems full of dead spots, but dodges the writer's duty to be original." Does this mean you really do not respond to, say, the monstrous manifestations of the sphinx in Yeats's "The Second Coming"? Or were you merely reacting against bookishness?

LARKIN. My objection to the use in new poems of properties or personae from older poems is not a moral one, but simply because they do not work, either because I have not read the poems in which they appear, or because I have read them and think of them as part of that poem and not a property to be dragged into a new poem as a substitute for securing the effect that is desired. I admit this argument could be pushed to absurd lengths, when a poet could not refer to anything that his readers might not have seen (such as snow, for instance), but in fact poets write for people with the same background and experiences as themselves, which might be taken as compelling argument in support of provincialism.

PHILLIPS. The use of archetypes can weaken rather than buttress a poem?

LARKIN. I am not going to fall on my face every time someone uses words such as "Orpheus" or "Faust" or "Judas." Writers should work for the effects they want to produce, and not to wheel out stale old Wardour Street lay figures.

PHILLIPS. What do you mainly read?

LARKIN. I don't read much. Books I'm sent to review. Otherwise, novels I've read before. Detective stories: Gladys Mitchell, Michael Innes, Dick Francis. I'm reading *Framley Parsonage* at the moment. Nothing difficult.

PHILLIPS. What do you think of the current state of poetry in England today? Are things better or worse in American poetry?

LARKIN. I'm afraid I know very little about American poetry. As regards England, well, before the war, when I was growing up, we had Yeats, Eliot, Graves, Auden, Dylan Thomas, John Betjeman—could you pick a comparable team today?

PHILLIPS. You haven't been to America, have you?

LARKIN. Oh, no, I've never been to America, nor to anywhere else, for that matter. Does that sound very snubbing? It isn't meant to. I suppose I'm pretty unadventurous by nature, partly because that isn't the way I earn my living—reading and lecturing and taking classes and so on. I should hate it.

And of course, I'm so deaf now that I shouldn't dare. Someone would say, "What about Ashbery," and I'd say, "I'd prefer strawberry," that kind of thing. I suppose everyone has his own dream of America. A writer once said to me, "If you ever go to America, go either to the East Coast or the West Coast: the rest is a desert full of bigots." That's what I think I'd like: where if you help a girl trim the Christmas tree, you're regarded as engaged, and her brothers start oiling their shotguns if you don't call on the minister. A version of pastoral.

PHILLIPS. How is your writing physically accomplished? At what stage does a poem go through the typewriter?

LARKIN. I write—or used to—in notebooks in pencil, trying to complete each stanza before going on to the next. Then when the poem is finished, I type it out, and sometimes make small alterations.

PHILLIPS. You use a lot of idioms and very common phrases—for irony, I'd guess, or to bear more meaning than usual, never for shock value. Do these phrases come late, to add texture or whatever, or are they integral from the beginning?

LARKIN. They occur naturally.

PHILLIPS. How important is enjambment for you? In certain lines, you seem to isolate lives by the very line breaks . . .

LARKIN. No device is important in itself. Writing poetry is playing off the natural rhythms and word order of speech against the artificialities of rhyme and meter. One has a few private rules: Never split an adjective and its noun, for instance.

PHILLIPS. How do you decide whether or not to rhyme?

LARKIN. Usually the idea of a poem comes with a line or two of it, and they determine the rest. Normally one does rhyme. Deciding *not* to is much harder.

PHILLIPS. Can you drink and write? Have you tried any consciousness-expanding drugs?

LARKIN. No, though of course those of my generation are drinkers. Not druggers.

PHILLIPS. Can you describe the genesis and working out of a poem based upon an image that most people would simply pass by? (A clear road between neighbors, an ambulance in city traffic?)

LARKIN. If I could answer this sort of question, I'd be a professor rather than a librarian. And in any case, I shouldn't want to. It's a thing you don't want to think about. It happens, or happened, and if it's something to be grateful for, you're grateful.

I remember saying once, "I can't understand these chaps who go around American universities explaining how they write poems: it's like going round explaining how you sleep with your wife." Whoever I was talking to said, "They'd do that, too, if their agents could fix it."

PHILLIPS. Do you throw away a lot of poems?

LARKIN. Some poems didn't get finished. Some didn't get published. I never throw anything away.

PHILLIPS. You only included six of your own poems in *The Oxford Book of Twentieth-Century English Verse* (as opposed, say, to twelve by John Betjeman).

LARKIN. My recollection is that I decided on six as a limit for my generation and anyone younger, to save hurt feelings. Mine were representative, as you say—one pretty one, one funny one, one long one, and so on. As editor, I couldn't give myself much space . . . could I?

PHILLIPS. In your introduction to that anthology, you make a fine point of saying that you didn't include any poems "requiring a glossary for their full understanding." Do you feel that your own lucid work has helped close the gap between poetry and the public, a gap which experiment and obscurity have widened?

LARKIN. This was to explain why I hadn't included dialect poems. We have poets who write in pretty dense Lallans. Nothing to do with obscurity in the sense you mean.

PHILLIPS. Okay, but your introduction to *All What Jazz?* takes a stance against experiment, citing the trio of Picasso, Pound, and Parker. Why do you distrust the new?

LARKIN. It seems to me undeniable that up to this century literature used language in the way we all use it, painting represented what anyone with normal vision sees, and music was an affair of nice noises rather than nasty ones. The innovation of "modernism" in the arts consisted of doing the opposite. I don't know why, I'm not a historian. You have to distinguish between things that seemed off when they were new but are now quite familiar, such as Ibsen and Wagner, and things that seemed crazy when they were new and seem crazy now, like *Finnegans Wake* and Picasso.

PHILLIPS. What's that got to do with jazz?

LARKIN. Everything. Jazz showed this very clearly because it is such a telescoped art, only as old as the century, if that. Charlie Parker wrecked jazz—or so they tell me—by using the chromatic rather than the diatonic scale. The diatonic scale is what you use if you want to write a national anthem, or a love song, or a lullaby. The chromatic scale is what you use to give the effect of drinking a quinine martini and having an enema simultaneously.

If I sound heated on this, it's because I love jazz—the jazz of Armstrong, and Bechet, and Ellington, and Bessie Smith, and Beiderbecke. To have it all destroyed by a paranoiac drug addict made me furious. Anyway, it's dead now, dead as Elizabethan madrigal singing. We can only treasure the records. And I do.

PHILLIPS. Let's return to the Oxford anthology for a moment. Some of its critics said your selections not only favored traditional poetic forms, but minor poets as well. How do you respond to that?

LARKIN. Since it was *The Oxford Book of Twentieth-Century English Verse,* I had of course to represent the principal poets of the century by their best or most typical works. I think I did this. The trouble is that if this is all you do, the result will be a worthy but boring book, since there are quite enough books doing this already, and I thought it would be diverting to put in less familiar poems that were good or typical in themselves, but by authors who didn't rank full representation. I saw them as unexpected flowers along an only too well trodden path. I think they upset people in a way I hadn't intended, although it's surprising how they are now being quoted and anthologized themselves.

Most people make anthologies out of other anthologies; I spent five years reading everyone's complete works, ending with six months in the basement of Bodleian Library handling all the twentieth-century poetry they had received. It was great fun. I don't say I made any major discoveries, but I hope I managed to suggest that there are good poems around that no one knows about. At any rate, I made a readable book. I made twentieth-century poetry sound nice. That's quite an achievement in itself.

PHILLIPS. Not many have commented upon the humor in your poetry, like the wonderful pun on "the stuff that dreams are made on" in "Toads." Do you consciously use humor to achieve a particular effect, or to avoid an opposite emotion?

LARKIN. One uses humor to make people laugh. In my case, I don't know whether they in fact do. The trouble is, it makes them think you aren't being serious. That's the risk you take.

PHILLIPS. Your most recent collection, *High Windows,* contains at least three poems I'd call satirical—"Posterity," "Homage to a Government," and "This Be The Verse." Do you consider yourself a satirist?

LARKIN. No, I shouldn't call myself a satirist, or any other sort of -*ist.* The poems you mention were conceived in the same way as the rest. That is to say, as poems. To be a satirist, you have to think you know better than everyone else. I've never done that.

PHILLIPS. An American poet-critic, Peter Davison, has characterized yours as a "diminutional talent," meaning that you make things clear by making them small—England reduced to "squares of wheat," and so forth. Is this a fair comment? Is it a technique you're aware of?

LARKIN. It's difficult to answer remarks like that. The line "Its postal districts packed like squares of wheat" refers to London, not England. It doesn't seem diminutional to me—rather the reverse, if anything. It's meant to make the postal districts seem rich and fruitful.

PHILLIPS. Davison also sees your favorite subject as failure and weakness.

LARKIN. I think a poet should be judged by what he does with his subjects, not by what his subjects are. Otherwise you're getting near the totalitarian attitude of wanting poems about steel-production figures rather than   *"Mais où sont les neiges d'antan?"* Poetry isn't a kind of paint spray you use to cover selected objects with. A good poem about failure is a success.

PHILLIPS. Is it intentional that the form of "Toads" is alternating uneven trimeters and dimeters, with alternating off-rhymes, whereas "Toads Revisited" is in trimeters and off-rhymed couplets? What determines the form of a poem for you? Is it the first line, with its attendant rhythms?

LARKIN. Well, yes: I think I've admitted this already. At this distance, I can't recall how far the second toad poem was planned as a companion to the first. It's more likely that I found it turning out to be a poem about work, but differently from the first, and it seemed amusing to link them.

PHILLIPS. How did you arrive upon the image of a toad for work or labor?

LARKIN. Sheer genius.

PHILLIPS. As a writer, what are your particular quirks? Do you feel that you have any conspicuous or secret flaw?

LARKIN. I really don't know. I supposed I've used the iambic pentameter a lot: some people find this oppressive and try to get away from it. My secret flaw is just not being very good, like everyone else. I've never been didactic, never tried to make poetry *do* things, never gone out to look for it. I waited for it to come to me, in whatever shape it chose.

PHILLIPS. Do you feel you belong to any particular tradition in English letters?

LARKIN. I seem to remember George Fraser saying that poetry was either "veeshion"—he was Scotch—or "moaral deescourse," and I was the second, and the first was better. A well-known publisher asked me how one punctuated poetry, and looked flabbergasted when I said, "The same as prose." By which I mean that I write, or wrote, as everyone did till the mad lads started, using words and syntax in the normal way to describe recognizable experiences as memorably as possible. That doesn't seem to me a tradition. The other stuff, the mad stuff, is more an aberration.

PHILLIPS. Do you have any thoughts on the office of poet laureate of England? Does it serve a valid function?

LARKIN. Poetry and sovereignty are very primitive things. I like to think of their being united in this way, in England. On the other hand, it's not clear what the Poet Laureate is, and does. Deliberately so, in a way: it isn't a job, there are no duties, no salary, and yet it isn't quite an honor, either, or not just an honor. I'm sure the worst thing about it, especially today, is the publicity it brings, the pressure to be involved publicly with poetry, which must be pretty inimical to any real writing.

Of course, the days when Tennyson would publish a sonnet telling Gladstone what to do about foreign policy are over. It's funny that Kipling, who is what most people think of as a poet as national spokesman, never was Poet Laureate. He should have had it when Bridges was appointed, but it's typical that he didn't—the post isn't thought of in that way. It really is a genuine attempt to honor someone. But the publicity having anything to do with the Palace is so fierce these days, it must be really more of an ordeal than an honor.

PHILLIPS. Your poetry volumes have appeared at the rate of one per decade. From what you say, though, is it unlikely we'll have another around 1984? Did you really only complete about three poems in any given year?

LARKIN. It's unlikely I shall write any more poems, but when I did, yes, I did write slowly. I was looking at "The Whitsun Weddings" just the other day, and found that I began it sometime in the summer of 1957. After three pages, I dropped it for another poem that in fact was finished but never published. I picked it up again, in March 1958, and worked on it until October, when it was finished. But when I look at the diary I was keeping at the time, I see that the kind of incident it describes happened in July 1955! Of course, that's an exception. But I did write slowly, partly because you're finding out what to say, as well as how to say it, and that takes time.

PHILLIPS. For someone who dislikes being interviewed, you've responded generously.

LARKIN. I'm afraid I haven't said anything very interesting. You must realize I've never had "ideas" about poetry. To me, it's always been a personal, almost physical, release or solution to a complex pressure of needs—wanting to create, to justify, to praise, to explain, to externalize, depending on the circumstances. And I've never been much interested in other people's poetry—one reason for writing, of course, is that no one's written what you want to read.

Probably my notion of poetry is very simple. Some time ago, I agreed to help judge a poetry competition—you know, the kind where they get about thirty-five thousand entries and you look at the best few thousand. After a bit, I said, "Where are all the love poems? And nature poems?" And they said, "Oh, we threw all those away." I expect they were the ones I should have liked.

(1982)

Joyce Carol Oates
Photograph by Layle Silbert

Joyce Carol Oates

This interview was commissioned at the author's request, after an initial attempt by another—assigned by the Paris Review*—failed to produce an adequate account. Oates and I have known each other since 1956, and she felt that the results would be more satisfactory.*

The interview began at the Windsor, Canada, home of Oates and her husband, professor-editor Raymond J. Smith, in the summer of 1976. Talks continued during a stroll by the bank of the Detroit River, which the Smith home overlooked. Oates described sitting for hours by that river, watching the horizon and the boats, dreaming her characters into existence. She set these dreams onto paper on a writing table in one corner of the master bedroom.

I asked additional questions in New York City during the winter of 1976, when Oates and Smith attended a seminar on her work that was part of that year's Modern Language Association Convention. Further questions were posed in Princeton, New Jersey, where the couple moved in fall 1978. Oates had assumed duties as writer-in-residence at Princeton University, and Smith had taken a teaching position at New York University. Having given up the Detroit River, Oates and Smith widened a pond on their new property. Despite the demands of students and writing, she continued to devote much energy to the Ontario Review, *a distinguished literary quarterly which the couple coedits. I asked my questions in their modern, glass-walled Princeton home and by the pond, where Oates sat in a wrought-iron lawn chair.*

It was in this Princeton residence that she first began writing on a word processor. But eventually she gave up computer technology for a return to pad and pen and electric typewriter. The shift does not seem to have affected her output.

Ms. Oates is striking—slender, with straight dark hair and large, inquiring eyes. She is not photogenic; no photo has ever done justice to her appearance, which conveys grace and high intelligence. (Of her photographed self, she has written in her unpublished journal, housed in the Joyce Carol Oates Archive at Syracuse University, "Oh why do I look so frail and tremulous when I feel so strong????"). Her voice is soft and her manner reticent. One gets the impression that she never speaks in anything but perfectly formed sentences. Slang is not a part of her argot. If she sometimes has been taken for aloof— and she has—it is the result of a shyness and deference which international fame has not displaced. She is an accomplished pianist and maker of drawings, enjoys jogging and picnicking, biking and tennis. She is a tireless letter writer and doting keeper of cats. And she is the most prolific author of the first rank in twentieth-century American literature.

•   •   •

PHILLIPS. We may as well get this one over with first: You're frequently charged with producing too much.

OATES. Productivity is a relative matter. And it's really insignificant. What is ultimately important is a writer's strongest books. It may be the case that we all must write many books in order to achieve a few lasting ones—just as a young writer or poet might have to write hundreds of poems before writing his first significant one. Each book as it is written, however, is a completely absorbing experience, and feels always as if it were *the* work I was born to write. Afterward, of course, as the years pass, it's possible to become more detached, more critical.

I really don't know what to say. I note and can to some extent sympathize with the obturator tone of certain critics who feel I write too much, because, quite wrongly, they believe they ought to have read most of my books before attempting to criticize a recently published one. (At least I *think* that's why they react a bit irritably.) Yet each book is a world unto itself, and must stand alone, and it should not matter whether a book is a writer's first, or tenth, or fiftieth.

PHILLIPS. About your critics—do you read them, usually? Have you ever learned anything from a book review or an essay on your work?

OATES. Sometimes I read reviews, and without exception I will read critical essays that are sent to me. The critical essays are interesting on their own terms. Of course, it's a pleasure simply to discover that someone has read and responded to one's work; being understood, and being praised, is beyond expectation most of the time. . . . The average review is a quickly written piece not meant to be definitive. So it would be misguided for a writer to read such reviews attentively. All writers without exception find themselves clapperclawed from time to time; I think the experience (provided one survives it) is wonderfully liberating: after the first death there is no other. . . . A writer who has published as many books as I have has developed, of necessity, a hide like a rhino's, while inside there dwells a frail, hopeful butterfly of a spirit.

PHILLIPS. Returning to the matter of your "productivity": Have you ever dictated into a machine?

OATES. No, oddly enough I've written my last several novels in longhand first. I had an enormous, rather frightening stack of pages and notes for *The Assassin*—probably eight hundred pages, or was it closer to a thousand? It alarms me to remember. *Childwold* needed to be written in longhand, of course. And now everything finds itself expressed in longhand, and the typewriter has become a rather alien thing—a thing of formality and impersonality. My first novels were all written on a typewriter: first draft straight through, then revisions, then final draft. But I can't do that any longer.

The thought of dictating into a machine doesn't appeal to me at all. Henry James's later works would have been better had he resisted that curious sort of self-indulgence, dictating to a secretary. The roaming garrulousness of ordinary speech is usually corrected when it's transcribed into written prose.

PHILLIPS. Do you ever worry—considering the vast body of your work—if you haven't written a particular scene before, or had a character say the same lines?

OATES. Evidently there are writers (John Cheever, Mavis Gallant come immediately to mind) who never reread their work, and there are others who reread constantly. I suspect I am somewhere in the middle. If I thought I *had* written a scene before, or written the same lines before, I would simply look it up.

PHILLIPS. What kind of work schedule do you follow?

OATES. I haven't any formal schedule, but I love to write in the morning before breakfast. Sometimes the writing goes so smoothly that I don't take a break for many hours—and consequently have breakfast at two or three in the afternoon on good days. On school days, days that I teach, I usually write for an hour and forty-five minutes in the morning, before my first class. But I don't have any formal schedule, and at the moment I am feeling rather melancholy, or derailed, or simply lost, because I completed a novel some weeks ago and I haven't begun another . . . except in scattered, stray notes.

PHILLIPS. Do you find emotional stability is necessary in order to write? Or can you get to work whatever your state of mind? Is your mood reflected in what you write? How do you describe that perfect state in which you can write from early morning into the afternoon?

OATES. One must be pitiless about this matter of "mood." In a sense, the writing will *create* the mood. If art is, as I believe it to be, a genuinely transcendental function—a means by which we rise out of limited parochial states of mind—then it should not matter very much what states of mind or emotion we are in. Generally, I've found this to be true: I have forced myself to begin writing when I've been utterly exhausted, when I've left my soul as thin as a playing card, when nothing has seemed worth enduring for another five minutes . . . and somehow the activity of writing changes everything. Or appears to do so. Joyce said of the underlying structure of *Ulysses*—the Odyssean parallel and parody—that he really didn't care whether it was plausible, so long as it served as a bridge to get his "soldiers" across. Once they were across, what does it matter if the bridge collapses? One might say the same thing about the use of one's self as a means for writing to get written. Once the soldiers are across the stream . . .

PHILLIPS. What does happen when you finish a novel? Is the next project one that has been waiting in line? Or is the choice more spontaneous?

OATES. When I complete a novel I set it aside, and begin work on short stories, and eventually another long work. When I complete *that* novel, I return to the earlier novel and rewrite much of it. In the meantime, the second novel lies in a desk drawer. Sometimes I work on two novels simultaneously, though one usually forces the other into the background. The rhythm of writing, revising, writing, revising, etc., seems to suit me. I am inclined to think that as I grow older I will come to be infatuated with the art of revision, and there may come a time when I will dread giving up a novel at all. My next novel, *Unholy Loves,* was written around the time of *Childwold,* for instance, and revised after the completion of that novel, and again revised this past spring and summer. My reputation for writing effortlessly notwithstanding, I am strongly in favor of intelligent, even fastidious, revision—which is, or certainly should be, an art in itself.

PHILLIPS. Do you keep a diary?

OATES. I began keeping a formal journal several years ago. It resembles a sort of ongoing letter to myself, mainly about literary matters. What interests me in the process of my own experience is the wide range of my feelings. For instance, after I finish a novel I tend to think of the experience of having written it as being largely pleasant and challenging. But in fact (for I keep records carefully) the experience is various: I do suffer temporary bouts of frustration and inertia and depression. There are pages in recent novels that I've rewritten as many as seventeen times, and a story, "The Widows," which I revised both before and after publication in the *Hudson Review,* and then revised slightly again before I included it in my next collection of stories—a fastidiousness that could go on into infinity.

Afterward, however, I simply forget. My feelings crystallize (or are mythologized) into something much less complex. All of us who keep journals do so for different reasons, I suppose, but we must have in common a fascination with the surprising patterns that emerge over the years—a sort of arabesque in which certain elements appear and reappear, like the designs in a well-wrought novel. The voice of my journal is very much like the one I find myself using in these replies to you—the voice in which I think or meditate when I'm not writing fiction.

PHILLIPS. Besides writing and teaching, what daily special activities are important to you? Travel, jogging, music? I hear you're an excellent pianist?

OATES. We travel a great deal, usually by car. We've driven slowly across the continent several times, and we've explored the South and New England and of course New York State with loving thoroughness. As a pianist I've defined myself as an "enthusiastic amateur," which is about the most merciful thing that can be said. I like to draw, I like to listen to music, and I spend an inordinate amount of time doing nothing. I don't even think it can be called daydreaming.

I also enjoy that much maligned occupation of housewifery, but hardly dare say so, things being what they are today. I like to cook, to tend plants, to garden (minimally), to do simple domestic things, to stroll around shopping malls and observe the qualities of people, overhearing snatches of conversations, noting people's appearances, their clothes, and so forth. Walking and driving a car are part of my life as a writer, really. I can't imagine myself apart from these activities.

PHILLIPS. Despite critical and financial success, you continue to teach. Why?

OATES. I teach a full load at the University of Windsor, which means three courses. One is creative writing, one is the graduate seminar (in the Modern Period), the third is an oversized (115 students) undergraduate course that is lively and stimulating but really too swollen to be satisfying to me. There is, generally, a closeness between students and faculty at Windsor that is very rewarding, however. Anyone who teaches knows that you don't *really* experience a text until you've taught it, in loving detail, with an intelligent and responsive class. At the present time, I'm going through Joyce's work with nine graduate students, and each seminar is very exciting (and draining), and I can't think, frankly, of anything else I would rather do.

PHILLIPS. It is a sometimes-publicized fact that your professor-husband does not read most of your work. Is there any practical reason for this?

OATES. Ray has such a busy life of his own— preparing classes, editing the *Ontario Review* and books for Ontario Review Press, and so forth—that he really hasn't time to read my work. I do, occasionally, show him reviews and he makes brief comments on them. I would have liked, I think, to have established an easygoing relationship with some other writers, but somehow that never came about. Two or three of us at Windsor do read one another's poems, but criticism as such is minimal. I've never been able to respond very fully to criticism, frankly, because I've usually been absorbed in another work by the time the criticism is available to me. Also, critics sometimes appear to be addressing themselves to works other than those I remember writing.

PHILLIPS. Do you feel in any way an expatriate or an exile, living in Canada?

OATES. We are certainly exiles of a sort. But we would be, I think, exiles if we lived in Detroit, as well. Fortunately, Windsor is really an international, cosmopolitan community, and our Canadian colleagues are not intensely and narrowly nationalistic.

But I wonder—doesn't everyone feel rather exiled? When I return home to Millerport, New York, and visit nearby Lockport, the extraordinary changes that have taken place make me feel like a stranger; the mere passage of time makes us all exiles. The situation is a comic one, perhaps, since it affirms the power of the evolving community over the individual, but I think we tend to feel it as tragic. Windsor is a relatively stable community, and my husband and I have come to feel, oddly, more at home here than we probably would anywhere else.

PHILLIPS. Have you ever consciously changed your lifestyle to help your work as a writer?

OATES. Not really. My nature is orderly and observant and scrupulous, and deeply introverted, so life wherever I attempt it turns out to be claustral. "Live like the bourgeois," Flaubert suggested, but I was living like that long before I came across Flaubert's remark.

PHILLIPS. You wrote *Do With Me What You Will* during your year living in London. While there, you met many writers such as Doris Lessing, Margaret Drabble, Colin Wilson, Iris Murdoch—writers you respect, as your reviews of their work indicate. Would you make any observations on the role of the writer in England versus that which you experience here?

OATES. The English novelist is almost without exception an observer of society. (I suppose I mean "society" in its most immediate, limited sense.) Apart from writers like Lawrence (who doesn't seem altogether *English,* in fact) there hasn't been an intense interest in subjectivity, in the psychology of living, breathing human beings. Of course, there have been marvelous novels. And there *is* Doris Lessing, who writes books that can no longer be categorized: fictional parable, autobiography, allegory. . . ? And John Fowles. And Iris Murdoch.

But there is a feel to the American novel that is radically different. We are willing to risk being called "formless" by people whose ideas of form are rigidly limited, and we are wilder, more exploratory, more ambitious, perhaps less easily shamed, less easily discouraged. The intellectual life as such we tend to keep out of our novels, fearing the sort of highly readable but ultimately disappointing cerebral quality of Huxley's work . . . or, on a somewhat lower level, C. P. Snow's.

PHILLIPS. The English edition of *Wonderland* has a different ending from the American. Why? Do you often rewrite published work?

OATES. I was forced to rewrite the ending of that particular novel because it struck me that the first ending was not the correct one. I have not rewritten any other published work (except, of course, for short stories, which sometimes get rewritten before inclusion in a book) and don't intend to if I can possibly help it.

PHILLIPS. You've written novels on highly specialized fields, such as brain surgery. How do you research such backgrounds?

OATES. A great deal of reading, mainly. Some years ago, I developed a few odd symptoms that necessitated my seeing a doctor, and since there was for a time talk of my being sent to a neurologist, I nervously and superstitiously began reading the relevant journals. What I came upon so chilled me that I must have gotten well as a result . . .

PHILLIPS. In addition to the novel about medicine, you've written one each on law, politics, religion, spectator sports. Are you consciously filling out a program—of novels about American life?

OATES. Not really consciously. The great concern with "medicine" really grew out of an experience of some duration that brought me into contact with certain thoughts of mortality—of the hospitals, illnesses, doctors, the world of death and dying and our human defenses against such phenomena. (A member of my family to whom I was very close died rather slowly of cancer.) I attempted to deal with my own very inchoate feelings about these matters by dramatizing what I saw to be contemporary responses to "mortality." My effort led me to wed myself with a fictional character, and our synthesis in turn with a larger almost allegorical condition. This resulted in a novel that was difficult to write, and also, I suspect, difficult to read.

A concern with law seemed to spring naturally out of the thinking many of us were doing in the sixties: what is the relationship between "law" and civilization, what hope has civilization without "law," and yet what hope has civilization *with* "law" as it has developed in our tradition? More personal matters blended together with the larger issues of "crime" and "guilt," so that I felt I was able to transcend a purely private and purely local drama that might have had emotional significance for me, but very little beyond that. Quite by accident, I found myself writing about a woman conditioned to be unnaturally "passive" in a world of hearty masculine combat—an issue that became topical even as the novel *Do With Me What You Will* was published, and is topical still, to some extent.

The "political" novel, *The Assassins,* grew out of two experiences I had some years ago, at high-level conferences involving politicians, academic specialists, lawyers, and a scattering—no, hardly that—of literary people. (I won't be more specific at the moment.) A certain vertiginous fascination with work, which I noted in my own nature, I was able to objectify (and, I think, exaggerate) in terms of the various characters' fanaticism involving their own "work"—most obviously in Andrew Petrie's obsession with "transforming the consciousness of America." *The Assassins* is about megalomania and its inevitable consequences, and it seemed necessary that the assassins be involved in politics, given the peculiar conditions of our era.

The new "religious" novel, *Son of the Morning,* is rather painfully autobiographical, in part—but only in part. The religion it explores is not institutional but rather subjective, intensely personal, so as a novel is perhaps like the earlier three I have mentioned, or the racing novel, *With*

Shuddering Fall. Rather, *Son of the Morning* is a novel that begins with wide ambitions and ends very, very humbly.

PHILLIPS. Somewhere in print, you called *The Assassins* the favorite of your novels. It received very mixed reviews. I've often thought that book was misread. For instance, I think the "martyr" in that novel arranged for his own assassination, true? And that his wife was never really attacked outside the country house; she never left it. Her maiming was all confined within her head.

OATES. What a fine surprise! You read the scene exactly as it was meant to be read. Even well-intentioned reviewers missed the point; so far as I know, only two or three people read Yvonne's scene as I had intended it to be read. Yet the hallucinatory nature of the "dismemberment" scene is explicit. And Andrew Petrie did, of course, arrange for his own assassination, as the novel makes clear in its concluding pages.

The novel has been misread, of course, partly because it's rather long, and I think reviewers, who are usually pressed for time, simply treated it in a perfunctory way. I'm not certain that it is my favorite novel. But it is, or was, my most ambitious. It involved a great deal of effort, the collating of the passages (and memories) that differ from or contradict one another. One becomes attached to such perverse, maddening ugly ducklings, but I can't really blame reviewers for being impatient with the novel. As my novels grow in complexity, they please me more and please the "literary world" hardly at all—a sad situation, but not a paralyzing one.

PHILLIPS. It's not merely a matter of complexity. One feels that your fiction has become more and more urgent, more subjective and less concerned with the outward details of this world—especially in *Childwold*. Was that novel a deliberate attempt to write a "poetic novel"? Or is it a long poem?

OATES. I don't see that *Childwold* is not concerned with the outward details of the world. In fact, it is made up almost entirely of visual details—of the natural world, of the farm the Bartletts own, and of the small city they gravitate to. But you are right, certainly, in suggesting that it is a "poetic novel." I had wanted to create a prose poem in the form of a novel, or a novel in the form of a prose poem: the exciting thing for me was to deal with the tension that arose between the image-centered structure of poetry, and the narrative-centered and linear structure of the interplay of personas that constitutes a novel. In other words, poetry focuses on the image, the particular thing, or emotion, or feeling; while prose fiction focuses upon motion through time and space. The one impulse is toward stasis, the other toward movement. Between the two impulses, there arose a certain tension that made the writing of the novel quite challenging. I suppose it is an experimental work, but I shy away from thinking of my work in those terms: it seems to me there is a certain self-consciousness about anyone who sets himself up as an "experimental" writer. All writing is experimental.

But experimentation for its own sake doesn't much interest me; it seems to belong to the early sixties, when Dadaism was being rediscovered. In a sense, we are all post-*Wake* writers, and it's Joyce, and only Joyce, who casts a long, terrifying shadow. . . . The problem is that virtuoso writing appeals to the intellect and tends to leave one's emotions untouched. When I read aloud to my students the last few pages of *Finnegans Wake,* and come to that glorious, heartbreaking final section ("But you're changing, acoolsha, you're changing from me, I can feel"), I think I'm able to communicate the almost overwhelmingly beautiful emotion behind it, and the experience certainly leaves *me* shaken. But it would be foolish to think that the average reader, even the average intelligent reader, would be willing to labor at the *Wake,* through those hundreds of dense pages, in order to attain an emotional and spiritual sense of the work's wholeness, as well as its genius. Joyce's *Ulysses* appeals to me more: that graceful synthesis of the "naturalistic" and the "symbolic" suits my temperament, also. . . . I try to write books that can be read in one way by a literal-minded reader, and in quite another way by a reader alert to symbolic abbreviation and paradisaic elements. And yet, it's the same book—or nearly. A trompe l'oeil, a work of *as if.*

PHILLIPS. Very little has been made of the humor in your work, the parody. Some of your books—like *Expensive People, The Hungry Ghosts,* and parts of *Wonderland*—seem almost Pinteresque in their absurd humor. Is Pinter an influence? Do you consider yourself a comedic writer?

OATES. There's been humor of a sort in my writing from the first, but it's understated, or deadpan. Pinter has never struck me as very funny. Doesn't he really write tragedy?

I liked Ionesco at one time. And Kafka. And Dickens (from whom Kafka learned certain effects, though he uses them, of course, for different ends). I respond to English satire, as I mentioned earlier. Absurdist, or "dark," or "black," or whatever: what isn't tragic belongs to the comic spirit. The novel is nourished by both and swallows both up greedily.

PHILLIPS. What have you learned from Kafka?

OATES. To make a jest of the horror. To take myself less seriously.

PHILLIPS. John Updike has been accused of a lack of violence in his work. You're often accused of portraying too much. What is the function of violence in your work?

OATES. Given the number of pages I have written, and the "violent" incidents dispersed throughout them, I rather doubt that I am a violent writer in any meaningful sense of the word. Certainly the violence is minimal in a novel like *them,* which purported to be a naturalistic work set in Detroit in the sixties; real life is much more chaotic.

PHILLIPS. Which of your books gave you the greatest trouble to write? And which gave you the greatest pleasure or pride?

OATES. Both *Wonderland* and *The Assassins* were difficult to write. *Expensive People* was the least difficult. I am personally very fond of *Childwold,* since it represents, in a kind of diffracted way, a complete world made of memory and imagination, a blending together of different times. It always surprises me that other people find that novel admirable, because to me it seems very private . . . the sort of thing a writer can only do once.

Aside from that, *Do With Me What You Will* gives me a fair amount of pleasure, and of course, I am closest to the novel I finished most recently, *Son of the Morning.* (In general, I think we are always fondest of the books we've just completed, aren't we? For obvious reasons.) But then I think of Jules and Maureen and Loretta of *them,* and I wonder if perhaps that isn't my favorite novel, after all.

PHILLIPS. For whom do you write—yourself, your friends, your "public"? Do you imagine an ideal reader for your work?

OATES. Well, there are certain stories, like those in *The Hungry Ghosts,* which I have written for an academic community and, in some cases, for specific people. But in general, the writing writes itself—I mean a character determines his or her "voice," and I must follow along. Had I my own way, the first section of *The Assassins* would be much abbreviated. But it was impossible to shut Hugh Petrie up once he got going; and, long and painful and unwieldy as his section is, it's nevertheless been shortened. The problem with creating such highly conscious and intuitive characters is that they tend to perceive the contours of the literary landscape in which they dwell and, like Kach of *Childwold,* try to guide or even take over the direction of the narrative. Hugh did not want to die, and so his section went on and on, and it isn't an exaggeration to say that I felt real dismay in dealing with him.

Son of the Morning is a first-person narration by a man who is addressing himself throughout to God. Hence the whole novel is a prayer. Hence the ideal reader is, then, God. Everyone else, myself included, is secondary.

PHILLIPS. Do you consider yourself religious? Do you feel that there is a firm religious base to your work?

OATES. I wish I knew how to answer this. Having completed a novel that is saturated with what Jung calls the God experience, I find that I know less than ever about myself and my own beliefs. I have beliefs, of course, like everyone—but I don't always believe in them. Faith comes and goes. God diffracts into a bewildering plenitude of elements—the environment, love, friends and family, career, profession, "fate," biochemical harmony or disharmony, whether the sky is slate gray or a bright, mesmerizing blue. These elements then coalesce again into something seemingly unified. But it's a human predilection, isn't it—our tendency to see, and to wish to see, what we've projected outward upon the universe from our own soul? I hope to continue to write about religious experience, but at the moment I feel quite drained, quite depleted. And as baffled as ever.

PHILLIPS. You mentioned Jung. Is Freud also an influence? Laing?

OATES. Freud I have always found rather limited and biased; Jung and Laing I've read only in recent years. As an undergraduate at Syracuse

University, I discovered Nietzsche and it may be the Nietzschean influence (which is certainly more provocative than Freud's) that characterizes some of my work. I don't really know consciously. For me, stories usually begin—or began, since I write so few of them now—out of some magical association with characters and their settings. There are some stories (I won't say which ones) which evolved almost entirely out of their settings, usually rural.

PHILLIPS. Your earliest stories and novels seem influenced by Faulkner and by Flannery O'Connor. Are these influences you acknowledge? Are there others?

OATES. I've been reading for so many years, and my influences must be so vast—it would be very difficult to answer. An influence I rarely mention is Thoreau, whom I read at a very impressionable age (my early teens). And Henry James, O'Connor, and Faulkner, certainly. Katherine Anne Porter and Dostoyevsky. An odd mixture.

PHILLIPS. The title *Wonderland,* and frequent other allusions in your work, point toward a knowledge of, if not an affinity for, Lewis Carroll. What is the connection, and is it an important one?

OATES. Lewis Carroll's *Alice in Wonderland* and *Through the Looking-Glass* were my very first books. Carroll's wonderful blend of illogic and humor and horror and justice has always appealed to me, and I had a marvelous time teaching the books last year in my undergraduate course.

PHILLIPS. Was there anything you were particularly afraid of, as a child?

OATES. Like most children, I was probably afraid of a variety of things. The unknown? The possibility of those queer, fortuitous metamorphoses that seem to overtake certain of Carroll's characters? Physical pain? Getting lost? . . . My proclivity for the irreverent and the nonsensical was either inspired by Carroll, or confirmed by him. I was always, and continue to be, an essentially mischievous child. This is one of my best-kept secrets.

PHILLIPS. You began writing at a very early age. Was it encouraged by your family? Was yours a family of artistic ambitions?

OATES. In later years, my parents have become "artistic," but when they were younger, and their children were younger, they had no time for anything much except work. I was always encouraged by my parents, my grandmother, and my teachers to be creative. I can't remember when I first began to tell stories—by drawing, it was then—but I must have been very young. It was an instinct I followed quite naturally.

PHILLIPS. Much of your work is set in the 1930s, a period during which you were merely an infant at best. Why is that decade so important to your work or vision?

OATES. Since I was born in 1938, the decade is of great significance to me. This was the world of my parents, who were young adults at the time, the world I was born into. The thirties seem in an odd way still "living" to me, partly in terms of my parents' and grandparents' memories, and partly in terms of its treatment in books and films. But the twenties is too remote—lost to me entirely! I simply haven't had the imaginative power to get that far back.

I identify very closely with my parents in ways I can't satisfactorily explain. The lives they lived before I was born seem somehow accessible to me. Not directly, of course, but imaginatively. A memory belonging to my mother or father seems almost to "belong" to me. In studying old photographs with my parents—as if I'd known them when they were, let's say, only teenagers. Is this odd? I wonder. I rather suspect others share in their family's experiences and memories without knowing quite how.

PHILLIPS. When we were undergraduates together at Syracuse, you already were something of a legend. It was said you'd finish a novel, turn it over, and immediately begin writing another on the backside. When both sides were covered, you'd throw it all out, and reach for clean paper. Was it at Syracuse that you first became aware you were going to be a writer?

OATES. I began writing in high school, consciously training myself by writing novel after novel, and always throwing them out when I completed them. I remember a three-hundred-page book of interrelated stories that must have been a modeling on Hemingway's *In Our Time* (I hadn't yet read *Dubliners*), though the subject matter was much more romantic than Hemingway's. I remember a bloated, trifurcated novel that had as its vague model *The Sound and the Fury*. . . . Fortunately these experiences were thrown away and I haven't remembered them until this moment.

Syracuse was a very exciting place academically and intellectually for me. I doubt that I missed more than half a dozen classes in my four years there—and none of them in English.

PHILLIPS. I remember you were in a sorority. It is incredible to contemplate you as a "sorority girl."

OATES. My experience in a sorority wasn't disastrous, but merely despairing. (I tried to resign but found out that upon joining I had signed some sort of legal contract.) However, I did make some close friends in the sorority, so the experience wasn't a total loss. I would never do it again, certainly. In fact, it's one of the three or four things in my entire life I would never do again.

PHILLIPS. Why was life in a Syracuse sorority so despairing? Have you written about it?

OATES. The racial and religious bigotry; the asininity of "secret ceremonies"; the moronic emphasis upon "activities" totally unrelated to—in fact antithetical to—intellectual exploration; the bullying of the presumably weak by the presumably strong; the deliberate pursuit of an attractive "image" for the group as a whole, no matter how cynical the individuals might have been; the aping of the worst American traits—boosterism, God-fearing-ism, smug ignorance, a craven worship of conformity; the sheer *mess* of the place once one got beyond downstairs. . . . I tried to escape my junior year, but a connection between sororities and the Dean of Women and the university housing office made escape all but impossible, and it seemed that, in my freshman naïveté, I had actually signed some sort of contract that had "legal" status . . . all of which quite cowed me. I remember a powdered and perfumed alum explaining the sorority's exclusion of Jews and blacks: "You see we have conferences at the Lake Placid Club, and wouldn't it be a shame if *all* our members couldn't attend. . . . Why, it would be embarrassing for them, wouldn't it?"

I was valedictorian of my class, the class of 1960. I fantasized beginning my address by saying: "I managed to do well academically at Syracuse despite the concerted efforts of my sorority to prevent me . . ."

I haven't written about it, and never will. It's simply too stupid and trivial a subject. To even *care* about such adolescent nonsense, one would have to have the sensitivity of a John O'Hara, who seemed to have taken it all seriously.

PHILLIPS. I recall you won the poetry contest at Syracuse in your senior year. But your books of poetry appear relatively later than your fiction. Were you always writing poetry?

OATES. No, really I began to write poetry later. The poetry still comes with difficulty, I must admit. Tiny lyric asides, droll wry enigmatic statements: they aren't easy, are they? I'm assembling a book which I think will be my last—of poems, I mean. No one wants to read a novelist's poetry. It's enough—too much, in fact—to deal with the novels. Strangely enough, my fellow poets have been magnanimous indeed in accepting me as a poet. I would not have been surprised had they ignored me, but in fact they've been wonderfully supportive and encouraging, which contradicts the general notion that poets are highly competitive and jealous of one another's accomplishments . . .

PHILLIPS. You say no one wants to read a novelist's poetry. What about Robert Penn Warren? John Updike? I supposed Allen Tate and James Dickey are poets who happen to write novels . . .

OATES. I suppose I was thinking only of hypothetical reactions to my own poetry. Robert Penn Warren aside, however, there *is* a tendency on the part of critics to want very much to categorize writers. Hence one is either a writer of prose or of poetry. If Lawrence hadn't written those novels, he would have been far more readily acclaimed as one of the greatest poets in the language. As it is, however, his poetry has been neglected (at least until recently).

PHILLIPS. *By the North Gate,* your first book, is a collection of short stories, and you continue to publish them. Is the short story your greatest love? Do you hold with the old adage that it is more difficult to write a good story than a novel?

OATES. Brief subjects require brief treatments. There is *nothing* so difficult as a novel, as anyone knows who has attempted one; a short story is bliss to write set beside a novel of even ordinary proportions.

But in recent years, I haven't been writing much short fiction. I don't quite know why. All my energies seem to be drawn in longer works. It's probably the case that my period of greatest productivity is behind me, and I'm becoming more interested in focusing upon a single work, usually a novel, and trying to "perfect" it section by section and page by page.

PHILLIPS. Nevertheless, you've published more short stories perhaps than any other writer in America today. I remember that when you chose the twenty-one stories that compose *The Wheel of Love,* you picked from some ninety that had been in magazines the two years since your previous collection. What will become of the seventy or so stories you didn't include in that collection? Were some added to later collections? Will you ever go back and pick up uncollected work?

OATES. If I'm serious about a story, I preserve it in book form: otherwise I intend it to be forgotten. This is true of course for poems and reviews and essays, as well. I went back and selected a number of stories that for thematic reasons were not included in *The Wheel of Love,* and put them into a collection called *The Seduction and Other Stories.* Each of the story collections is organized around a central theme and is meant to be read as a whole—the arrangement of the stories being a rigorous one, not at all haphazard.

PHILLIPS. You don't drink. Have you tried any consciousness-expanding drugs?

OATES. No. Even tea (because of caffeine) is too strong for me. I must have been born with a rather sensitive constitution.

PHILLIPS. Earlier you mentioned Hugh Petrie in *The Assassins.* He is but one of many deranged characters in your books. Have you known any genuine madmen?

OATES. Unfortunately, I have been with a small number of persons who might be considered mentally disturbed. And others, strangers, are sometimes drawn my way; I don't know why.

Last week when I went to the university, I wasn't allowed to teach my large lecture class because, during the night, one of my graduate students had received a telephone call from a very angry, distraught man who announced that he intended to kill me. So I had to spend several hours sequestered away with the head of our department and the head of security at the university and two special investigators from the Windsor City

Police. The situation was more embarrassing than disturbing. It's the first time anyone has so explicitly and publicly threatened my life—there have been sly, indirect threats made in the past, which I've known enough not to take seriously.

(The man who called my student is a stranger to us all, not even a resident of Windsor. I have no idea why he's so angry with me. But does a disturbed person need a reason. . . ?)

PHILLIPS. How about the less threatening, but nonetheless hurtful, reactions of friends and relatives—any reactions to conscious or unconscious portraits in your work?

OATES. My parents (and I, as a child) appear very briefly in *Wonderland,* glimpsed by the harassed young hero on his way to, or from, Buffalo. Otherwise, there are no portraits of family or relatives in my writing. My mother and father both respond (rather touchingly at times) to the setting of my stories and novels, which they recognize. But since there is nothing of a personal nature in the writing, I have not experienced any difficulties along those lines.

PHILLIPS. Aside from the singular incident at the university, what are the disadvantages of being famous?

OATES. I'm not aware of being famous, especially in Windsor, where the two major bookstores, Coles', don't even stock my books. The number of people who are "aware" of me, let alone who read my writing, is very small. Consequently, I enjoy a certain degree of invisibility and anonymity at the university, which I might not have at an American university—which is one of the reasons I am so much at home here.

PHILLIPS. Are you aware of any personal limitations?

OATES. Shyness has prevented me from doing many things; also the amount of work and responsibility here at Windsor.

PHILLIPS. Do you feel that you have any conspicuous or secret flaw as a writer?

OATES. My most conspicuous flaw is . . . well, it's so conspicuous that anyone could discern it. And my secret flaw is happily secret.

PHILLIPS. What are the advantages of being a woman writer?

OATES. Advantages! Too many to enumerate, probably. Since, being a woman, I can't be taken altogether *seriously* by the sort of male critics who rank writers 1, 2, 3 in the public press, I am free, I suppose, to do as I like. I haven't much sense of, or interest in, competition; I can't even grasp what Hemingway and the epigonic Mailer mean by battling it out with the other talent in the ring. A work of art has never, to my knowledge, displaced another work of art. The living are no more in competition with the dead than they are with the living. . . . Being a woman allows me a certain invisibility. Like Ellison's *Invisible Man*. (My long journal, which must be several hundred pages by how, has the title "Invisible Woman." Because a woman, being so mechanically judged by her appearance, has the advantage of hiding within it—of being absolutely whatever she knows herself to be, in contrast with what others imagine her to be. I feel no connection at all with my physical appearance and have often wondered whether this was a freedom any man—writer or not—might enjoy.)

PHILLIPS. Do you find it difficult to write from the point of view of the male?

OATES. Absolutely not. I am as sympathetic with any of my male characters as I am with any of my female characters. In many respects, I am closest in temperament to certain of my male characters—Nathan Vickery of *Son of the Morning*, for instance. I feel an absolute kinship with him. "The Kingdom of God *is* within."

PHILLIPS. Can you tell the sex of a writer from the prose?

OATES. Never.

PHILLIPS. What male writers have been especially effective, do you think, in their depiction of women?

OATES. Tolstoy, Lawrence, Shakespeare, Flaubert . . . very few, really. But then very few women have been effective in their depiction of men.

PHILLIPS. Do you enjoy writing?

OATES. I do enjoy writing, yes. A great deal. And I feel somewhat at a loss, aimless and foolishly sentimental, and disconnected, when I've finished one work and haven't yet become absorbed in another. All of us who write work out a conviction that we are participating in some sort of communal activity. Whether my role is writing, or reading and responding, might not be very important. I take seriously Flaubert's statement that we must love one another in our art as the mystics love one another in God. By honoring one another's creation, we honor something that deeply connects us all and goes beyond us.

Of course, writing is only one activity out of a vast number of activities that constitute our lives. It seems to be the one that some of us have concentrated on, as if we were fated for it. Since I have a great deal of faith in the processes and the wisdom of the unconscious, and have learned from experience to take lightly the judgments of the ego, and its inevitable doubts, I never find myself constrained to answer such questions. Life is energy, and energy is creativity. And even when we as individuals pass on, the energy is retained in the work of art, locked in it and awaiting release if only someone will take the time and the care to unlock it . . .

(1978)

Karl Shapiro
Photograph by Layle Silbert

Karl Shapiro

At the time of the interview in 1984, Karl Shapiro was living half the year in Davis, California (where he had taught before retirement), and half the year on New York's Upper West Side, twenty blocks north of Zabar's, the landmark food emporium, and ten blocks south of Columbia University. This interview took place in his Morningside Heights apartment, where he lived with his third wife, the distinguished translator and editor Sophie Wilkins. The view from their roomy apartment overlooks the enormous Cathedral of St. John the Divine. During this period, Shapiro was busy with two projects—putting together his thirteenth book of poems, New & Selected Poems 1940–1986 *(1987), and finishing his two-volume autobiography.*

During his lifetime, Shapiro received numerous honors, including the Pulitzer Prize in 1945 for his second volume of verse, V-Letter and Other Poems; *the Bollingen Prize in Poetry in 1960 for his* Selected Poems—*a 333-page collection culled from thirty years' work; appointment as consultant in poetry to the Library of Congress (the position now called Poet Laureate); and membership in the American Academy and Institute of Arts and Letters. Perhaps his best-known volumes of outspoken criticism are* To Abolish Children and Other Essays *(1968) and* The Poetry Wreck: Selected Essays 1950–1970 *(1975).*

Then seventy-two, Shapiro appeared energetic and handsome, with a full head of white hair and expressive dark eyes behind black plastic-rimmed glasses. One was struck by his gentleness, his fine manners, and his soft voice. From his essays, one would have expected a bit of a wild man. During the course of the interview—done over one long December day—he chain-smoked and sipped white wine. His apartment

*was lined with books, and he would reach out for titles to illustrate
points.*

•   •   •

PHILLIPS. You were in the army during World War II when your first
two books of poems, *Person, Place and Thing* and *V-Letter and Other
Poems,* came out in this country. When you returned from the war, were
you aware of having become the literary spokesman of your generation?

SHAPIRO. Words like "spokesman" and "touchstone" took me
completely by surprise. For very real reasons. Not only had I been out of
the country when my first two books were published, but I have always
been "out of the country" in the sense that I never had what ordinarily is
thought of as a literary life, or been part of a literary group. What psy-
chiatrists nowadays call a support system. I never had any of that and
still don't. I've never magnetized toward centers like New York. I never
even thought of living in New York. When I first started to publish single
poems, the place I thought of was Chicago, since *Poetry* magazine was
there. And you didn't have to live in Chicago to have something printed
by them. I thought *Poetry* was preferable to any magazine that I knew of
in New York, except perhaps *Partisan Review,* and that was relatively
new and wasn't specifically poetry, anyway. So when I was in the army in
New Guinea, and finally got the reviews that people sent of my first
book, they were all very heady to me. Using words like "spokesman." I
was baffled. I wasn't sure what the reviewers were talking about, because
I had no association with anybody. I had never met a poet in my life before winning the Pulitzer in 1945. Well, that's not strictly true; when I
went to Johns Hopkins in 1939, W. H. Auden gave a private reading to a
group of special literature students, and I was one. I shook hands with
him. As it happened, at that time he was my idol, above all others as a
modern poet, and that experience was a very sustaining one. But I could
hardly say I "knew" him.

PHILLIPS. How old was Auden then?

SHAPIRO. Well, in 1939—he was born in 1907—he was quite
young. He looked it. And he did something that impressed me to no end.
He read at this club called the Tudor and Stuart, at Johns Hopkins, and

he didn't have his book with him. He recited almost the whole book beautifully, and it included the elegy on Freud and the one on Yeats. That was a magnificent experience! But from my point of view, it was something like a rustic going to the opera. At that time, I hadn't published a thing except a privately printed book.

PHILLIPS. Is it true that your wife put your first and second books together in your absence during the war?

SHAPIRO. The first really was an adaptation of a long group of poems that James Laughlin at New Directions had printed in an anthology called *Five Young American Poets*. Those were published at the time I was about to be sent overseas, and I begged Laughlin to publish a separate book of mine instead of putting them in that anthology. Well, I was unknown and he wouldn't do it. He never did a book of mine. But that anthology was the occasion of my first reviews, and they were good ones. After I went overseas, my wife, Evalyn, in fact moved from Baltimore to New York for the purpose of getting more of my work published. She was working as a secretary in some office in Baltimore and had no real ties. She did have friends in Manhattan. I'd send Evalyn individual poems as they were finished. I had no way of sending them to magazines. We were on the move all the time and mail was heavily censored and all mail at that time was sent by ship, which took three to four months. It wasn't until later in the war that they began to photograph letters, those letters called "V-letters," which gave the title to my second collection. Then the mail became faster. Anyway, Evalyn did meet publishers, especially Reynal and Hitchcock, who were then a new firm. Albert Erskine, my lifelong editor, was the editor there and he accepted the book that I called *Person, Place and Thing*. And when that firm died, I followed Erskine to Random House.

PHILLIPS. What were the physical circumstances during the war? Did you have much time off?

SHAPIRO. I was drafted a year before the war, when it was a one-year, peacetime draft that people have forgotten about now. And I was in almost a year when Pearl Harbor happened, so I couldn't get out. But because I was from Baltimore, I was sent to the Medical Corps—all of us who were drafted from Baltimore that first day were sent to the Medical

Corps. I guess they knew the war was coming and were trying to build it up. A lot of us were orderlies from hospitals, but many were clerks, stenographers, and so on. I was studying in a library school at the time—I was going to be a librarian. But I couldn't take the final exam because I was drafted. Nobody had ever heard of student deferment in those days. Because of my background of two years of college at Johns Hopkins, they put me in the company headquarters and gave me a typewriter.

PHILLIPS. Did you have access to a typewriter throughout the war?

SHAPIRO. I did. Because I became the company clerk and even in very bad situations, like combat, my job was to be on the typewriter. Although I carried a .45 and a carbine like everyone else.

PHILLIPS. But what about the availability of a library? You also wrote *Essay on Rime* when you were stationed in the South Pacific. It's full of quotes from Eliot, Auden, Yeats, Cummings, Crane . . .

SHAPIRO. There weren't that many quotes. Besides, I had a book. I'd met William Van O'Connor [later a literary critic] in New Guinea, and we became friends right away. He was stationed at Fort Morely and so was I. We were waiting to go someplace else, and Bill gave me his copy of *The Oxford Book of Modern Verse,* which Yeats had edited. I had that book and I had quotes in my head and there was always a Bible. And that was about it. I later heard there was an army library nearby, but if there was I had never heard of it. Anyway, I wrote *Essay on Rime* to amuse myself. We had been told that we were going to be in one spot for ninety days with nothing to do. So we were just sitting there waiting to be shipped to the Dutch East Indies. Well, I had the office and the typewriter and the paper, so I blocked out a poem. I figured I wanted to write a poem about poetry, an essay like Pope's. I actually diagrammed it—I had never done that before in my life. But I diagrammed how many sections there would be, how many lines per section, how much on prosody and how much on language, and so on. I figured precisely how many lines I would write a day to get the book done in ninety days, and I did it. It was thirty lines a day, and I went to the office every day and wrote those thirty lines. I had no reports to write. The office was deserted.

PHILLIPS. It's a prodigious feat.

SHAPIRO. Well, yes, but you see, I had it all in my head—I had read everything on prosody before I was drafted. Don't forget I'd been working in a big library and I knew a lot about prosody. Nobody ever read prosody books except me. And the rest of the stuff in the poem was simply my ideas about Auden and Williams and the rest.

PHILLIPS. Then you mailed the book off to your wife?

SHAPIRO. Not all at once. I sent her sections, and a piece appeared in the *Kenyon Review* and another in the *Southern Review.*

PHILLIPS. This was in the days before duplicating machines. Did anything ever get lost in the mail?

SHAPIRO. I don't recall that it did. I kept carbons. But it took a year for the bound copy of my first book to reach me. It nearly drove me crazy, waiting.

PHILLIPS. When did you realize you were going to become a writer?

SHAPIRO. Probably when I was in high school, because I already had a reputation for being a poet. The English teachers always liked what I did and put my stuff up on the bulletin boards. I never had any idea of publication, though. In high school, in Baltimore, I wrote a sonnet about Mahatma Gandhi. From which I can only remember one line, "Dim adumbrations of a dim intent." Not bad for high school, but it was supposed to be a favorable poem about Gandhi! I would play hooky from school in Baltimore, which is an historic place, and go to places like Federal Hill, where you can see where the American flag was that inspired Francis Scott Key to write "The Star Spangled Banner." I would go there and write love poems. I was seventeen or eighteen—a little late for high school, because I had to transfer to three different schools because of my family moving about.

PHILLIPS. Somewhere in print, you've said that you only had a "half-education."

SHAPIRO. Well, "half" is an exaggeration. I went to the University of Virginia and quit after the first semester. Then five years later, I went to Johns Hopkins and studied English literature, Greek, Latin, French, and history. I was there only two years. I was in some kind of accelerated thing. I was supposed to go for two years, then enter the graduate school. But I had to drop out. So what I don't have is a formal education in a sense that I could pass the Graduate Record Exam, or whatever they call it. My education is at best spotty.

PHILLIPS. What did your father do?

SHAPIRO. He was a salesman. So many fathers of American writers were—Arthur Miller's, Tennessee Williams's. My father was ingenious. He made special products out of the waste products of oil. I think he was the first one whose idea it was to put motor oil into cans and sell them in grocery stores. He did things like that and got people to produce his ideas for him. Before Baltimore, we lived in Virginia, in Norfolk, where he had his own business. But during the Depression, I never was able to find a job. My father would beg me to, but it was impossible. So until he finally invented jobs for my brother and me, I was allowed to stay home and write.

PHILLIPS. Most war poems aren't remembered. But several of yours are among your best. Is war still a factor in your dreams or outlook? Did the war permanently change you?

SHAPIRO. Oh, yes, I think it did. It probably does to anybody who was ever in a war. The first book review I ever wrote was for *Poetry* magazine, in the thirties. They asked me to write a review of the poets of the First World War who had just published new collections. There was Siegfried Sassoon, and Edmund Blunden, and others. And I went and dug their old books out of the library and noticed they hadn't been read since the First World War. It struck me as very sad that these men, who were now probably in their fifties or so and had never gotten over their experiences, were forgotten. Passed over. They were all in the trenches, too. I remarked in my review that war seems to be a permanent tattoo, or scar, on those who have been in it.

PHILLIPS. Some of your later poems— "The Phenomenon" and "In the Waxworks"—seem concerned with nightmares, whereas your earlier work is very rational, almost idealistic. Are you aware of undergoing any personality changes that could account for that?

SHAPIRO. I'm not aware of any changes in personality or outlook. "The Phenomenon" might be called a war poem, too. I was very surprised when the *New Yorker* accepted it. The other one was about the honky-tonk in Baltimore, where the low bars and cheap hotels and burlesque houses are. I was writing about the unconscious part of a civilized city. Of all the stuff that drifts to the bottom.

PHILLIPS. In your early poems, it strikes me that you were somewhat of a verbal voluptuary. I think of a poem like "Buick," for instance, which I love to read aloud just for the sounds of it. Were Hopkins or Hart Crane influences?

SHAPIRO. Oh, definitely, both of them. And even to this day, I have never lost my admiration for and involvement with them. I very much resented the critical treatment of Crane by people like Yvor Winters. "Buick" was a love poem, so I was trying to make it as sensuous as possible. I always felt that poem was perhaps the first Pop poem: you know, taking a beer can and making it six feet high. I was taking the image of this car, the Buick itself, which is still a voluptuous automobile, I tell you—I was in one recently.

PHILLIPS. The Buick in your poem—was that a car you owned?

SHAPIRO. I never owned one. If you want to know how I got the idea of writing that poem, I was hitchhiking back to the army base one night between Petersburg, Virginia, and Baltimore, and an officer from my camp stopped for me. He drove what appeared to be a new Buick. Now there is a straight road that goes from Richmond to Fredericksburg, and at that time of night there were no cars on it. He got this thing up to 100 mph. And that was like flying—all those beautiful lights on the dashboard moving around.

PHILLIPS. Do you still hold Auden's work in as high esteem as you did?

SHAPIRO. Yes, I do. And unlike most critics I've read, I think that Auden's later work is his best—those poems written in a kind of adaptation of the Horatian odes which he did so well and which served him so well—all the poems he wrote while he lived in Austria at the end of his life. I think they are certainly among his finest. They are not the big, portentous poems, like "For the Time Being," though things like "For the Time Being" are magnificent.

PHILLIPS. In the middle or late fifties, Whitman became very important to you—almost in religious terms. Can you comment on that? And what about Poe?

SHAPIRO. As a matter of fact, I was born under the same roof where Poe died, the same Baltimore hospital where there is a plaque on the wall. Whenever people came from out of town, I would always take them to Poe's grave, which was in a slum of the city even when I lived there. It is a very ugly tombstone. The decorations on it were sent from France.

PHILLIPS. Why did the French love Poe?

SHAPIRO. Because Baudelaire discovered him and, well, his symbolism. Poe was the father of symbolism. Now, I am on the other side of the railroad tracks from symbolism, so Poe never appealed to me. Every kid read his stories and his poems. We used to memorize "The Bells." I could never take Poe seriously. On the other hand, there was Whitman. Whitman to me is the most fascinating of American poets. Whitman started to write the great poetry from scratch after he had written all that junk for newspapers, the sentimental lyrical poems. All of a sudden, he wrote *Leaves of Grass*. When I was teaching at the University of Nebraska, my friend James Miller was chairman of the English Department. He wrote the first book attempting to make a parallel between the structure of *Leaves of Grass* and the steps of the mystical experience, as in St. John of the Cross. I was completely bowled over by this, not having been able to explain how Whitman came to write "Song of Myself," which is unlike anything not only in American literature, but unique in all the world. The parallels to it are mystical literature. Miller tried to show that there was actually evidence for this kind of experience, which evidently happens at a particular moment in someone's life.

PHILLIPS. Whitman wasn't fashionable at the time you took him up.

SHAPIRO. When I saw the negative reaction to Whitman with the great ruling critics of the time, I couldn't believe it. Eliot never really gave up hammering away on Whitman—neither did Pound. Although Pound makes little concessions. Whitman, you know, didn't have any influence in this country until Allen Ginsberg came along. I am not crazy about the Whitman element in Ginsberg; it seems to me Ginsberg knew what Whitman was doing, but Ginsberg is a programmer and a propagandist and a politician. His poetry has suffered very badly. There's some great stuff—poetry of lamentation and so on—but so much of it is theatrical and phony.

PHILLIPS. We can see the Cathedral of St. John the Divine from here. I saw you at the dedication of the new Poets' Corner there. Who would you honor next, if it were up to you?

SHAPIRO. Let's see . . . who were the first three? Emily Dickinson, Walt Whitman, and Washington Irving, for some reason. Poe would have to be in there, and Melville and Emerson. And they should certainly install T. S. Eliot first among the moderns.

PHILLIPS. What about Wallace Stevens?

SHAPIRO. Oh, yes. I'd put him neck and neck with Eliot.

PHILLIPS. Robert Lowell?

SHAPIRO. Well, yes, if it comes to that.

PHILLIPS. We forgot Pound.

SHAPIRO. If I have an objection to Pound, it is that he remained more of a novice. He never really achieved what he set out to do. There is a very strange thing that happened to the modern poets, the famous ones. They all had one goal in common—to discover a form, or *the* form. Something like alchemists looking for the secret. Auden found his form—the ode. And William Carlos Williams wrote his best work in that kind of tercet form that he stumbled on after many years. But Eliot and Pound never succeeded in discovering the form in which they could write naturally. *The Cantos* remain a scaffolding for a structure that was never built.

PHILLIPS. Can you think of a good poet who has a bad ear?

SHAPIRO. Yes, but I can't say this on tape. The author of *All the King's Men.*

PHILLIPS. You didn't name him.

SHAPIRO. Of course not! It astonishes me that this can be—that there's a poet who has a tin ear. Some people say this is also true of Thomas Hardy. Hardy was a wonderful poet, but I don't think he was as tone deaf to the musicality of words as the other gentleman I alluded to. It happens infrequently, but it does happen. I imagine the Victorians said it about Browning. But it's certainly not true of the famous modern poets like Williams and Eliot and so on.

PHILLIPS. You once wrote that an astonishing fact about the twentieth century is that it is without its poet. Do you feel that is still true today?

SHAPIRO. Oh, no, I've changed my position on that. As some others already have said, in terms of English and American poets, it would be quite just to call this the Age of Auden. Not only because Auden was such a dominant and successful poet, but because he went through all the contradictory ideological phases, from Marx to God. He really is a representative in that sense. When Auden and his colleagues were writing their social revolutionary stuff in the late thirties, they were really representative of what the good poets were doing at the time—with the exception of Eliot and Pound. And Auden finally capitulated to the Church of England and Christianity and all that. I think he was the poor shadow of the kind of ideology which in one way or another pervades the poetic atmosphere today. We have a lot of politically biased poetry, even when it is political feminist. So the Age of Auden is as good as any name for where we are now. It could hardly be called the Age of Eliot or Pound or Williams or Ginsberg. Because they didn't have an umbrella.

PHILLIPS. In 1964, when you published *The Bourgeois Poet,* you made a clean break—not only with the poems of your past, but it seemed with all European art before the Renaissance. When did you recognize the futility of the well-made formal poem? And did you have a model—Ginsberg?

SHAPIRO. Certainly not Ginsberg! Influence is strange. Because one can be influenced powerfully in every way but technique. For instance, I would think Walt Whitman probably had more influence on my whole poetic thinking than anybody, but I never dreamed of trying to write in the Whitman manner. My precedent for the style of *The Bourgeois Poet* is French poetry. When I shipped out overseas, from Boston to Australia, it took forty days. I carried a baggage sack full of books, which is an awful thing to do because I had to carry them. There were no porters for a private or a corporal. Among the books I took was Baudelaire's *Flowers of Evil* in a bilingual edition. I also had a French dictionary and did some translations of my own on the ship. I think it was then and there that I fastened on the manner of *The Bourgeois Poet* poems. When I got to Australia, I published a privately printed book in which my first poems appeared. They're in that style. In fact, I still keep two of those poems in my latest collected poems: "The Dirty Word" and "The New Ring." I liked writing in that style very much, but at the time it seemed a dead end. It wasn't until the early sixties that I returned to the model and did more.

PHILLIPS. Was *The Bourgeois Poet* conceived and written as a book, or as individual poems that somehow came together?

SHAPIRO. No, no, as a book. I had a Guggenheim, to go to Europe, and I wanted to write an autobiography in verse. But I didn't know exactly how to do it. I took all the letters I had written to Evalyn. I carried them in a metal case. She still has those letters, incidentally—she's trying to sell them. With my permission, of course. Anyhow, I was trying to write about becoming a poet, using some of those letters as a basis. I found I could not write in Italy. I've since discovered that I can't write when I'm traveling. Later trips to Rome, London, all ended the same way. I love Europe, but whenever I go there, I feel I'm catching a disease. So I cut that trip short and came home. I lived in Nebraska then, and I had a study built in my garage. When it was done, I sat down and wrote *The Bourgeois Poet* poems straight off. I wrote one every day. There were ninety-four in the book, some quite long.

PHILLIPS. Did you complete more than the ninety-four?

SHAPIRO. God, yes. I had quite a lot I wanted to say then—either about the past or the present or from the point of view of a middle-class American poet, Jewish, and living in the middle of the United States and having come through certain things.

PHILLIPS. Will you publish some of the unpublished ones?

SHAPIRO. Probably not. I had given all that stuff to the Library of Congress a few years ago, and when I put together my recent volume of new and selected poems, I sent to the library and asked to see what was there. They sent me a stack a foot high. But I found almost nothing I would subsequently use. Albert Erskine thought I'd sent him too much to begin with. I don't think he ever really liked the book, although he published it. There was no real editing involved. He just told me to put the poems into some kind of sequence. It was too random at the beginning, he said. "This *is* Random House, isn't it?" I replied. He was not amused. So I found an order, and it was a book. My best selling one, I believe.

PHILLIPS. You wrote in that book that "the audience brings me news of my death." Have you been conscious of try-ing to overcome the critical decline, or to live up to your early reputation?

SHAPIRO. Well, no. When I wrote that I was, you know, very well received. I think I took that expression from Freud. Certain people were wrecked by success, like Dylan Thomas and Delmore Schwartz. I continued. In fact, I'm not so sure when I used that phrase, in that context, that I meant the race of Jews and not the race of poets.

PHILLIPS. I took it to mean poets.

SHAPIRO. Good. Because I always had this feeling—I've heard other Jews say—that when you can't find any other explanation for Jews, you say, "Well, they are poets." There are a great many similarities. This is a theme running all through my stuff from the very beginning. The poet is in exile whether he is or he is not. Because of what everybody knows about society's idea of the artist as a peripheral character and potential bum. Or troublemaker. Well, the Jews began their career of troublemaking by inventing the God whom Wallace Stevens considers the ultimate poetic idea. And so I always thought of myself as being both in and out of society at the same time. Like the way most artists probably feel in order to survive—you have to at least pretend that you are "seriously" in the world. Or actually perform in it while you know that in your own soul you are not in it at all. You are outside, observing it. You must know exactly what I mean.

PHILLIPS. I do. What does it mean to you to be a Jew? Christ is certainly one of your myths. What has being Jewish done to your work?

SHAPIRO. Just everything. I went through a period, like many middle-class Jews, in which I consciously drew away from the religion and everything Jewish in my life. And I think for a long time, say in the 1930s, I felt completely cured of the religious virus. And of course at that time, everybody was enveloped in radical politics and nobody took religion seriously. Even among poets—except Eliot. During the war, I became more interested in Christianity. I had a friend who used to write me enormously long letters. She was a very religious Catholic who wanted to become a nun. And she tried to convert me. She sent me a missal and a rosary, the works. I think I was hypnotized—she almost succeeded. I actually went to the Catholic chaplain at the time and asked for instruction. But he was too busy or didn't want to be bothered. That was the end of that. I think this is a phase many Jews go through. When I came back from the war, I returned to my original position of neutrality. I didn't think about religion and I didn't care. I felt I didn't have any personal stake in that kind of thinking. I had by then become known as a poet and was given very good jobs—teaching at universities, consultant in poetry at the Library of Congress. I considered myself above religion.

PHILLIPS. This doesn't sound like the author of *Poems of a Jew* speaking.

SHAPIRO. The actual turning point in my life was the voting of the Bollingen Prize to Ezra Pound. This sounds real crackpot, but it is true! I was one of the people on that jury, and I was the only one who voted against giving the prize to Pound. There was an enormous amount of publicity about it. It was a great blow to me, the publicity and the scandal. I was suddenly forced into a conscious decision to stand up and be counted as a Jew. Jewish organizations got in touch with me, Jewish papers wanted me to write things for them, make me a spokesman.

PHILLIPS. Were you against his getting the prize because you didn't think the *Pisan Cantos* good poetry, or because you abhorred Pound's politics?

SHAPIRO. Both. But I would have voted for the *Pisan Cantos* if it hadn't been for all the anti-Semitic and anti-American propaganda in them. Well, when the Bollingen Prize was kicked out of the Library of Congress and went to Yale, I was kept on the committee for two years, then dropped. From that point on, I began to write essays, like my book *In Defense of Ignorance,* in which I pointed to the politics in poetry. For instance, there is no question that Allen Tate and Eliot were attempting to set up an equivalent of the French Academy in the Library of Congress. They seemed to have the backing, people like Robert Lowell, who was young but definitely on the make as a critical culturalist and wanted to be in charge. From that point on, I became a kind of guerrilla fighter and sniper.

PHILLIPS. That does seem to be your reputation!

SHAPIRO. I was at Notre Dame just a few years ago, and one of the professors there said to me, "You don't know what effect *In Defense of Ignorance* had. It ripped the whole academic community in half!" I'm glad I wrote the book. I like it, and I still stand by my observations, although I wouldn't write it so violently now. I guess I really *am* in the Whitman tradition. The Eliot lecture I gave in Cincinnati also caused an uproar. Some of the professors got up and walked out in the middle of it. Then, when the piece was published in the *Saturday Review,* it caused another stir. All I did was call Eliot a theologian gone astray, a failed poet who hates originality. I said his importance exists only in the minds of a few critics. That's all. Oh, yes—I also called *Four Quartets* a deliberately bad book.

PHILLIPS. Do you feel upset when people walk out of your lectures?

SHAPIRO. I don't think about it. For two reasons. First, I have a sort of special status around English departments. I'm not really a professor, but a sort of mad guest. Second, I really wasn't alone in my feelings about Eliot and Modernism. When I was at the University of Nebraska, there was a core of people who felt the way I did—James Miller, Bernice Slote, others.

PHILLIPS. Do you deliver your lectures off the cuff?

SHAPIRO. Hardly. I write them out very carefully, the product of much rumination. Except for my Henry Miller piece. I did that one just a couple of days before I had to deliver it. I was sitting in a beautiful house overlooking a golf course and drinking Scotch. I wrote it while I was bombed, but it came out just the way I wanted. The woman who lived in the house left and put a whole bottle of Scotch in front of me. Which I drank. I had to get drunk to write that essay, because Evalyn couldn't stand the name of Henry Miller. She didn't want any of his books around the house. And she was with me at the time, so I couldn't write the essay in the hotel where we were staying. So I wrote it on the side, in a borrowed house. It's a kind of secret lecture.

PHILLIPS. You regarded Miller as a holy man. You called him "Gandhi with a penis." Do you still think of him in that way?

SHAPIRO. As a matter of fact, I don't. But you have to remember that when I wrote about Henry Miller, he was completely banned. I had always been a crusader against censorship. That was part of the reason for my strong stand. The books of Miller's that I owned were all smuggled into the States by friends who would visit Switzerland and get them past customs. I had illegal books, and this is great fun. But it was very important to me, because Miller never claimed that he was a writer. Henry James was a writer; Miller was a gabber, a prophet. And as far as pornography goes, he didn't aim to write erotica. He aimed to write the whole truth about the life he knew, which included sex. As a matter of fact, it is Miller who was the twentieth-century reincarnation of Whitman, not Ginsberg.

PHILLIPS. Let's return to *The Bourgeois Poet* one last time. That was your first and last thematic book of poems?

SHAPIRO. That was the only one of its kind, and I knew when I had come to the end of it, too. Actually, there is a plot in that book. It has to do with a female graduate student I was involved with.

PHILLIPS. It sounds as if the subject matter spilled over into your novel, *Edsel.*

SHAPIRO. Subject matter, yes. But the technique of *The Bourgeois Poet* I'd invented for myself, out of Baudelaire. And I invented the typographical form, which I got partly from a poet named Byron Vazakas. Do you remember him? Williams liked his stuff. He wrote prose poems in the shape of Oklahoma. And when I did the book, I didn't want my paragraphs to look exactly like prose, so I reversed the indentation process and had the body of the poems indented and the initial line extended to the left-hand margin. Like a pan handle.

PHILLIPS. So you call that book prose?

SHAPIRO. No, no. A lot of it is the sort of old-fashioned free verse of the King James Bible. It was an unconscious imitation of the Old Testament declamatory poetry. But that is a step backwards from the straight prose style in terms of versification. What I was sure of at the time was that the two traditional attributes of poetry—rhyme and versification— were not only nonessential, but artificial impediments to the poetic process.

PHILLIPS. But in your next book after that, *White-Haired Lover,* you returned to traditional verse forms.

SHAPIRO. I did and didn't. Most of them are conventional forms like a sonnet, but they're not what anyone would call good sonnet form. The meters are too bumpy. And there's no intent to conform to, say, the iambic patter. There's no inversion in the second foot, and that kind of thing. I didn't pay attention to that. In fact, I was doing what Eliot succeeded in doing when he discovered his own kind of iambic and free verse, which he called Websterian. Whether or not Webster was just a bad versifier, or trying to make the line conform to whatever speech was in his time, I don't know. But Eliot succeeded in adapting Webster to get a line which both is and is not iambic. And so, in other words, is loose.

PHILLIPS. Did the critics know what you were up to?

SHAPIRO. Not really. Those who liked the *"Bourgeois Poet"* style criticized the sonnet business, and said, "Who the hell writes sonnets in 1968?" That sort of thing.

PHILLIPS. A religious magazine once called you the "Mort Sahl of literary criticism." Do you take your critics seriously?

SHAPIRO. I try to avoid reading them. I forget who made that crack about Mort Sahl. It must have been during the time I was writing inflammatory stuff. There are a lot of critics who are very offended and irritated by my kind of criticism, and they attack me. I naturally expect that. Cleanth Brooks published a book in which he said he didn't know how to categorize me. I thought that was very flattering.

PHILLIPS. Do you want to talk about Dylan MaGoon?

SHAPIRO. Oh, sure. That was perhaps naïve of me, but I was very upset when I saw that Random House—my publisher—was publishing Rod McKuen, too. I had been invited to talk at the American Library Association, and I used that as an example of the degeneration of publishing poetry. I didn't want to throw in his real name, so I made him a mixture of Bob Dylan and Rod McKuen. In fact, McKuen's agent heard about it and got angry. He didn't do anything, though.

PHILLIPS. Have you ever been involved in a lawsuit?

SHAPIRO. Only over my suicide. Put "suicide" in quotes.

PHILLIPS. One would hope.

SHAPIRO. Yes, I'd like to get this in. I beat the American Medical Association in a lawsuit because of a libelous accusation. When I signed the settlement with their lawyers, there was a clause that said I would never publish anything about this. So let's publish it by all means! Here's what happened. Someone sent me a copy of the *Journal of the American Medical Association*. In it, a professor of psychiatry had published an article about Sylvia Plath and the plight of American authors and poets who commit suicide. At the beginning she gave a list, including Hart Crane, Hemingway, John Berryman, Randall Jarrell (which is risky—he may not have jumped), and so on. And I was on the list of suicides. I wrote this woman a letter demanding an explanation. She replied saying she hoped I still had my sense of humor. I did. She was a graduate student who got a Ph.D. in English and then an M.D.—very ambitious. So I forgot all about it, because I didn't know anybody who read the *Journal of the American Medical Association*. I just asked her to retract my name or take it out in case the thing was ever reprinted. A year later, she sold the article—intact—to the *Saturday Evening Post*. She'd never taken my name out. Now, I never see that magazine, either, but one of my students came to me waving it and said, "Have you seen this?" I was so upset and furious, I got a lawyer. It dragged on for two years. I had my local country lawyer, and the American Medical Association had a battery of Chicago lawyers. I sued the University of Iowa Medical School and the woman who wrote the article; I sued the *Saturday Evening Post* and the Curtis Publishing Company. My lawyer was even thinking of sending me to actors' school to learn how to act on the witness stand. I thought, my God, I can't take this. I lost twenty pounds in about two weeks. I had night sweats and all the symptoms of TB without spitting blood. It was the first serious illness I ever had in my life, all apparently psychosomatic. We finally made a settlement and it was enough for Teri, my second wife, to buy two houses and get into the real estate business. And the woman who wrote the article was promoted.

PHILLIPS. Of course. In addition to teaching, you've edited two magazines. Was editing better for your writing than teaching?

SHAPIRO. My editing was fortuitous. I had no training in it—does anybody? I worked purely by instinct. Writers told me I was a good editor, and I know I had some success in people and pieces I discovered. But when I was happy teaching, it was because I was teaching things like modern poetry, not teaching writing at all. But as it happened, more of the nonwriting academics moved in on the teaching of modern poetry and squeezed us out. They figured this was their business and I should shut up about teaching literature and let them do it. So for years and years, I taught nothing but this creative writing class—which disturbed me a lot. Because there was so little I could do, and there was no necessity for it except conviviality. It was a very pleasant way to spend the day. I used to have the students come to my house and we'd have wine. They'd read their poems and I'd attempt to comment. Recently, I went down to Philadelphia to give a writers' workshop, and it was all adults. I felt I failed them completely. I read their poems carefully, I said what I had to say about them, but I didn't have that much to say. And the conversation degenerated into, "Do you think this word will be better than that word?" I felt I hadn't earned my money.

PHILLIPS. What about when you edited *Poetry* in Chicago?

SHAPIRO. It wasn't good for my writing. For five years there was a constant involvement with poets from all over the world, not only corresponding with me, but coming to the office, too. But, you know, when I did write, I accomplished some of my best poems while working at *Poetry*— "Adam and Eve" and "The Bathers" and "The Alphabet." Actually, I have never written poetry with the view of having a book. I guess that is true of most poets who write our kind of poetry. You write the individual poem. This is unlike Yeats, who was a thematic poet. And he knew he was. Each book was going to represent some great mythological whatever.

PHILLIPS. Wasn't there some unpleasantness during the latter days when you edited *Prairie Schooner*?

SHAPIRO. A bit. It involved local morality. I was an editor in the middle of Nebraska. I accepted a short story by a man who was quite good, named Irving Drauss. It was a very good, clean story about a man who had been a graduate student who comes through a town similar to Lincoln, Nebraska, and stops off to see a woman he used to make love to. She is a beauty parlor operator. (That's where I got the idea for the beauty parlor operator in *Edsel*.) During the course of the story, the ex-graduate student recollects that, when he used to sit in the coffee room of the English department, the homosexual professors would gather to talk and gossip. I was going away, and had accepted the story, and it was in galley proof. When I returned, there was a note from the administration (who weren't supposed to have anything to do with this publication). They said the story had to be removed. I went to see them and said, "Hey—what's this?" They said, "The homosexual business." There were quite a few people in the closet at the time, and they didn't want to risk an investigation. They threatened to withdraw funds for the publication. I told the vice chancellor I had accepted the story and I was committed to print it. Since they thought it was so perilous or something, I was going to read it on the radio. (There was an FM station in Lincoln that played good music and even read some poems.) The station manager was delighted. And again I was threatened that I'd be arrested if I read it on the air. When I arrived, the sheriff's car was there, and everybody in Lincoln listened to their radios. I went ahead and read this story, which was rather sweet. And nothing happened. But after that, the handwriting was on the wall for me at the University of Nebraska. I looked for another job.

PHILLIPS. You seem to thrive on controversy. Your essay on the desirability of abolishing children, for instance. Do you ever get hate mail?

SHAPIRO. Not really hate mail. During the 1960s some students and young instructors at the University of California referred to me as a fascist. And when I published in *Esquire* some poems making fun of the protest movement, one of the San Francisco poets wrote me saying, "I see you're now publishing in men's fashion magazines." Pretty tame stuff.

PHILLIPS. How was your experience as consultant in poetry at the Library of Congress?

SHAPIRO. Very stormy, as a matter of fact. There was no job as such, because there were no duties as such. It was really at the beginning of the appointments. I think I'm the one who turned it from an honorific into a job. I created work.

PHILLIPS. You refused membership when you were first elected to the American Academy and Institute of Arts and Letters. Why?

SHAPIRO. No particular reason, except I didn't see what it was for. I disliked the idea of cultural academies. In a democracy, it can easily turn into something else. I gave the example of Thomas Jefferson stopping

George Washington when George founded the Society of Cincinnatus, which was going to be an hereditary officer corps. Jefferson said, "You can't do that, George." You can't, by God!

PHILLIPS. Who are your best friends? Other writers?

SHAPIRO. Not necessarily. Most of my friends have been made outside the occupation. I enjoy writers I think more than anybody else, any other kind of people. But I never go out of my way to be in a writers' situation. I've never accepted an invitation to go to a writers' colony, for instance. I don't see the point. I'm always writing what I want where I happen to be.

PHILLIPS. Then you can write anywhere?

SHAPIRO. Yes, except in a foreign country, as I said.

PHILLIPS. What are your normal working hours?

SHAPIRO. I don't have normal working hours. Although since I've been writing my autobiography, I've been working about three or four hours a day. Usually in the late morning or early afternoons.

PHILLIPS. At the typewriter?

SHAPIRO. I write prose at the typewriter. I don't like to work in the evening or after, partly because I use the typewriter. I think I'm keeping people awake upstairs.

PHILLIPS. This apartment must be a good working environment for you.

SHAPIRO. Oh, it's just perfect. It's got everything.

PHILLIPS. I haven't heard other people in the building.

SHAPIRO. There are children upstairs and sometimes they trample around on Sunday morning. But that's rare. Do you know what woke me up this morning? Somebody got a saxophone for Christmas. A saxophone is such a city sound. It's quite wonderful.

PHILLIPS. Was writing a novel a different process from writing poems?

SHAPIRO. Completely. It had nothing to do with poetry and I—never having written fiction, just one short story—didn't have any inhibitions. I wrote *Edsel* so fast. I wrote parts of it sitting on a beach with a portable typewriter in Tampa, Florida. There were some friends who were on that trip with us, and they would wait for me to finish a chapter. Then they would run across the sand and get to read it.

PHILLIPS. It's a very inventive novel, very unpredictable. The reader can't guess where he's going next.

SHAPIRO. That's because I didn't know. It was written that fast. I once read that E. M. Forster said, when interviewed about *A Passage to India*, that he knew when those people got into the cave, something terrible was going to happen. He just didn't know what. I felt the same way about *Edsel*. The fascination, you know. It was a marvelous experience for me—I had something I wanted to say, and I think I said it.

PHILLIPS. In the novel, Edsel says that there is nothing more ridiculous or moving than a poet on the podium. Do you feel that way about poetry readings?

SHAPIRO. In the beginning I was terrified. Then I got to like them. It's hard now to remember when there were practically no poetry readings. People used to invite Archibald MacLeish, but only because he was sort of undersecretary of state. When I grew up, poetry readings consisted of maybe ten people in a living room. Later, when Eliot read at Minnesota, he filled the football stadium! Imagine.

PHILLIPS. Edsel also says, "I don't see how anybody gets past adolescence without committing suicide at least twice." Was your own adolescence so bad?

SHAPIRO. Worse. Terrible. It might have been because I was brought up in a rather strict Jewish family, and didn't have enough intercourse—if that's the word—with girls. Social intercourse, I mean.

PHILLIPS. Of course, of course. Is Edsel the definitive schlemihl?

SHAPIRO. I thought of him more as the schlimazel. You know the difference? The schlemihl spills the soup in the schlimazel's lap. In other words, the schlimazel is someone with chronic, dependable bad luck. That's not the same as the schlemihl, who is maladroit, whose trouble is his own lack of coordination, social grace, whatever. Edsel's problem is his foreignness, his being a foreign body in academia—he doesn't fit in, and he doesn't fit out, either. So that his schlimazelism is partly a comic tragedy of his situation.

PHILLIPS. In the novel you say the hardest thing for a poet is to separate his actual feelings from his poetic feelings. Is there that distinction?

SHAPIRO. There is. I might have had in mind Eliot's statement about aesthetic distance and personal emotion. It's a question of judgment and taste. I suppose I liked Kate Smith and Bing Crosby. At the same time, I feel disgusted with myself for liking them. You see?

PHILLIPS. But you would admit to liking them in public?

SHAPIRO. Oh, sure. Old Kate Smith records bowl me over.

PHILLIPS. Edsel described his poems as all jagged glass and rusty nails. Is that how you viewed your own poems at the time?

SHAPIRO. Some. That's how I viewed American poetry generally. You know Louis Simpson's poem on the subject: "Whatever it is, it must have / A stomach that can digest / Rubber, coal, uranium, moons, poems. . ."

PHILLIPS. In the one poetry textbook you edited, you represent yourself only by the "Adam and Eve" sequence. Is that the favorite of your poems, and if so, why?

SHAPIRO. It's the only thing of its kind I ever wrote. There's nothing else even remotely similar. I don't know really how or why I wrote it. I am genuinely fond of it. I like to read it at readings. I remember while I was writing it, I was editing *Poetry,* and some friends of mine (one was an artist and had a gallery) asked if I would read at the opening of his show. And I said, "Okay, I have a poem that I'll finish." And I finished it for his deadline. I write very well for deadlines.

PHILLIPS. Do you keep a notebook?

SHAPIRO. No. I used to, for years, and one time when I was about twenty-three I destroyed all my notebooks. I've been pretty sorry ever since. They were full of poems, and I put them all in the furnace.

PHILLIPS. Why did you do that?

SHAPIRO. I think at the time I was writing stuff that annoyed me. Imitation Elizabethan plays and tragedies. It was probably a good idea to burn the lot.

PHILLIPS. What are you working on now?

SHAPIRO. For about two years, I've been writing this autobiography of sorts. It's funny how I began the book. My brother, Irvin, who was a child prodigy, asked me on the telephone, "Karl, how did you become a poet?" And I didn't know the answer. So I started trying to find the answer in this book. The first thing I wrote about was meeting a professor in a railroad station, trying to get a scholarship to the university after I'd already dropped out of school. So you can see, the thing has no chronology. It's not thematic. It may even be a new form. I'm doing something which I think is interesting. I didn't want to name people, let alone drop names—I didn't even want to name myself. So I talk about myself in the third person, as "The Poet," which I think of as the fourth person, because it's the poet standing outside himself, looking at all these other people, which include him. I'm getting somewhere. I've got enough material now to know that I have the makings of the creation of a character—the self-creation of a character who becomes a poet and discovers his identity that way. I've read parts of it to audiences and they really like it. Because it's like conversation. It's not like writing.

PHILLIPS. Does it have a title?

SHAPIRO. At the beginning I called it *Scratchings,* and I still like that. Then I thought of *Auto-mobile,* with a hyphen. And I think I like that better—referring to my car poems, of course—the Buick, the Cadillac, the ambulance, the auto wreck, as well as myself. Of course, I may be kidding myself, thinking people know those poems today.

PHILLIPS. Some do. But how bad is cultural illiteracy, based on your teaching experience?

SHAPIRO. It's very bad. I used to write about it and get flak from the writing professors, the ones who were teaching boneheading. It's begun to improve a little in the last five years. But I don't think we'll ever get back to the point at which college students used to know English when they got to the universities. The discipline has not only disappeared, it's changed so completely that there's now a greater tolerance for nonstructured teaching of language. And the so-called linguists themselves, in trying to create a new vocabulary of grammar and so on, have interfered with the pedagogy of the whole thing. You can no longer make a student learn a definition of an adverb, because the theorists will tell you that those definitions are spurious. It's like the shake-up caused by the New Math, if you remember that. I'm of two minds about whether we should go back to the old Latin discipline of teaching English the way I learned it—English on the basis of Latin grammar and roots. Maybe that day is past. But I don't know who's going to provide norms or standards for the ordinary language of communication if there is not a model.

PHILLIPS. How does this affect your creative writing classes?

SHAPIRO. My "creative" writing classes which I abhor? The subject of linguistic knowledge among the poets is something that really bothers me. It seems to me they not only read very little, but they also have no ambition to increase vocabulary and subtle grammatical structures. They don't study the niceties and the subtleties of language the way it's supposed to be their business to do. And once they get to the level in the colleges and universities where they're always taking creative writing, it's insulting to them to say, "You don't know your own language." Which in most cases is God's truth.

PHILLIPS. Do you have a sense of a public for your own work, for whom you write poems?

SHAPIRO. I'm surprised from time to time when I find evidence that people have learned something from me, or when people tell me they have. I've always tried to achieve a certain tone of voice, which I think I now have under control. It's not simply a question of locution and syntax, it's a question of hearing the tones in which people communicate with each other on various levels. And that generally involves idiom—if idiom is a synonym for a rich, spontaneous kind of language. Randall Jarrell was extremely good at this, although if you write like Jarrell, you're only imitating him. And Delmore Schwartz, as in his poem, "The Beautiful American Word, Sure."

PHILLIPS. Would you encourage young people to adopt writing as a way of life?

SHAPIRO. I've never encouraged *anybody* to do that. I think it's not only presumptuous, it's dangerous. When I first started teaching, I encouraged a few students in a couple of cases. But you can change the whole course of their career—a terrible responsibility. I wouldn't do it now. But if I ran across a talented student, I'd encourage him or her as much as I could. I used to try to direct those writing students to a job or a profession. I had a student at Davis who was very good, who said to me one day, "I'm going to go to the Academy of the Merchant Marine and be a ship's captain." I said, "Gee, that's wonderful! That'll be terrific for your poetry." Well, he went and he's still a captain of a ship somewhere. I haven't seen any more poetry from him. That still may be better than hanging around the academy all one's life.

PHILLIPS. Are you about to become a New Yorker?

SHAPIRO. Perhaps a part-time New Yorker. Because of Baltimore, and having lived my entire life in other parts of the country—Chicago, Nebraska, California—I find it hard to think of being here full time. The thing I love best about living in New York is that you can be as isolated as if you were in Iowa if you want to be, but if you get the sudden urge to go to a concert, it's right there. You live in Iowa, you could drive two hundred miles each way just to find something to do that night! We're also thinking of moving to San Francisco. Next to New York, that's the liveliest place.

PHILLIPS. The last question: Why do you write?

SHAPIRO. I don't know why, but it's a compulsion. I feel that after working a long time, I've really learned how to do what I do. I enjoy it. I don't think there's anything more satisfying than turning out a good stanza or a good piece of prose. And when you're satisfied enough, you want to show it to other people. That's called publication.

(1986)

William Goyen

Photograph by J. Gary Dontzig

William Goyen

The interview with William Goyen took place on a sunny Saturday after-noon in June 1975—the spring of Goyen's sixtieth birthday and also of the publication of the Twenty-fifth Anniversary Edition of his first novel, The House of Breath, *a book which became a literary sensation upon its first appearance in 1950. Since that time, he had published* Ghost and Flesh *(1952),* In a Farther Country *(1955),* The Faces of Blood Kindred *(1960),* The Fair Sister *(1962),* A Book of Jesus *(nonfiction, 1973),* Come, the Restorer *(1974), and* Nine Poems *(1976). Goyen's* Selected Writings *appeared in 1974, his* Collected Stories *late in 1975. Four of his plays had been produced. During 1976–1977, he was writer-in-residence at Princeton University. He was married to the actress Doris Roberts.*

The interview was taped over a three-hour period in my former home in Katonah, New York. The house was of French country architecture, and sunlight streamed through six tall casement windows overlooking the Cross River Reservoir. Mr. Goyen remained seated on a sofa through-out, sipping a soft drink. He requested that Baroque music be played over the stereo, "to break the silences." There were silences—long, con-sidering pauses between thoughts.

William Goyen was a slender, lanky, and handsome figure at sixty. His aspect was intense and patrician, his manner gracious and courtly, except when he launched into an infrequent harangue. His hair was sil-ver; he spoke with a strong Southwestern accent which years of living in Manhattan had not erased. He wore a navy blue blazer, khaki slacks, and an open-neck, faded blue chambray shirt.

. . .

PHILLIPS. In the introduction to your *Selected Writings,* you state that you began writing at the age of sixteen, at a time when you were also interested in composing and dancing and other art forms. Why writing as a career rather than one of the other arts?

GOYEN. My foremost ambition, as a very young person, was to be a composer, but my father was strongly opposed to my studying music— that was for girls. He was from a sawmill family that made strict a division between men's and women's work. (The result was quite a confusion of sex roles in later life: incapable men and oversexed women among his own brothers and sisters.) He was so violently against my studying music that he would not allow me even to play the piano in our house. Only my sister was allowed to put a finger to the keyboard. . . . The piano had been bought for her. My sister quickly tired of her instrument, and when my father was away from the house, I merrily played away, improving upon my sister's études—which I had learned by ear—and indulging in grand Mozartian fantasies. In the novel *The House of Breath,* Boy Ganchion secretly plays a "cardboard piano," a hidden paper keyboard pasted on a piece of cardboard in a hidden corner. I actually did this as a boy. My mother secretly cut it out of the local newspaper and sent off a coupon for beginners' music lessons. I straightaway devised Liszt-like concerti and romantic overtures. And so, silent arts were mine: I began writing. No one could hear that, or know that I was doing it, even as with the cardboard piano.

PHILLIPS. You weren't having to write under the sheets with a flashlight, were you?

GOYEN. You know, I *was* playing my music under the quilt at night, quite literally. I had a little record player and I played what music I could under the quilt, and later wrote that way. So I did write under the sheets.

PHILLIPS. What was your father's reaction to writing?

GOYEN. Something of the same. He discovered it some years later, when I was an undergraduate at Rice University in Houston. He found me writing plays, and to him the theater, like the piano, was an engine of corruption that bred effeminate men (God knows he was generally right, I came to see), sexual libertines (right again!), and a band of gypsies flaunting their shadowed eyes and tinseled tights at reality. When my first novel was published, my father's fears and accusations were justified—despite the success of the book—and he was outraged to the point of not speaking to me for nearly a year.

This could, of course, have been because the book mostly was about his own family—the sawmill family I spoke of earlier. My father, his brothers, his father, everybody else were lumber people, around mills . . . and forests. I went around the sawmills with him, you see, and saw all that. He loved trees! My God, he would . . . he'd just *touch* trees. . . . They were human beings. He would smell wood and trees. He just loved them. He knew wood. He was really meant for that.

Poor beloved man, though—he later came around to my side and became the scourge of local bookstores, making weekly rounds to check their stock of my book. He must have bought a hundred copies for his lumbermen friends. God knows what *they* thought of it. Before he died he had become my ardent admirer, and my *Selected Writings* is dedicated to him.

PHILLIPS. Do you agree with the theory that an unhappy childhood is essential to the formation of exceptional gifts? Were you genuinely unhappy?

GOYEN. How could it have been any other way? My own nature was one that would have made it that way. It was a melancholy childhood. It was a childhood that was searching for—or that *needed*—every kind of compensation it could get. I think that's what makes an artist. So that I looked for compensation to fulfill what was not there.

PHILLIPS. How have the physical conditions of your writing changed over the years? What is the relation between the creative act and privacy for you, today? In your "Note" on the Twenty-fifth Anniversary Edition of *The House of Breath,* you stated that part of the novel was written on an aircraft carrier in the Pacific.

GOYEN. Since my writing began in the air of secrecy, indeed, of alienation—as the work had to be done without anyone knowing it—forever after my work has had about it the air of someone in solitude having done it, alienated from the press of society and the everyday movements of life.

On the ship, where I continued working, I found that there are many hidden places on an aircraft carrier where one can hide out and do secret work. And this was easily achieved. Also on the night watches and so forth, there was a lot of time. There is a great deal of free time aboard a ship in wartime, ironically. This kind of tradition in my work has been mine all my life, and I have generally lived in hidden places. In New Mexico, it was at the beautiful foot of a mountain (the Sangre de Cristo in the primitive village of El Prado), and also in a mysterious mountain (Kiowa Mountain—the D. H. Lawrence Ranch called Kiowa Ranch, over San Cristobal, New Mexico, near Taos). And in Europe—Zurich, Rome—I worked in backstreet *pensions*.

Yet more and more, as I get more worldly and have the security of having survived, I feel that it is not necessary to be *that* far removed from the workings of daily life and the daily lives of people. Indeed, the older I get and the more I write, the more I feel it important to be a part of daily life . . . to know that it surrounds me as I work. I presently live in a large apartment on the West Side of New York City. One of those rooms is mine, and it's an absolute hideaway, yet all around me in the other rooms the life of a family goes on, and I like to know that. I also like to know that twelve flights down I can step onto the street in the midst of a lot of human beings and feel a part of them. Whereas, in the old days, in New Mexico, I was brought up—taught by—Frieda Lawrence to see that simple manual endeavor is a part of art. I would work in gardens and dig water ditches and walk in mountains and along rivers when I was not writing, and I felt that it was absolutely essential to my work. That's changing for me now. I'm more city-prone. Maybe the world is changing, too. Maybe solitude is best had in the midst of multitudes.

It's amazing how quickly something gets written. Now, when it comes, it can be on a bus, or in a store. I've stopped in Macy's and written on a dry-goods counter, and then suddenly had a whole piece of writing for myself that was accomplished; where earlier in my life, I felt I had to spend a week in a house somewhere in the country in order to get that. Conditions change.

PHILLIPS. Some say that poverty is ennobling to the soul. Is economic stability helpful to a writer? On the other hand, do you think wealth can be harmful?

GOYEN. It can be harmful. This depends on the stage in a writer's life, of course. As a young man, for me . . . I speak now not as a wealthy or an impoverished man, but as a man looking back when he was younger . . . it was imperative that I live *very* simply and economically. Living in Taos, where—who would have believed it then that fifteen or twenty years later a whole migration of young hippies would come to live and meditate in the desert just where I had lived—I was totally solitary. It was imperative for me and my work that I keep everything simple and have practically nothing at all. I lived in just a mud house with a dirt floor on land that Frieda Lawrence gave me out of friendship. I built it with a friend and a couple of Indians. Yet, to live in absolute poverty all his life could harm a writer's work. The hardship and worry over money in writers, as they get older, is a social horror; grants given to writers should be *sufficient,* so that they are able to live with amplitude and, yes, some dignity.

PHILLIPS. The genesis of it all goes back to that aircraft carrier, doesn't it?

GOYEN. I thought I was going to die in the war. I was on a terrible ship. It was the *Casablanca,* the first baby flattop. There were always holes in it, and people dying, and it was the just the worst place for me to be. I was really desperate. I just wanted to jump off. I thought I was going to die anyway, be killed, and I wanted to die because I couldn't endure what looked like an endless way of life with which I had nothing to do— the war, the ship, and the water. . . . I have been terrified of water all my life. I would have fits when I got close to it.

Suddenly—it was out on a deck in the cold—I saw the breath that had come from me. And I thought that the simplest thing that I know is what I belong to and where I came from, and I just called out to my family as I stood there that night, and . . . I saw this breath come from me and I thought, "In that breath, in that call, is *their* existence, is their reality . . . and I must shape that and I must write about them." *The House of Breath.*

I saw this whole thing. I saw what was going to be four-five years' work. Isn't that amazing? But I knew it was there. Many of my stories happen that way. It's dangerous to tell my students this, because then these young people say, "Gee, all I've got to do, if I really want to write, is wait around for some ship in the cold night, and I'll blow out my breath and I've got my thing."

PHILLIPS. So this sustained you?

GOYEN. It brought my life back to me. I saw my relationships—it was extraordinary. Lost times come for us in our lives if we're not phony and if we just listen; it hurts, but it's also very joyous and beautiful . . . it's a redemption . . . it's all those things that we try to find and the world seems to be looking for. As a matter of fact, that's the hunger of the world. So there it was on the ship, and it just came to me. I saw so much . . . that I wouldn't have to go home, and they wouldn't have to suffocate me; they wouldn't kill me; I'd find other relationships.

PHILLIPS. So after the war you didn't go home.

GOYEN. When the war was over, I just dipped into Texas and got my stuff and left and headed towards San Francisco. I had come to love San Francisco when it was the home port for my ship, the aircraft carrier, and I thought that it would be a good place to live. But I passed through Taos, New Mexico, in winter, in February, and I was enchanted. It really was like an Arthurian situation. . . . I couldn't leave. It was beautiful and re-mote, like a Himalayan village, untouched, with this adobe color that was ruby-colored and yellow, all the magical colors of mud. It's not all one color. It's like Rome. Rome looks like that. And the sunlight and the snow . . . just about everyone on foot . . . a few cars . . . high, seventy-five hundred feet.

PHILLIPS. Did the D. H. Lawrence commune in Taos have anything to do with your staying?

GOYEN. I didn't know anything about the Lawrence legend. Had I, I might not have stayed at all. But I did, and right away I thought that I'd better get a little more money for myself before I settled in to work. So I got a job as a waiter at a very fashionable inn called the Sagebrush Inn. I worked as a waiter for a few months until I met Frieda, who came in one night and I waited on her. The whole Lawrence world came to dinner there: Dorothy Brett and Mabel Dodge, Spud Johnson, Tennessee Williams. He was living up at the ranch. They all came to my table. And then the owner of the inn had to come out and say, "This young man is just out of the war and he wants to be a writer." The *worst* thing I wanted said about me; it almost paralyzed me. Well, of course, Tennessee thought, "Oh, God, who cares about *another* writer." But Frieda said, "You must come and have tea with me." She said it right away. I went, and from that moment . . . we just hit it off. It was almost a love affair. It was the whole world.

So it wasn't Lawrence that brought me to her; circumstances brought me to Frieda, and I found her a great pal and a luminous figure in my life on her own terms.

I would go to teas with her. She would have high teas. In Texas we have a Coke. But here it was the first time I met someone who baked bread, you know? She made a cake and brought it out. . . . It was wonderful. She wore German clothes, like dirndls, and peasant outfits, and an apron. She was a kitchen Frau. A few people came. . . . Mabel Dodge had given her this great three-hundred-acre ranch in return for the manuscript of *Sons and Lovers*. That was the exchange. Except she never took *Sons and Lovers* away, so that the manuscript and many others, *Women in Love,* . . . all holograph . . . were there in a little cupboard at the ranch. I could read them and look at them in amazement.

PHILLIPS. What sort of things did you talk about?

GOYEN. We talked about the simplest things . . . well, really about love, about men and women and about sex, about *physical* living. Of course, I didn't know that I was hearing what Lawrence had heard. Because it was Frieda who gave Lawrence this whole thing, and it overwhelmed me.

The various people would come up in the summer and spend time with us, all kinds of people. Just simple people . . . Indians. She was close to Indians. I got very close to three Indians who were really like my family and helped me build my house.

PHILLIPS. And then people like Tennessee Williams came.

GOYEN. Yes, Tennessee stayed up there with his friend, Frank Merlo. Tennessee told us that he heard Lawrence's voice. . . . He was a haunted poor thing, but he did go a little too far. D. H. Lawrence was whispering things to him. Suddenly, Tennessee had a terrible stomach ache, and it turned out that he had a very bad appendix and had to be brought down to Mabel Dodge. Mabel owned the only hospital—built it and owned it. It was like a European town and we were the only Americans, and I went to this hospital to witness Tennessee's dying. . . . He was always dying, you know. He was dying in this Catholic hospital screaming four-letter words and all kinds of things, with the nuns running around wearing the most enormous habits, most unsanitary for a hospital. Mabel was wringing her hands and saying, "He's a genius, he's a genius." The doctor said, "I don't care—he's going to die. He's got gangrene. His appendix has burst. We have to operate at once." Tennessee said, "Not until I make my will." The doctor said, "How long will the will be?" "Well, everything's going to Frankie." So they sat down, with Frank going though an inventory of all Tennessee's possessions. "What about the house in Rome? You left that out." Tennessee was just writhing in pain. So they made a list of all the things. And then they wheeled him off, and he indeed had this operation, which to everyone's surprise he managed to recover from. Eventually he got out of there . . .

PHILLIPS. All this time you were working on *The House of Breath.* How did you get it published?

GOYEN. It got published through Stephen Spender, indirectly. He came to that little village where I was living. I had sent a piece of it to *Accent,* a wonderful early magazine; it caused quite a kind of thing. I began to get letters. Random House wrote me a letter and said that they hoped this was "part of a book." (All editors do that, I later learned.) They'll say that even if it's just a "letter to the editor" they've seen. That's what editors do, God bless them, and I'm glad they do. About that time, Spender, a man I scarcely knew, whose *poetry* I scarcely knew, arrived in Taos on a reading tour. A wealthy lady named Helene Wurlitzer—of the family who made the organs—lived there and brought people into that strange territory to read, and give chamber concerts and so on. I never went to those things because . . . well, I didn't have any shoes; I really was living on mud floors in an adobe house that I had built, utterly primitive, which I loved. I was isolated and terrified with all those things going on in me . . . but I was writing that book. Well, Spender heard that I was there. . . . He heard through Frieda, who went to the reading, and so then he asked me if he could come to see me; he treated me as though I were an important writer. He had just read that piece in *Accent,* and he asked if there was more that he could read. I showed him some other pieces and he sent those around. They were published, and then somebody at Random House sent me a contract right away of $250.00 advance for the book, and then promptly was fired. But Spender was very moved by the way I was living there; he wrote a well-known essay called "The Isolation of the American Writer" about my situation there. Nothing would do until Mr. Spender would have me come to London, because he thought I was too isolated, too Texan, too hicky. . . . He really took it upon himself to make that kind of decision for me. It was a wonderful thing that he did. The stipulation was that I would bring a girl who had come into my life (this blessed girl has passed on among the leaves of autumn), and she was very much a part of my life there in London, and together we were real vagabonds, embarrassing everybody—people like Stephen, and Cyril Connolly, and Elizabeth Bowen, Rose Macaulay, I mean, all of them . . .

PHILLIPS. You stayed in Spender's house?

GOYEN. I had a room at the top, and Dorothy had a room in the basement, with the stairs between us, creaking stairs. It was an elegant house, an eighteenth-century house in St. John's Wood. At 4:00 P.M. teatime in the winter it was dark, and they pulled Florentine-brocaded curtains and turned on lights; it was a time of austerity still, but people came to tea. Veronica Wedgwood would arrive. Dorothy wouldn't come up from the basement. She really hated this kind of thing. She vanished. She just wouldn't participate. So I was really quite alone with this. I guess I must have kept her under wraps. I must have been very bad to her. I don't know. I have to think about that some time. But here they would come. Natasha, Stephen's wife, was a gifted pianist and wanted to be a concert pianist, and so musicians came, and painters. Cyril Connolly was often there because he and Stephen were working together. Dame Edith Sitwell came. We went to her house and she read one night; she sat behind a screen because she wouldn't read facing anyone or a group . . . behind a marvelous Chinese screen, and you would hear this voice coming through the screen . . . all those people . . . that was a world that Spender gave me, and it was a great influence in my life and on my work.

PHILLIPS. What an extraordinary change.

GOYEN. I was thrown into this elegant surround which was precisely the opposite of what I had been doing. It was right for me because my character, Folner, yearned for elegance. Suddenly, my country people were singing out their despair in those great elegant houses. I saw cathedrals for the first time. . . . I'd not really seen cathedrals. I was able to get to Paris and all around there. All this went into *The House of Breath*. I saw the Sistine Chapel—well, that's the first page of *The House of Breath,* "on the dome of my skull, paradises and infernos and annunciations," and so forth. Europe just put it all right—everything that started in a little town in Texas, you see. It saved the book, I think. Because it made that cry, you know . . . an *elegant* cry. There's nothing better than an elegant cry of despair . . .

PHILLIPS. Did people worry what this tremendous change in venue—from Taos to Europe—would do to *The House of Breath*?

GOYEN. Some people worried about it. James Laughlin of New Directions, when I had published a bit, wrote me: "You are ruining your work fast; the influences you are coming into are coming too soon, and you're allowing your personality to overwhelm your talent. Obviously, people find your *Texas* personality charming" (and he could be a snide guy, too), "and you might be of interest to them for a little while. But you are writing a very serious book, and this will be permanently damaging to your work." He really wanted me to get out of there.

PHILLIPS. Were there other Cassandras about *The House of Breath*?

GOYEN. Well, Auden had kind of looked down his nose at me. He said it's the kind of writing where the next page is more beautiful than the one just read. "One is just breathless for fear that you're not going to be able to do it," he said, "and that makes me too nervous. I prefer James."

Christopher Isherwood said, "You know, my dear boy, you'll never make it. That is what one feels when one reads you. You'll never survive with this kind of sensibility unless you change, get some armor on yourself." As a matter of fact, he wrote me and warned me again. . . . He put it all down in a letter. And that *did* scare me. I was young and I was scared. But I knew that I had no choice. Then that feeling of doom *really* came on me . . . because I had no choice. I knew that I couldn't write any other way.

PHILLIPS. When you began writing *The House of Breath* did you expect to be published? Were you writing for publication?

GOYEN. I was most surely not "writing for publication." But I don't think there is any piece of the novel except one that was not published in magazines before the book itself was published.

PHILLIPS. You said earlier that your father was upset by the book when it was published. Had you been concerned about the family and hometown reaction?

GOYEN. Concerned, yes. I fell out of favor with many people in the town, let's put it that way, and just about disinherited by my own family. I had nasty letters, bad letters from home and heartbroken letters from my mother and my father. Generally, the attitude was one of hurt and shock. It was not until fifteen years later that I was able to go back to the town! And even then, rather snide remarks were made to me by the funeral director and the head of the bank. We met on the street.

PHILLIPS. So when you apply for a loan, you won't do it in that town?

GOYEN. No, and I won't die there, either.

PHILLIPS. How long did you and your girlfriend stay as Spender's guests in England?

GOYEN. I settled in for the whole year of 1949 . . . and I finished the book in that house at St. John's Wood, in Stephen's house. Dorothy was there until it got very bad; we had problems and so she moved to Paris; that made me have to go to Paris to see her there, and we had this kind of thing that was going on. When I came back, bringing my manuscript on the *Queen Mary,* she came with me to New York. But then we had one visit with Bob Linscott, my editor, who said to her, "My dear, do you like to eat? Do you like a roof over your head? You'll never have it; he's an artist. I feed him and Random House has kept him alive and probably will have to from now on. Don't marry him, don't even fall in love." And he broke her heart. He really did. Poor Dorothy. He was right; I wasn't about to be saddled down. And so it broke away and that's okay. Many years later, I found a woman exactly like her. Her name was Doris, and so often I say to Doris, "Dorothy," and I'm in trouble.

PHILLIPS. That was quite a step for an editor to take. What do you think their particular function should be?

GOYEN. Well, really caring for authors . . . not meddling with what they did, but loving them so much and letting them know that he cares. Generally, at that point, when you're starting, you feel that nobody does. Linscott looked after you, and if you had no money, he gave you money. Once, Truman Capote met me at the Oak Room of the Plaza. "I'm embarrassed to sit with you," he said when I sat down, "your suit is terrible." I hadn't really thought about what I was wearing. He said, "I'm not going to have you wear that suit anymore. But," he said, "I've ordered drinks for us, and if you'll just wait, I'm going to call Bob and tell him that he must buy you a suit that costs at least $250." And he did. Bob gave me the money and he told me, "Well, I guess he's right." He was lovable, Truman. He did sweet, lovely things then.

PHILLIPS. Carson McCullers was one of Linscott's authors, wasn't she?

GOYEN. I had first known her in this nest that Linscott had up there for these little birdlings of writers. Carson had great vitality and she was quite beautiful in that already decaying way. She was like a fairy. She had the most delicate kind of tinkling, dazzling little way about her . . . like a little star. Like a Christmas . . . she was like an ornament of a king. She had no mind and she could make no philosophical statements about anything; she didn't need to. She said far-out, wonderfully mad things that were totally disarming, and for a while people would say, "I'll go wherever you go." She'd knock them straight out the window.

PHILLIPS. What sort of people interested her?

GOYEN. She had a devastating crush on Elizabeth Bowen. She actually got to Bowen's Court: she shambled over there to England and spent a fortnight. I heard from Elizabeth that Carson appeared at dinner the first night in her shorts—tennis shorts. That poor body, you know, in tennis shorts, and she came down the stairs; that was her debut. It didn't last long. But that was Carson.

PHILLIPS. What was distinctive about her stories—as compared, say, to the other Southern "magnolia" writers?

GOYEN. She would try to make her stories scary, and the word "haunted" was used, of course, by the literary critics, the "haunted domain." I think that was the French title for Truman's first novel . . . *Other Voices, Other Rooms. Les Domaines Hantés.* But Carson was . . . she was a really truly lost, haunted wonder-creature. It's hard to be that and grow old, because of course you either go mad out of what you see, or I guess you try to imitate that kind of purity. She was a bad imitator. So it was just a bore.

PHILLIPS. She was not a person to have as an enemy.

GOYEN. She was . . . not tough but she had a nasty . . . well, she had a way of absolutely devastating you—the kind that hurt, that little kind of peeping, "drop dead" sort of thing. She had an eye for human frailty and would go right to that; that's why people fled her. They thought, "Who needs this? Why be around her?"

Then, of course, she was terribly affected by not being able to write. It was a murderous thing, a death blow, that block. She said she just didn't have anything to write. And really, it was as though she had never written. This happens to writers when there are dead spells. We die sometimes. And it's as though we're in a tomb; it's a death. That's what we all fear, and that's why so many of us become alcoholics or suicides or insane—or just no-good philanderers. It's amazing that we survive, though I think survival in some cases is kind of misgiven, and it's a bore. It was written recently about Saul Bellow that one of the best things about him is that he survived, he didn't become an alcoholic, he didn't go mad, and so forth. And that the true heroism of him lies simply in his endurance. That's the way we look at artists in America. People said to me when I was sixty, "My God, you're one of the ones—how are you? But you look *wonderful.* We didn't know where you were." They thought I was dead, or in an institution or something.

PHILLIPS. Could her editor, Linscott, help McCullers at all?

GOYEN. Poor Linscott couldn't get any more out of her, and then he died before he could help her. I doubt whether he could have; no one could have. She was hopeless. She was just kind of a little expendable thing, you know. She would stay with me days at a time. I put her to bed; she had a little nightgown. I was playing sort of dolly; I was playing house. I sat with her while her ExLax worked. Two or three ExLaxes and three wine glasses, and about three Seconal. And I would sit by her bed and see that it all worked, or at least it all got going in her. And then she was off to sleep.

She had some awful cancer of the nerve ends. This caused the strokes, and she had a stroke finally on the other side, until she was very badly paralyzed, and then she had just a massive killing stroke. She was absolutely skin and bones. They took her down there to Georgia, not far from where Flannery O'Connor lived, where they buried her.

PHILLIPS. Could she have written an autobiography?

GOYEN. She did not "have a hold of herself," as a person would say, enough to look back and see herself in situations. She never could have written her autobiography; it would be impossible for her. . . . She had disguised herself so much. And what a past, you know? Her mother . . . the mother of *all* these people. . . . Thank God mine seems to be quite okay—I'd be raving mad at this point. Carson's mother was an aggressive lady, all over the place, and she came here once and worked at *Mademoiselle*. She had a notorious time as a fiction editor there. She did the oddest things . . . rejecting stories in her own Georgian way, generally in terms of cooking. I think she wrote to a writer once, "The crust of this story holds its contents well" (she was off on a pie) "but, my dear, by the time we get to the custard, it runs." The pie image went on and on. "This pie won't do," she said, "came out of the oven too soon." She was a self-educated lady from the South who very early on had read Katherine Mansfield, for instance, and had told Carson about Mansfield, which was the worst thing she could have done. Once, I went with her to meet Carson's plane. When she saw her daughter step out of the plane, she turned to me and said, "I seen the little lamp." I thought, "That's some allusion I'm going to have to find out about." When Carson reached us, she said, "Carson, you know what I told Bill when you appeared?" (She was the kind of lady who would repeat a thing she'd said.) "I told him that I seen the little lamp." Carson burst into tears. I said, "Please tell me what that is that hurts you so." She said, "Well, it's that beautiful story called 'The Doll's House' by Katherine Mansfield. It's the last line of the story. A poor little girl peeks in a garden at a doll's house owned by a snobbish family, and she sees this glowing little lamp inside. Later, when the little girl's sister asks why there is a curious glow in her eye, she says, 'I seen the little lamp.' "

PHILLIPS. What about your own mother?

GOYEN. As a literary person, I truly am the offspring of my mother and women like my mother. There's no woman like a Texas woman in her eighties. It's not Southern. She wouldn't have a clue as to what a "Southern lady" was. Hers was a singing way of expressing things, and this I heard so very early that it became my own speech: that's the way I write. I love spending money to talk to her on the phone in Texas an hour at a time, because it's just as though the curtain that came down on an opera last night goes right up when I call her tonight. The aria goes right on; it's just wonderful.

PHILLIPS. What do you talk about?

GOYEN. About how Houston has grown, and how she wants to go back to the little town she left fifty years ago. I write her expressions down. I have to do that to understand what they really mean; it's almost another language. But she keeps breeding it. I mean, she's writing all the time. I may not be writing, but she is. She's alive . . .

PHILLIPS. Do you carry a notebook with you to put these things in? Or keep a diary?

GOYEN. Oh, yes, I always carry paper with me . . . something to write on, always. And I keep not so much a formal diary any longer, but, well, a notebook, and in it I keep most things.

PHILLIPS. What do you do with those ideas that strike you in the middle of Macy's, say, and you can't record them fully or easily? Are they often unrelated to what you currently are working on?

GOYEN. It's rarely unrelated. When one's really engaged deeply in a piece of work, truly writing it, it takes over almost everything else, and you find you're thinking about it constantly, and it's part of everything that happens. Even the clerk in Macy's suddenly speaks out of the novel that you are writing, it seems, or is a character in it. All the people in the world are suddenly characters in the novel you are writing. Everything contributes. The created piece of work has suddenly replaced what is called real life . . . life as it really is, whatever *that* means . . . so that it's not surprising to have it come at one from all angles.

Therefore, I know that if I've been writing all morning and I've got to buy groceries at noon, I better take paper with me, because I'm going to *keep* writing as I go down the street; you can write on the sack that your groceries come in, and I have!

PHILLIPS. What about the six years you were an editor at Mc-Graw-Hill? Were you able to write, or did this interfere with your work?

GOYEN. The whole McGraw-Hill period is one that I want to write about. I have been writing about it in my "Memoirs" (my next book). The writer in the world of publishing, and particularly *me* in the world of publishing, who had been so disillusioned and embittered by publishers . . .

PHILLIPS. You were disillusioned with your own publishers?

GOYEN. Not my own, per se. Just publishing in general—the making of books and the life of the making of books. All these things seemed so dead end to me, without meaning. In this great place, this huge publishing house, I was a special person, in that I was a special editor. I was brought there to concern myself with serious writers and with new writers and what would be called "Good Books"—quality writing. I was so concerned with the writing of my own authors that I considered their books my own and treated them as such. I entered into their creative process. Nevertheless, I was caught in the competitive crush and thrust of commercial publishing. There was no question of my own writing. I was relieved not to have to worry about my own writing. I scarcely grieved it, or mourned it. It had brought me so little—no more than itself.

I suddenly was not a man who I had known. I was on the phone. . . . I hate phones. I really can't manage phones well. I won't answer it, generally, and if I do I can't talk very long; I just can't do it. But here I was, having to live and negotiate on the phone. Editors live that way. With agents and all that. Here I was, doing this for the first two or three years. I was drawing up contracts, and I never knew what a contract was; I didn't know what they were about.

But I began to fail after the fourth year. I got very disturbed for all kinds of reasons. . . . Publishing, that's a corrupt thing sometimes. I had my way for a while, but then pretty soon night must fall, and I was back in the old budgets and best-selling books and a lot of crap.

PHILLIPS. I take it your interest in your own writing increased during those six years?

GOYEN. Yes, that was bound to happen. As years passed, I began to be hungry and I wasn't quite sure what that hunger was. Well, of course, it was that I was not writing, and the more I exhausted myself with other writers, the more hungry I became to do my own work. This is an exhausting thing, being an editor, and I had no time left for my own work, no matter how much I wanted it. The demands made on me were almost unbearable. And that was when I left McGraw-Hill—or was asked to do so by Albert Leventhal.

PHILLIPS. That was in the sixties. In the fifties you were teaching at the New School. Did you find teaching just as demanding? Or was this a more satisfactory way to earn an income while doing your own writing?

GOYEN. Teaching writing is draining, too, of course. Especially the way I do it. You see, I believe that everybody can write. And in believing and teaching this, what happens, of course, is enormous productivity on the part of many students. One's students produce so much that he is followed down the street by the mass of stuff he's encouraged. I mean, he's overtaken by it. And there's that much more work to do, and more conferences to hold, and it's a depleting and exhausting thing. Just as exhausting as editing.

PHILLIPS. Is there an ideal occupation for the writer, then? Other than teaching?

GOYEN. Probably teaching is ideal. Because there's a community of writers there, and because the writer is respected and understood as a writer in colleges now. He's brought there as a writer, so it's understood why he's behaving the way he does, and what he's doing when he's not around; he's *expected* to write. It's well paid now, too—universities are paying writers well. It's probably the best. It takes a lot of discipline for a writer to teach writing, though. But in the end, leading writing seminars and workshops is refreshing and exhilarating and creative and in touch with life. I consider teaching one of my callings.

PHILLIPS. What do you think of your students?

GOYEN. The young people I've been involved with in my classes seem to have no sense of place. It bewildered me at first, and then it caused me no little alarm. We've talked about it, and what they tell me is often what I've presumed . . . that there isn't much of a place where they come from. I mean, every place looks like every other place. Even suburban places—around here or in Ohio or wherever—all look alike . . . a shopping center, a McDonald's, the bank with the frosted globes on the facade—you know, that's a given building. The repertory theaters all look alike. So that they really don't have a sense of place except through literature. But when they begin to write, they can't write about Flaubert's place. So what they're writing about is the Princeton campus, and I've told them I don't want to hear about that. I ask them, "But didn't you live somewhere before? Wasn't there a room somewhere, a house? A street? A tree? Can't you remember?"

There was always a sense of belonging to a place in my childhood. The place. We call the house, "the place." "Let's go back to the place," we'd say. I loved that. There was such a strong sense of family and generation and my ancestors in it. It was like a monument—that's what my impression was, and I wrote about it as that. It was a Parthenon to me . . . with that enduring monumentality to it. But these students . . . they've had terrible family problems—they are dissociated. They're so disoriented . . . divorce, my God, divorce is a way of life in these generations. I ask them, "Don't you have a grandmother? Do you ever go to your grandmother's? Where does she live?" "Oh," they say, "she lives with us," or, "she lives in an apartment; she lives in a condominium." These elegant old ladies—they don't live in places anymore, either.

PHILLIPS. To get back to your own work, do you feel that music is reflected in your writing?

GOYEN. It's an absolute, basic part of my work—there's no question. And I think of my writing as music, often . . . and of my stories as little songs.

PHILLIPS. "Little songs," of course, is the literal meaning of the word "sonnet." The Albondocani Press has just published an edition of your early poems, poems written before your first novel. What made you abandon poetry for fiction? Faulkner said that all short story writers are failed poets. Do you feel this is so?

GOYEN. I think an awful lot of them are. I'm not a failed poet—I'm just a poet who made another choice, at a certain point, very early. Actually, I'm so taken by the dramatic form that I'm really a playwright manqué! I still consider myself, after having written and seen produced four plays in the professional theater, manqué in the theater. And yet I continue to love the form and fear it more than love it.

PHILLIPS. Do you think your playwriting has been beneficial to your fiction writing?

GOYEN. I think it has. I think it has made me care more about writing fiction, for one thing.

PHILLIPS. Do you feel compromised in the collaborations between director and producer and writer?

GOYEN. No, no, that's welcome to me, all that. I need all the help I can get! I never accept playwriting as a solitary thing. Once you do, you're ruined: because from the beginning it's a collaborative affair, and the sooner you can get it on to a stage, the better. The more you write at the table on a play, alone, the farther away you're going to get from the play. So far as the theater is concerned, it becomes a *literary* work the more you work on it. But writing for the theater has made me understand plot. It's helped me with plot in fiction writing.

PHILLIPS. What European authors and what American authors have meant the most to you?

GOYEN. As for American authors, Hawthorne and Melville have meant a great deal. And Henry James. And two poets—Ezra Pound and T. S. Eliot—have influenced me.

PHILLIPS. In what ways? They seem odd choices for a Southwestern fiction writer . . .

GOYEN. I still read, I still study, the *Cantos* of Pound. I found Pound in Texas when I was eighteen or nineteen, through a young friend named William Hart. Hart was one of those prodigies, enfants terribles, that materialize in small towns—naturally as others bore the instinct to compete and to copulate. He had a great deal to do with my early enlightenment and spiritual salvation in a lower-middle-class environment, in an isolated (then) Texas town, where a boy's father considered him a sissy if he played the piano, as I've said, and questioned the sexual orientation of any youth who read poetry.

William Hart was a true pioneer; he brought me Pound, Eliot, and Auden. He was self-taught, finding things for himself out of hunger. He had a high-school education, barely, but afterwards he came and sat in my classes at Rice and listened. He knew more than the professors did sometimes—he really did . . . about Elizabethan drama, and medieval romances. He knew these things. He was a delicate boy, obviously, but not effete. He was French Cajun, from a poor family, and he was on the streets, and could have been in trouble a lot. But he ended up in the library. They felt they had a revolutionary in there. In the Houston Public Library, at nineteen, he would get up and speak about literature, and Archibald MacLeish, of all people. And oh, how this man Hart spoke. The whole library would turn and listen. He became that kind of town creature, one of those who go down in cities, unheralded. . . . They go down into beds of ashes. Well, he brought me Pound.

Pound's *Cantos* hold for me madness and beauty, darkness and mystery, pain, heartbreak, nostalgia. Some of the most beautiful and most haunting were written as a prisoner. He made, above all, *songs,* and he told his stories lyrically, as I have felt driven to tell mine. By ordinary speech, ordinary people. I mean that it seems to me that Pound sometimes speaks from a sort of "subtone" in his poems, like a con man, a backstreet hustler, using pieces of several languages, bits of myth, literary quotations and mixed dialects and plain beguiling nonsense. There is a stream, flowing and broken, of *voices* in Pound—echoes, town speech, songs—that deeply brought me back to my own predicament, in the home of my parents and in the town where I lived. He helped show me a way to sing about it—it was, as most influences have been for me, as much a *tone* as sound, a quality, than anything else.

The same for T. S. Eliot. He seemed then so much more American than Pound—but then Pound has the Chinese calligraphy and the heavy Greek and Latin. Eliot's wan songs, broken suddenly by a crude word or a street phrase, directly influenced me as a way to tell *The House of Breath.* And doom cut through by caprice shocked me, and helped me survive in my own place until I could escape—showed me a way of managing the powerful life that I felt tearing through me and trying to kill me. I saw a way: Eliot's *Waste Land* narrator stopping the man by crying, "Stetson! / You were with me in the ships at Mylae!" Oh, Eliot got hold of me at that early age with his dark, biblical overtones, and helped me speak for my own place.

The storytelling method of Eliot and Pound—darting, elliptical, circular, repetitive, lyric, self-revealing; simple speech within grand cadence and hyperbole—educated me and showed me a way to be taken out of my place, away from my obsessing relations—saved me from locality, from "regionalism." I knew then that it was "style" that would save me. I saw Pound as the most elegant of poets and the most elemental. Both. His madness partakes of both (elegance and elementalness) and is a quality of his poetry:

> Hast 'ou seen the rose in the steel dust
> (or swansdown ever?)
> so light is the urging, so ordered the dark petals of iron
> we who have passed over Lethe.

That's Canto 74, from the *Pisan Cantos*.

PHILLIPS. What of the Europeans?

GOYEN. Balzac above all, if just for the sheer fullness of story in him, for the life-giving detail in his novels. The daily *stuff* and the *fact* of his writing helped me struggle against a tendency toward the ornate and fantastical and abstract. Then come Flaubert, Proust. Of the English, Milton—a curious choice, right? The minor poems of Milton, but *Paradise Lost* above all. Milton's richness and grandness—his *scope*. I had an *epic* sense of my story, my material, and he helped me see it. Then Dante—the *Inferno*. Heine's poems—their sweet madness. The beautiful lyric poems of Goethe. Thomas Mann's stories, especially "Disorder and Early Sorrow," and *Buddenbrooks*. And some of the lyrical poems of Wordsworth. Poetry has been a strong influence on me, you see. I read it often as fiction.

PHILLIPS. You weren't influenced by Faulkner in any way?

GOYEN. No, not at all. His work is monumental, and extremely important to me, but not in any way an influence. It goes along beside me—*Light in August, Absalom, Absalom*—but not through me. I can't say why, but I know that that's true. Maybe he's too *Southern*. If that is a tradition . . . I'm not part of that. Thank God for my Southwestern-ness . . . that Texan thing. My father, I'm afraid, is a Southerner, a Mississippian, but my mother and her family for generations were native Texas people . . . so that was a strong influence. I knew a lot of my father's family; they're the people I've really written about in *The House of Breath*. But something kept me away from those sicknesses and terrors that come from that Deep South.

PHILLIPS. *The House of Breath* came out at the same time as other celebrated works—Styron's, Capote's, Mailer's. Did you feel part of a writing generation?

GOYEN. I felt immensely apart. And most certainly did not belong to any "writing generation." I remember, indeed, saying, in an interview with Harvey Breit in 1950 in the *New York Times,* that I felt excited about joining the company of those writers, but that I had not before that time been aware of any of them! I stayed to myself. I read nothing of "the literary world" when writing *The House of Breath.*

PHILLIPS. Subsequently, did you any do reviews of your contemporaries?

GOYEN. I reviewed *Breakfast at Tiffany's* for the *New York Times Book Review.* Actually, it was a fair review . . . but it was critical. I called Capote a valentine maker and said I thought he was the last of the valentine makers. Well, this just seemed to shake his life for the longest time.

PHILLIPS. Do your contemporaries interest you now?

GOYEN. They really don't interest me very much. I still feel apart and, well, I *am* apart from my contemporaries. And they don't know what to *do* about me, or they ignore me. I am led to believe they ignore me.

PHILLIPS. Hasn't that perhaps to do with your books having been out of print for a decade or more, until recently?

GOYEN. No, I don't think so. How could it? My books have been in libraries, on reading lists at universities. Somebody was always writing a thesis or paper on my work and writing to me for my help.

But: if I am so full of the books of all these people—Doris Lessing and John Updike and X and Y and Z—how will I have a clear head for anything of my *own*? I'm really not very interested in contemporary fiction, anyway. I consider my fiction absolutely separate and apart from and unrelated to "contemporary American fiction."

PHILLIPS. You feel closer to the European literary tradition?

GOYEN. I do.

PHILLIPS. Your books continued to remain in print in European editions long after they were unavailable here. Do you have any notion why that is?

GOYEN. No, unless it was because my books were translated by such eminent translators—Ernst Robert Curtius and Elizabeth Schnack in Germany, Maurice Edgar Coindreau in France.

PHILLIPS. All your novels have a rather unique form: they do not follow a linear line, for one thing. Did *The House of Breath* ever take form as a straightforward narrative and then later get broken down into monologues?

GOYEN. No, no, no. The form of that novel is the way it was written. It was slow, although it poured from me, and a whole lot of it was simply *given* to me, absolutely put in my mouth. There were great stretches when nothing came. Then it poured out . . . in pieces, if that's possible. So, I thought of it as fragments—that was what established its form. I once called it "Cries Down a Well," and then I called it "Six Elegies." Later it was "Six American Portraits." So it came in pieces, but I knew that they were linked.

PHILLIPS. What do you have against the linear novel?

GOYEN. I always *intend* to write a linear novel when I begin. It's my greatest ambition to write a straightforward novel, and I always feel that I am, you know. I get very close. I thought *Come, the Restorer* was very close to being a linear novel. Then people laughed at me when I finished and said that's not true at all.

PHILLIPS. What people?

GOYEN. Friends or interviewers, I suppose. What I end up writing each time, you see, is a kind of opera. It's a series of arias and the form is musical, despite myself, and it is lyrical. The outcry is lyrical, despite myself. These novels have come to me at their height, passages have come to me in exaltation. So that the gaps between have been my problem and the . . . I was going to say *quieter* spaces and moments . . . but I don't mean that, because there are *many* quiet spaces in these books. But the less *intense* spaces seem to be hard for me to manage, somehow. What seems meant for me to do is always to begin what's called the linear novel, and try and try and try . . .

PHILLIPS. Going back to form: Do you think of the novel as a lot of short stories, or as one big story? Or does it depend upon the novel?

GOYEN. It might. But it seems to me that the unified novel, the organic entity that we call a novel, is a series of parts. How could it not be? I generally make the parts the way you make those individual medallions that go into quilts—all separate and as perfect as I can make them, but knowing that my quilt becomes a whole when I have finished the parts. It is the *design* that's the hardest. Sometimes it takes me a long time to see, or discover, what the parts are to form or make.

PHILLIPS. Does the completion of one "medallion" lead to another?

GOYEN. No, the completion of one medallion does not usually lead to another. They seem to generate, or materialize, out of themselves and are self-sufficient, not coupled to, or often, related to, any other piece. That seems to be what my writing job is: to discover this relationship of parts. Madness, of course, comes from not being able to discover any connection, any relationship at all! And the most disastrous thing that can happen is to *make up*, to *fake*, connections. In a beautiful quilt, it looks like the medallions really grow out of one another, organic, the way petals and leaves grow. The problem, then, is to graft the living pieces to one another so that they finally become a living whole. That is the way I've had to work, whatever that means.

PHILLIPS. Have you made medallions that did not fit into the final quilt?

GOYEN. There's rarely been anything left over, that is, medallions that didn't fit into the final quilt. If the pieces didn't all come together, the whole failed. It's really as though all the pieces were around, hidden, waiting to be discovered, and there were just enough for the design on hand. If, in rare cases, something was left over, one tried to use it as some sort of preamble or "postlude"—that sort of fussy thing. It never worked, even when one felt it was such "fine" writing that it should be kept in. It's this kind of exhibitionism of bad taste that's harmed some good work by good writers.

PHILLIPS. So you started writing under a quilt and you came out producing quilts.

GOYEN. Producing them is right.

PHILLIPS. How else would you describe your own writing, or your style?

GOYEN. As a kind of singing. I don't say this because others have said it. But we've spoken of my work as a song, earlier, the musicality of my writing and its form. It's impossible for me not to write that way. I write in cadence—that could be very bad. Just as in the theater, when an actor in rehearsal discovers that lines in a speech rhyme, he or the director is horrified. Someone in the back of the theater will scream out, "Couplet! Couplet!" meaning, "It rhymes! It rhymes!"

PHILLIPS. Are you concentrating now on short stories or novels?

GOYEN. I have less an urge to write the short story, and more of a concern with writing the book. It has nothing to do with anything but my own lack of a need for the very short form, and a deep love for the book itself, for a longer piece of writing.

PHILLIPS. Some may say you achieved both in *Ghost and Flesh*—a book of short stories which, on rereading, seems a total book rather than a collection of pieces. Was it conceived as a book, or was it a true gathering?

GOYEN. No, it was conceived as a book, it truly was. A sort of song cycle, really, that made up a single, unified work, a thematic unity like Schubert's *Die Winterreise* (which influenced *The House of Breath*—an early Marian Anderson recording. Frieda Lawrence first made it known to me, that is, the poem on which the songs were based).

Ghost and Flesh . . . you can see in those stories . . . wow . . . quite surreal, and I loved those, and when that was finished and published, I kind of went off the beam. I think the book made me quite mad—writing it, the obsession of that book. But on the other hand, *The House of Breath* did not. And that's an obsessed book, you see. It's hard to say these things, but something always pulled me through. Of course, my critics might say, "He *should* have gone mad."

PHILLIPS. What sort of madness was it?

GOYEN. While I wasn't that sane, I knew that madness—that's the word I use, but I don't know if it's quite right—that dangerous thing . . . that terror, and I knew that. I guess I knew when to let it alone.

It comes in a loss of reality. If we say madness, that sounds funny. But let's say an "other-worldness." It has to do with identity. I go through phases of not knowing my own history. It's amnesiac almost. I've known this all my life; as a child I've known that. The loss of the sense of the world around me, of the reality. It means that I just have to isolate myself, and then I'm okay.

Also, I've found a very strong wife. So my choices must have been blessed. God knows, when I brought her home to Texas, people gathered to meet her and congratulate us, and one woman came over to me who had known me all my life and said, "My God, I can't tell you how relieved we all are. We thought you were going to bring home some *poetess!*"

PHILLIPS. Is writing a work of nonfiction markedly different for you from writing fiction? Did you derive equal satisfaction from reconstructing the life of Jesus (in *A Book of Jesus*) as you do composing a novel?

GOYEN. Oh, yes. The excitement was tremendous in writing that book. There was no difference in feeling between that and what I felt when I had written fiction. It was as though I were creating a character in this man. A marvelous experience. Astonishing. A very real man began to live with me, of flesh and blood. He did the same work on me that He did on the people of the New Testament that He walked among: He won me over, enchanted and captured me, finally possessed me. I went rather crazy with the love from Him that I felt. I carried a little New Testament around with me in my pocket and would flip it open and read what He said, at cocktail parties or at dinner tables. A surprising reaction from my listeners generally followed: they were struck by the simplicity and beauty of what the man said to others, particularly the wonderful woman at the well.

PHILLIPS. How do you react to the charges of being a regional writer?

GOYEN. For me, environment is all. Place—as I was saying about my students—is absolutely essential. I know that the vogue for the "non-place," the placeless place, à la Beckett, is very much an influence on writing these days. It has been said that places don't exist anymore. That everything looks alike. There is the same Howard Johnson on your turnpike in Kansas as there is in Miami and in the state of Washington. And the same kind of architecture dominates the new office building and the skyscraper. What is a writer to do? Free the "reality" of his environment? To lament loss of place, to search for it in memory? Because within place is culture, style. We speak of a lost way of life. In many of my books and stories, I've felt the need to re-create, to restore lost ways, lost places, lost styles of living.

PHILLIPS. Isn't this what Marietta did in *In a Farther Country*? And what was expected of Mr. DePersia in *Come, the Restorer*?

GOYEN. Exactly. So to this extent, then, I *am* a regional writer, in that my writing begins by being of a region, of a real place. It begins with real people talking like real people from that place, and looking like them. Very often, regional reality ends there, and these people become other people, and this place becomes another place. The tiny town of Charity, in *The House of Breath,* is really Trinity, Texas, accurately described. Once described, however, it ceases to be Charity or Trinity and becomes, well, London or Rome. The pasture in front of the house in Charity, where a cow named Roma grazed, becomes the Elysian Fields, and Orpheus and Eurydice flee across it. The house itself becomes a kind of Parthenon, with friezes of ancient kin.

I think there are moments when I exceed myself as a human being, and become Ulysses, perhaps, or Zeus. It is the point of time at which the human exceeds himself, is transformed beyond himself, that I most care about writing about. This is the lyrical, the apocalyptic, the visionary, the fantastic, the symbolic, the metaphorical, the transfiguratory, transfigurational—all those terms which have been applied to my work.

Now, by "exceeding myself as a human being," I mean in *life*—epiphany moments in life—not in *writing*. I mean, those moments when human beings experience an epiphany, a transfiguration (that's the word) are the moments that most excite me. I've seen it in supreme artists who sang or danced or acted, in people who've told me they loved me, in those whose souls have suddenly been reborn before my eyes. These are moments and people I most care about writing about, no matter how small the moment, how humble the person. "I seen the little lamp," the transfigured child said at the end of the Katherine Mansfield story.

PHILLIPS. Are your closest friends writers? Is talking to other writers helpful or harmful to your work?

GOYEN. My closest friends are theater people. Painters were once closest to me. For some years I lived among painters. But that changed. Now it's either performers or directors. I love theater people—they give me a great deal. I don't particularly like writers, and I am not prone to talk about writing. Since they're solitary workers, writers tend to *act out* in public, I believe. They seem to carry more hostility, maybe because they are responsible to more people (their characters), to a whole world—like God—than painters or actors. Maybe it's because writers are caught in the English language—which sometimes seems like a sticky web you can't pull your antennae out of, like insects I've watched in webs—and are, in public and when they're with other people, still thrashing about in an invisible web. It is *enraging* to work in words, sometimes—no wonder writers are often nervous and crazy. Paint seems to be a more benevolent, a more soothing and serene-making medium.

Musicians always want to play for you, which is wonderful and wordless; painters seem to want to talk only about sex, or point out to you the hidden genital configurations in their canvas! Since the writer is truly a seminal person (he spits out his own web, as Yeats said, and then, as I just said, gets caught in it), the truly creative writer, I mean, he's full of the fear and the pride that a maker of *new* things feels. So it's seemed to me.

PHILLIPS. After one of your books is done, do you divorce yourself from the characters, or do you seem somehow to maintain a contact with them?

GOYEN. Oh, the characters in my first novel haunt me to this day! Actually *haunt* me. And characters like Oil King (from *Come, the Restorer*), who's been in my life a long, long time. I've lived with him and loved him and written about him for many, many years. They stay with me, yes indeed they do. They stay. They not only enter my life, but I begin to see them in life, here, there. I see Marietta McGee quite frequently, in several cities. I had not dreamt she was down in Ensenada, Mexico, until recently when I was there. They seem absolutely to exist in life. When I've seen some of them transferred to the stage—like Oil King in *The Diamond Rattler*—it's as though they read for the part and got it—read for their own role. And Swimma Starnes crops up a lot.

PHILLIPS. How much of a plan do you have before you begin a novel or a play?

GOYEN. I plan quite a bit. But I'm not too aware of it. That is, I've not got it all down, but I've got a good deal of it thought through, or *felt* through, before I begin writing. So that the whole world of it is very much alive and urgent for me. I'm surrounded by it—almost like a saturating scent. I feel it like a heat. The world that I'm going to write has already been created, somehow, in physical sensation before I go about writing it, shaping it, organizing it. My writing begins physically, in *flesh* ways. The writing process, for me, is the business of taking it *from* the flesh state into the spiritual, the letter, the Word.

PHILLIPS. Do you see a progression from *The House of Breath* to your latest novel? Do you see any new directions forthcoming?

GOYEN. There *is* a progression. I'm much freer. And I see a liberation of certain obsessive concerns in my work, a liberation towards joy! I feel that I'm much freer to talk about certain aspects of human relationships than I once was. . . . What was the other question?

PHILLIPS. Do you see any new directions in your subjects or forms?

GOYEN. That's very hard to say. I'd find that only as I write on. I *do* want very much to write a heavily plotted novel, a melodramatic novel.

PHILLIPS. One last question: Why do you write?

GOYEN. And the easiest to answer! I can't imagine *not* writing. Writing simply is a way of life for me. The older I get, the more a way of life it is. At the beginning, it was totally a way of life excluding everything else. Now it's gathered to it marriage and children and other responsibilities. But still, it is simply a way of life before all other ways, a way to observe the world and to move through life, among human beings, and above all, to record it all and to shape it, to give it sense, and to express something of myself in it. Writing is something I cannot imagine living without, nor scarcely would want to. Not to live daily as a writing person is inconceivable to me.

(1976)

NOTE: *Despite Goyen's convictions to the contrary, Carson McCullers did attempt an autobiography. Unfinished at her death, it was published as* Illumination and Night Glare, *edited by Carlos L. Dews (Madison: University of Wisconsin Press, 1999).—R. P.*

Marya Zaturenska
Photograph by Helen Merrill

Marya Zaturenska

Marya Zaturenska lived with her husband, the poet, critic, and translator Horace Gregory, and their black-and-white cat, Picolo, in a charming white pre-Revolutionary house in Palisades, Rockland County, New York, on the Hudson River. Day lilies and roses flourished in season in front of the house, which had turquoise shutters and a picket fence. The house was lined with the books of two lifetimes of reading, collecting, reviewing, and judging contests. Even the attic had built-in bookcases on all sides. The first-floor walls were hung with original art, including two watercolors by their friend E. E. Cummings. Inscribed books by Cummings and other friends—among them Samuel Beckett, Edith Sitwell, Robinson Jeffers, and Robert Lowell—were in the dining room. In the "drawing room," as she called it, Ms. Zaturenska lit a fire and served me tea and smoked oysters on crackers. Mr. Gregory's den was an enclosed back porch off the dining room, where he remained throughout his wife's interview. Zaturenska explained that she did all her writing upstairs in her bedroom, and showed me the room. The bed was covered with a spread replicating one of the unicorn tapestries at the Musée de Cluny.

The interview took place on an October afternoon in 1977. The poet's most recent (and final) collection, The Hidden Waterfall, *had appeared three years earlier. As a young woman Ms. Zaturenska had been slight. Now, at age seventy-five, she was stocky, her dark hair thinning. She wore a pink cotton dress and a white cardigan. Her manner was extremely outgoing—she admitted to being a "talker." She had a racking cigarette cough and a deep laugh. Her conversation, like her poems, was fascinating and full of wit. The interview was later augmented and clarified by correspondence and telephone calls.*

· · ·

PHILLIPS. You were born in Kiev, as was another distinguished American woman artist, Louise Nevelson, and your "Variations on a Polish Folk Song" reveals some of your cultural heritage. Do you think there is a strong Russian or Polish influence in your work?

ZATURENSKA. There must be, because I am haunted by Russian and Polish folk songs. Even before I could read I used to make up songs—folk songs.

PHILLIPS. Your parents were not "literary"?

ZATURENSKA. Of course not! It could not be expected. They were not adjusted to the United States, as many immigrants were not.

PHILLIPS. Have you any childhood memories of Europe?

ZATURENSKA. I remember hearing that my mother started to work at the age of eight. For generations, her family had worked for the princes of the Radziwill family, and lived on their estate. She used to earn money by making doll clothes for the Radziwill children. They took an interest in her and in me, even after we had arrived in America. I also remember being taken to the castle to kiss the hands of the Princess Radziwill, a descendant of Talleyrand, I discovered much later. She gave me my first and only doll.

PHILLIPS. What was it like, growing up in New York City at that time?

ZATURENSKA. Difficult. I went to night school and found odd jobs in a publishing house. I also worked at Brentano's bookshop in my teens. I also took jobs embroidering—my mother had taught me to do that.

PHILLIPS. When did you start writing poetry?

ZATURENSKA. As a teenager. I was in my early teens when I first had my poems published. Some of the magazines in which they appeared are now forgotten, but they published a number of the best-known poets of the day. I received much encouragement from the beginning. About that time, I met a poet so completely forgotten now that I can almost weep. Her name was Edith M. Thomas, a last survivor of what in our *History of American Poetry* we call the "Twilight Interval." She was a good poet, but goodness requires more than competence to survive. She was completely against the new poets coming up in what can be called the "Poetry Renaissance." Eliot filled her with horror; Pound and Amy Lowell ought to have been suppressed! H. D. [Hilda Doolittle] she thought such a nice girl gone wrong. . . . Miss Thomas was an editor of *Harper's,* especially the poetry pages, and she approved of my poems until she discovered I also contributed to Harriet Monroe's *Poetry* magazine, which she considered the source of all evil. Miss Thomas also considered Edna Millay an evil force on women writing poetry, incidentally. Some of her criticism was not unjust, as when she spoke of Millay's coyness, coquettishness, and kittenish cuteness.

PHILLIPS. Who else helped you in those days?

ZATURENSKA. An old gentleman, William Webster Ellsworth—a well-known lecturer on literature in his day—who was a descendent of the dictionary man. Mr. Ellsworth took an interest in my work. He introduced me to some of his literary friends, of whom he had many, all distinguished. He introduced me to Willa Cather. It was Miss Cather who secured a fellowship for me at Valparaiso University, which in her day was noted as "the Poor Man's Harvard." At Valparaiso, everyone was supposed to work his way through. I was glad to escape from there when, through Harriet Monroe, I was able to get a Zona Gale Scholarship at the University of Wisconsin.

PHILLIPS. When was this?

ZATURENSKA. In 1923. But you asked about other people who helped. Among the people I met in New York, before Valparaiso, was a famous beauty of her day, a Mrs. Jeanne Robert Foster, who was the friend of William Butler Yeats and his father, and the famous patron of the arts John Quinn (who later bequeathed his fabulous art collection to her). Through Mrs. Foster, I met John Jay Chapman, and the interesting Irish Group then settled in New York. I even met De Valera once at her house, but I was too young and uninformed to find him interesting. About this time, I began to contribute poetry to New York magazines.

PHILLIPS. "Variations on a Polish Folk Song" and "Woman at the Piano" show a good knowledge of music. Did you study music at any time?

ZATURENSKA. Not formally, though I did everything I could at

Wisconsin, including exposing myself to events at the music school from time to time. All lyric poetry, of course, has its source in music, and I am a pure, I hope, lyric poet. There are few of us around these days. I write my poems as if I were writing a song. I think lyric poetry is the poetry which is best remembered by most people. My poems are mainly, I think, in the tradition of early Italian and early English music.

PHILLIPS. Most of today's younger poets seem to have university positions. Do you think teaching is a good livelihood for a poet?

ZATURENSKA. I think teaching is the least helpful to a poet. Teaching is not essential to writing. It is another gift entirely. At the University of Wisconsin, I took up library work as a livelihood. I would have preferred to go on in history, but I couldn't afford to go on.

PHILLIPS. It was at the University of Wisconsin that you first met Horace Gregory? You and he edited the same literary magazine there, I remember.

ZATURENSKA. No, I first met Horace in New York. I never met him at Wisconsin. I had heard much of Horace Gregory from William Ellery Leonard, my adviser at Wisconsin, who thought very highly of Horace and made me wish to meet him. Horace edited the literary magazine before I did, then moved on to New York. My coeditor was Kenneth Fearing, who later introduced me to Horace when we were all in New York at the same time. I was twenty-two when we married.

PHILLIPS. How old were you when you put together your first book?

ZATURENSKA. When I was at Yaddo in 1933. That would make me thirty-one. Harriet Monroe asked me to put together poems for a book. I had really thought of a book, someday, but it seemed too exalted a dream. I wrote not to acquire fame, fortune, or a place in the sun, but because I couldn't help it. From time to time, I wrote a poem and sent it out, and it was usually accepted. But I thought little of a book: my children were very small, our circumstances during the Depression were depressing, I had little time. But then my neighbor in Sunnyside, Long Island, where we lived at the time, and Harriet Monroe and Mark Van Doren encouraged me to put my poems together. Miss Monroe and Van Doren were both editors at Macmillan, and they accepted my first book when I completed it, at Yaddo.

PHILLIPS. Despite these early friendships with such notables as Willa Cather and Harriet Monroe, I sense you've avoided the literary scene for the most part?

ZATURENSKA. I don't know what you mean by the "literary scene." As I said, Horace as well as I wrote because we couldn't help it. Dr. Johnson, the wisest of men, once said that poets ought to avoid each other: "It is dangerous to court the rivalry of wit accentuated by malice." But, to be frank, the *best* poets we've ever Known—E. E. Cummings, T. S. Eliot, Samuel Beckett (I insist on him as a poet)—never showed pettiness or rivalries. Even Robert Frost, whose difficult life made him bitter, had moments of great impersonal generosity. Dr. Johnson had the great luck—and insight—to discover Boswell, who was considered an amusing fool. But Johnson sensed Boswell's genius, and Boswell saved Johnson— and eventually himself—for posterity.

PHILLIPS. Having avoided the limelight, how did you react to being granted an honorary doctorate from the University of Wisconsin in 1977?

ZATURENSKA. The Wisconsin thing set me up greatly. I was pleased at the honor and respect shown to both Horace and myself. (He also received an honorary degree the same day.)

PHILLIPS. I'm interested in your highly successful literary collaborations with Mr. Gregory. How much of the *History of American Poetry* did you write?

ZATURENSKA. About half—very evenly measured out between us. I like to think the seams don't show. Eliot phoned us when the book came out in New York (he was visiting the States at the time), and he thanked Horace so much for the piece on him; the best on himself he had ever seen, he said. Horace told him I had written that piece.

PHILLIPS. One of you was especially hard on Louise Bogan in that book.

ZATURENSKA. I wrote that. I was extremely naïve. In the past, before I'd received the Pulitzer Prize, Louise was friendly to both of us. It so happened that at the time I received it, Louise had expected it to go to her, though I was quite unaware of all this. When the prize came to me, it was a very great surprise. Later, I learned through a newspaper column (by Leonard Lyons) in the *New York Post* that Louise Bogan's publisher was so certain of the Pulitzer that he had placed ads in advance of the actual award, congratulating her. . . . Well, Miss Bogan and her friends became violently angry that I had been awarded the prize. I had never written or said anything unkind. Later in the *History,* I did write that she had the voice and manner of a lady commando, and that she lacked real generosity and self-control. Which was true. She lacked *mature* emotions. She was as girlish in feeling at sixty as at twenty.

PHILLIPS. You and Mr. Gregory put together two anthologies for young people—*The Silver Swan* and *The Crystal Cabinet.* Did you find that to be a creative act?

ZATURENSKA. I don't like the words "creative act." It sounds too large and grand. Those books are a reflection of our taste and judgment. Give a young person the right poems to read and he will naturally appreciate whatever is good.

PHILLIPS. How do you work? Are there any conditions you need to write a poem?

ZATURENSKA. I work whenever I can find leisure, which is not often. I am very grateful for Yaddo and the MacDowell Colony, where I wrote the first drafts of several books of poems.

PHILLIPS. In the past, I've heard you mention your Muse . . .

ZATURENSKA. I have a number of them. My gifts, whatever they may be, are very secret and strange, even to me. They come from the subconscious or supernatural inspiration!

PHILLIPS. That's another thing. Poems like "The White Dress," "The Seance," "Four Ghosts," "House of Chimeras," and "The Haunted House" have strong supernatural strains. Is there any particular reason for this fascination? Do you believe strongly in the supernatural?

ZATURENSKA. Yes, very much so. Those are all *good* poems, by the way. I've had some strong psychic experiences.

PHILLIPS. In this house?

ZATURENSKA. In this house especially! I may write about it some time.

PHILLIPS. With your frequent mythic allusions, your poetry often could be interpreted in a Jungian light. On the other hand, your work seems totally to resist Freudian interpretation. Is this conscious? What do you think of the influence of Freud on today's literature?

ZATURENSKA. I prefer Jung to Freud, but I have no feeling for psychoanalysis. In most cases, it has done more harm than good. And when it acts as a substitution for religion, it can do harm. Someone in the eighteenth century—I think it was Dr. Johnson, again—wrote prophetically that the churches had neglected their great healing and spiritual functions. The psychological causes of many diseases, of mental disturbances, he said, should have been a profound area of study by the church. Someday, he said, a clever and learned *doctor* would probe deeply into the human soul (naturally, he didn't use the word "psyche") and come up with a *materialistic* interpretation of these things.

PHILLIPS. You never had an analyst?

ZATURENSKA. I don't feel I need anything but truthful interpretations of the world around me, and the mysterious Muse that sometimes leads us to the right places (if the Muse is genuine). Byron, who *might* have been a bad poet (but became one great enough to become one of the most powerful poets who ever lived), wrote that he had "that within me that can tire / Fortune, and Fame, and live when I expire." Not that I am Byron. But in a small way, I too have this inner inspiration.

PHILLIPS. How does a poem start for you—with a line, a message, an image?

ZATURENSKA. With an image. I work on that image, and let it expand. I am a *spontaneous* poet. The images I use come from the world—narrow and intense—that I have felt, experienced, or observed. Sometimes I feel they come from a world I have lost or forgotten.

PHILLIPS. When does meter come in?

ZATURENSKA. When I have the poem in my mind, I sing it to myself over and over and over. I've written my best pieces that way.

PHILLIPS. Do your poems start longer than they finish?

ZATURENSKA. Oh, much longer. Then I cut them ruthlessly. A lyric can't be too long. I've never heard of a good lyric that went on forever. Auden's longer pieces start out well, then peter out.

PHILLIPS. Have you ever written a truly long poem? All your published lyrics are brief.

ZATURENSKA. Of course the lyrics are brief. All true lyrics are. It requires great art to do the marvelous short poem. As someone else has said, "People write long poems, lacking the skill to write short ones." Ezra Pound, that master of technique and lyricism, said, "Poetry begins to atrophy when it gets too far from the Muse."

PHILLIPS. Have you ever written free verse?

ZATURENSKA. Rarely. Poetry without music—not necessarily rhyme—is like painting without color.

PHILLIPS. Are you conscious of using symbols in your work? The snowfall in your recent marriage poem, from *The Hidden Waterfall,* for instance? The islands throughout the book?

ZATURENSKA. When I use "snow," I mean *snow.* It's a lovely, beautiful element. I prefer the sensuous perception of cold and warmth to that old imagistic bromide about the "exact image," et cetera. The poem, "Another Snowfall," *is* a study of our marriage—the hardships we've gone through together. It's a song of survival that ends on that philosophical bromide, quite deliberately, of "the pain and pleasure principle." Rather stoically, too, I think. When I speak of islands, I want to convey large free horizons, the opposite of closed-in spaces . . . the richer, fuller life.

PHILLIPS. In "Night Music" and "The Castaways"—two of your finest poems—you seem to champion the underdog or the insecure. At least, you seem to find beauty in modest or diminished things, as you did also in "Song" and "The Daisy." Does this relate to your world view or philosophy?

ZATURENSKA. Yes, but it isn't "sociology." It's something more than that. Sociology is too shallow. I'm glad you like "The Castaways." Auden thought it was one of my best.

PHILLIPS. You seem evasive in that answer. Would you care to say *what* you've been trying to do?

ZATURENSKA. If people can't find out what I've been writing about, there's something wrong with what I'm doing. Isn't that so? Sometimes, if I've been good enough in my writing, the meaning slowly reveals itself. I've never sought for the metaphysical obscurities. I work for a strong, intelligible inner clarity.

PHILLIPS. Who are the poets you most admire?

ZATURENSKA. The poet I've come to admire most is Emily Dickinson. Then there is always Christina Rossetti. Both of these women kept an inner purity and intensity, and a disregard for everything but the final truth they found in a rich inner life.

PHILLIPS. I assume you included both in the manuscript of your new prose book, "A Gallery of Poets"?

ZATURENSKA. Yes, and a few other women besides. I wished to add more. Genius of the first rank is not their attribute, but they were genuine poets, distinguished, true, and mistresses—or shall I say masters?—of a personal style. I included Sara Teasdale and Edith Sitwell in my "Gallery," too.

PHILLIPS. What other women poets do you admire but didn't write about?

ZATURENSKA. In English, I would mention among recent poets Ruth Pitter, Lizette Reese, Alice Meynell. And why does somebody not mention Elinor Wylie—a poet of great distinction and creative intelligence? I like her sonnets much better than Millay's.

PHILLIPS. And who are the male lyric poets you admire?

ZATURENSKA. There is E. E. Cummings, Dylan Thomas, Robert Frost—in some respects a fine lyric poet of a particular kind. Walter de la Mare (one of the best). Edwin Muir. And occasionally, T. S. Eliot rises to fine bursts of lyricism. So does Auden. And of course, there is William Butler Yeats, the greatest of them all.

PHILLIPS. Are there any underrated poets you'd care to talk about?

ZATURENSKA. I would mention Robinson Jeffers—a highly original and independent poet. He is more mature, more culturally significant and profound than, say, Dr. William Carlos Williams. Jeffers's use of classical themes adds a depth and profundity and meaning. Unlike Williams, he is neither arty nor merely provincial, nor a receptacle for homespun virtues. It has been Williams's misfortune to live in the shadow of the flawed genius of Ezra Pound. Then I would mention Sir John Betjeman, who is not appreciated enough in this country, but is the one shining light in English poetry today, as I see it. He has made a fine art of parody, and he is writing out of the best tradition of English light verse. He has also written *Summoned by Bells,* one of the best examples of confessional verse written in our times.

PHILLIPS. Anyone else?

ZATURENSKA. I mentioned Ruth Pitter, whose lyric poetry at her best is worth studying as a model for what is called "formal verse." And I should also like to mention Horace Gregory, whose latest book, *Another Look,* contains some of his finest work and has not received the attention it deserves.

PHILLIPS. I gather that you don't care for much of what is happening in modern American poetry?

ZATURENSKA. I feel like a nun who has walked into a rock-and-roll festival.

PHILLIPS. At the last New York dinner party given for W. H. Auden, you were seated at his right. Were you close friends?

ZATURENSKA. The question is somewhat irrelevant. The party was given because Auden had given a reading to benefit the Horace Gregory Award, a grant given by a woman who is interested in poetry. The fund is given every year for writers and poets who keep on writing well after retirement. Auden approved of the grant and its recipients, and wanted to give a gratis reading. He was always respectful and kind to both of us, and used our work for his splendid anthologies. When he first came to this country, he praised my work highly. As a human being, Auden was wise, shrewd, and that rare thing nowadays—a gentleman. He was courteous, kindly, and sympathetic. He was also a rare intellectual among poets, and there have always been very few intellectuals among the English poets. Donne was one, perhaps Milton. And I may add Matthew Arnold, who keeps surviving in spite of sneers. I have a weakness—if one has to call it that—for the poetry of Matthew Arnold.

PHILLIPS. All the photographs agree: You have been a great beauty.

Did this ever conflict with your ambitions to create lyric poetry? Can you think of any instances where it helped or hindered your career?

ZATURENSKA. I never thought of myself as a great beauty. If some of my friends thought so, I thank them very much. The only real beauty I knew among poets was H. D., who was surely one, if her early portraits are to be believed. You mention my "career." I never thought in terms of one. I've been very lucky with the people who had faith in me and who wanted to help me. Vachel Lindsay was one—why didn't I mention him earlier? Also Alice Meynell, whom I met when I was a young girl in London. Willa Cather, who always thought I had promise. That charming and cultivated man, Morton Dauwen Zabel. And James T. Farrell, the novelist, who believed in me. It may have been looks; it may have been something else. The Muse was with me from the beginning, I guess.

PHILLIPS. Have you ever written fiction?

ZATURENSKA. I tried it once. I have a fragment of it, about six chapters on my childhood in Russia. It could be a small book if rewritten. Anyway, I would like to write more prose. I have standards in prose. I envy Emily Brontë her one prose masterpiece, *Wuthering Heights,* which was also her best poem.

PHILLIPS. What about your translations from the Italian: Why do you do them?

ZATURENSKA. My interest in Italian translation first stemmed from Dante Gabriel Rossetti's fine translation of the Renaissance Italian poets. Ezra Pound thought highly of them, by the way. I began to translate when I began to love a certain poem and wished to reproduce it perfectly in English. I believe that a good poem in any language should be as good an English poem as it was in the original language. Prove that the poem you translate is a masterpiece, or almost one!

PHILLIPS. Do you think writing can be taught?

ZATURENSKA. No. We must teach ourselves. If one wants to write poetry, one can do worse than study the classics. I am sure that many of the newcomers are already on the way out, unless they grow up fast. Despite their sense of liberation, they have not one ounce of the *real* eroticism of Catullus or even of Goethe, who, in his old age, wrote poems that are both beautiful and erotic. Colette is another writer of brilliant erotica who was civilized in a way that Greeks and Latins knew.

PHILLIPS. When you put together your *Collected Poems,* you left out all the war poems you'd published earlier. Why?

ZATURENSKA. I didn't think they were good enough. And I hated politics. I'd lived through the 1930s and wanted to run away from it all. My parents ran away from the Russian Revolution, don't forget. I do like my World War I poem "The Unsepulchred."

PHILLIPS. Is there any particular advice you would give to a young poet starting out today?

ZATURENSKA. It's a hard life. They have to stick it out and grow up to it. They shouldn't expect too much from it. Neither money nor fame. Just do it because they have to. And they should work their way through to what is *real* poetry. Real poetry is hard to define. What is good for one could be fatal for another. But the *real* thing is ultimately made clear. This is not mere mysticism. I know it to be true.

PHILLIPS. You have a half-finished study of Swinburne literally in the trunk. Do you think you'll finish it?

ZATURENSKA. Why should I? Nobody wants it. And I'm not wild about Swinburne anymore. Aside from his poetry, he had no life. And yet, on second thought, no life is without meaning. Swinburne did have a crazy romantic splendor.

PHILLIPS. What is it you'd like to finish, then?

ZATURENSKA. Poems that are more profound and better. And a good prose book. But first, all I ask is to complete a new book of poems. Someone has proposed to gather all my translations from the Italian into a small book, too. That would be nice. Above all, I wish to prove to the Muse who befriended me that I am not a disobedient servant.

(1978)

NOTE: *Zaturenska's "A Gallery of Poets" remains unpublished.*—R. P.

Elizabeth Spencer

Photograph by Sam Tata

Elizabeth Spencer

Elizabeth Spencer has published a large body of work, yet she became fa-
mous for a novella she wrote in a month (The Light in the Piazza). *The*
irony does not escape her. At the time of the first interview session, in
1975, she lived in a modern high-rise apartment overlooking downtown
Montreal. A Southerner who loves the rural South, this irony did not es-
cape her, either. She had moved to Canada for reasons relating to her
husband's career.

Theirs was an apartment full of light and plants and books, many
of the volumes inscribed to Ms. Spencer by author-friends, for the most
part American writers in the Southern tradition—Eudora Welty,
Reynolds Price, Doris Betts, William Goyen. It is to this Southern tradi-
tion that, by most critical accounts, Spencer is said to belong, despite
years spent living in Italy and Canada and the subsequent fiction she has
set in both locales, including three Italian novellas. The apartment had
no separate den or study; her writing was accomplished in the corner of
the dining room, the typewriter being put away every evening when her
husband returned from work. Some time after the first interview session,
Spencer's husband, John Rusher, retired. In the summer of 1986, the cou-
ple moved to Chapel Hill, where Spencer had accepted a position teach-
ing creative writing at the University of North Carolina. The interview
was updated once in Montreal and again during a visit to her publisher
in New York City in 1989.

Ms. Spencer is a tall, fashionable figure. During the initial interview,
she wore a leopard-skin print blouse and silver jewelry. Her hair had a sil-
ver-streaked forelock. Despite her fame, Spencer possesses a shy smile,
and her soft voice carries traces of her Mississippi roots. In Montreal she

drove a stylish, racing-green Peugeot, and took me to a fine restaurant in the Old Town section.

·   ·   ·

PHILLIPS. How do you work, and at what hours?

SPENCER. I'm a morning person. The minute my husband is out the door to work, out comes the paper, the typewriter, the manuscript I'm working on. I knock off at about two, eat and take a nap if possible, then I'm out for groceries, socializing, whatever.

PHILLIPS. You didn't teach until recently. Has that been a good experience?

SPENCER. Oh, but I did! I taught early on, at a girls' school, and later I taught creative writing at the University of Mississippi. Then I went abroad, met John, and I wasn't teaching after that. It's something I got back into in 1976, on the request of a writer, Clark Blaise, who was then at Concordia University here in Montreal. He was due for a sabbatical. I did one course for him that year and liked it, liked the students, was amazed at the variety of their backgrounds. The next year, the department invited me back as a writer-in-residence. And the *next* year, they were stuck for someone to do two advanced workshops, so I did those. This year I'm only doing one. I've found the work stimulating. I always complain about anything that takes time from writing, of course, but it is equally true that one can't write all the time. On balance, so far, it's been worth it. A five-day-a-week job saps up all the time. Teaching has many advantages this way, in that time is more spaced out.

PHILLIPS. Can writing be taught?

SPENCER. Was it Jean Stafford who had the best word on that? Writing can't be taught, but it can be learned. I think so.

PHILLIPS. You were a reporter on the *Nashville Tennesseean* as a young woman.

SPENCER. The year I spent as a reporter was marvelous for me! It took me out of the genteel world, gave me enlightening glimpses into how things went on. I wouldn't have wanted it permanently; it got to be drudgery like any job, only without much uplift. Some who got the more interesting top positions maybe felt differently, but I didn't aspire to those.

PHILLIPS. Unlike your first two novels, *The Voice at the Back Door* seems drawn from headlines rather than personal history. Was this book influenced by your newspaper work?

SPENCER. There's some truth in that, though I never thought of it. It was, at least in part, "topical." I was under some sort of pressure within myself to clarify my own thinking about racial matters; many of my attitudes had been simply inherited, taken on good faith from those of good faith whom I loved. It seemed like blasphemy to question *them,* so I had to question myself. I could do that out of materials—incidents, people—which I already knew about. It was just in the melodramatic arrangement of the novel that I may have stepped things up a bit.

PHILLIPS. I've wondered how that novel was received in the South, particularly in your home region. Is that why you ran off to Italy?

SPENCER. Oh, I'm sure a lot of people in my hometown and elsewhere objected. Some of the objections I heard about: I hadn't been "fair to the South," and so forth. But, no, nobody wanted to run me out of Mississippi. At least, nobody I know of wanted to. I don't mean to make too light of this; it is doubtless still known that I went against the white supremacy thing. The people who think like that will use anything against you that comes their way. They've nothing against you except *that,* but it happens to be everything. It's the same thinking as that of the Inquisition.

PHILLIPS. There's a passage in that novel I marked—here it is: "In the South, it's nothing but family, family. We couldn't breathe, even, until we left." Was this your feeling, and is that perhaps why you no longer live in the South?

SPENCER. Oh, Lord. Okay—while family is interesting for the range of characters it offers a writer, and for the stability it may, at best, offer to the individual, it is in many, many cases stifling and destructive. There is always bound to be, at the least, *suppressed* conflict. The price is high. Someone much wiser than I once told me that Southern families were cannibals. He was an enthusiastic Southerner himself, so I felt even more the weight of that judgment. The family assigns unfair roles, and never forgives the one who does not fulfill them. Of course, a sense of freedom is a large part of my own nature. I can't be strait-jacketed.

Maybe they ask no more than all traditional societies do, one way or another.

PHILLIPS. When did you start writing?

SPENCER. I started as a child, for me a time of total unconsciousness about the "South" in literary terms. I knew we had lost the war, that was about all. We had not so much a close-knit as a jumbled-up family, lots of them living right in the vicinity—Carroll County, Mississippi—and the moved-away ones kept coming back to visit. On my mother's side of the connection, writing was a natural thing. My rough, tough uncles had all written poetry and studied Latin, too. Imagine that today! They quoted poetry in great, memorized blocks, and what they wrote sounded like Kipling or Browning. Scraps of it were to be found around the house in old school notebooks. They all thought of literary things as meriting attention.

PHILLIPS. So your family was supportive?

SPENCER. My mother's family was. Not my father's. My mother's family bought books, kept books, referred to books, read incessantly. I often heard my aunts and my mother talk of characters as though they were really living people—it was a shame Fantine in *Les Misérables* had to sell her hair and teeth; they wept over Dora in *David Copperfield,* but quoted Dickens that it was better for her to die; my aunt fell for Darcy in *Pride and Prejudice,* and so on. Others in Carrollton, my little hometown, were equally strong on reading. I did, I do believe, get the impression that here was a pursuit for good families with their minds not exclusively on money, gossip, illness, marriages, and the crops. And unlike recipes, vegetable canning, fruit preserving, sewing, and going to church, it made for talk I was interested in overhearing. I was also interested in political talk, and in that sort of reminiscence about people that led to long, partly speculative stories. Dickens, Thackeray, and Victor Hugo were in no way contradicted by the spirit of such talk, which in most cases was done with kindness, compassion, and even love, with regard to human mystery. But I'm rattling about the older generation.

PHILLIPS. What about your own crowd? Anyone with a literary bent?

SPENCER. Well, there was a cousin, just up the street—a brilliant boy slightly older than I, who talked a lot about books, music, poetry, the best movies, and got the rest of us—tennis players, tree climbers, creek swimmers, pony riders, and stamp collectors—more inclined to these things as personal experience than we otherwise might have been. He could come in while we were sitting barefoot on the piano bench playing "Chopsticks," and, shooing us away, strike up the "Anvil Chorus" from *Il Trovatore,* or a Chopin étude. His mother, like mine, had given private lessons in piano, but he—unlike me—had musical talent. He wrote some very good poetry later on, and published one volume which I still admire.

PHILLIPS. What about you? Why do you write?

SPENCER. Writing, for me, I am trying to say, was *prepared for* in various ways, but just the same, I always looked on it as a natural impulse, one I would have had anyway. It had nothing to do with William Faulkner, Eudora Welty, and the other writers of the South, though I discovered them later with great joy. My true course was already set by the culture that was happily mine from the day I was born. When I started writing stories, my mother, my aunt, uncles, and others were immediately interested—I found a quick audience and some praise, a living kind of response. I take my experience as more typical of the Southern writers than not. I don't think Southerners were as culturally isolated as is common to think. We had an "oral tradition," true, but we also had an intellectual tradition. Translations from Greek and Latin were on our shelves, and some originals, and if anybody mentioned Dante, he was there, too. In addition to the novelists I mentioned, and their like, there were also Melville, Hawthorne, Poe, and the New England poets. A host of children's classics were read aloud to me, and one was expected to know the Bible backwards and forwards.

PHILLIPS. Why do you write the way you do?

SPENCER. When I started writing I fell into a certain way of expression that was natural to me and that I liked to put down and read over. I used to sit up in a tree and write. Really. Just because you've nothing on your feet doesn't mean you've nothing in your head! I would also write stories in study hall to pass the time after I raced through my homework. Or sit up in bed on winter nights, scribbling into tablets held on my knees. Then I was getting the feeling I've always kept as the best part of it, that I was not so much writing as *letting something come through me.* This is a strange delight, but maybe many writers have it. I see it more strongly in some of my work than others, so it does not always prevail, but when it does I feel I am writing best. It comes from an inner way of seeing things in their plainest but truest way—not only seeing but hearing, smelling, feeling. The words go toward that. This can be refined, but its origin is obscure.

PHILLIPS. Could you say a little more about Faulkner? He's associated now with those same times in Mississippi . . .

SPENCER. That same cousin who played the piano and wrote poetry did tell me before I got to Vanderbilt that Faulkner was a great writer. I think I was in college, though, before I heard him say this. It was a marvelous discovery, but I don't recall reading Faulkner extensively until some years later. It was well known that he was over there at Oxford writing books. But it was widely thought that he, along with Erskine Caldwell, was busy "giving the South a bad name" in order to "make money." This opinion did not spring from literary innocence so much as from a rather more complex reaction which I won't go into here, though I think I understand it. I remember when *Gone With the Wind* came out, there were immediate readers in our town who came up with strong opinions. It was thought that the book left a good bit to be desired as fiction of the first rank, but that at least nationwide interest was drawn to the South by a popular novel sympathetic to our history. For this, they said, we could be grateful.

PHILLIPS. What other American writers impressed you?

SPENCER. My cousin also talked about Willa Cather, and I still admire Cather more than certain "complicated" Southern women writers like, say, Ellen Glasgow. Cather seems at first simple, but the simplicity has its own difficulties—like some large natural phenomenon out West that you can look at and contemplate for a long time. I knew Melville from my early days, because *Moby Dick* was my brother's favorite book. He, unlike me, did not incline toward much reading that I know of, but he read that one over and over. He thought it was about whale hunting. Of course, people who say it isn't are wrong, too. Then, I'd always read Mark Twain, and was too scared to sleep after Tom Sawyer got lost in the cave or something. I was surprised to find Mark Twain was taught in graduate school! Poe and Hawthorne were taught in the public schools—I still get a textbook feeling whenever I open them.

PHILLIPS. What about Henry James? Some have mentioned him as an influence for your later fiction, especially *The Light in the Piazza* and *Knights and Dragons*.

SPENCER. Henry James I started reading at Vanderbilt, along with many of the "modern" English writers, like Virginia Woolf. It was an interesting labyrinth, enormous skill directed toward ends that did not seem then to be all that important.

PHILLIPS. James was not an influence, then?

SPENCER. Listen, if you write a novel in Mississippi—North Mississippi at that—you are bound to be compared to Faulkner. If you write about Americans abroad in some sort of confrontation with Europeans, then you are bound to be compared to James. I couldn't escape the Mississippi subject matter—I was brought up in it. When I went to Europe, as anyone might, I couldn't help loving Italy. . . . I just adored it, everything, and went back as soon as I could. That is, when I was awarded a Guggenheim. I wrote about it because I loved it, and had stayed there so long that I thought I knew it well enough. But I always wrote from an outsider's point of view. I think it must be clear that one has to do that, out of honesty. Well, right away, here came "Henry James" in every single review.

The only odd thing was that I never once thought about it. It did occur to me, and still seems obvious, that the correct comparison for *The Light in the Piazza* might have been Boccaccio. Here was the kind of situation outlandish enough to have delighted him. Can't you hear one of his *Decameron* ladies beginning this tale: "Chancing to travel to Florence was a little countess from a town in France who had as a daughter a beautiful young girl, a cause of great unhappiness. For, since an unfortunate accident had overtaken her at an early age, she had no little trouble with reasoning, reading being beyond her to learn, and ciphering also, so that no doctor could tell her parents that she could never be cured, and no young nobleman, being exposed to her conversation, could dream of offering a serious proposal. Nonetheless, she was of so charming a nature, and so unaffected in her responses, which were all sweetness and delight, that anyone not knowing of her defect might take true pleasure in her company," and so on, through to a satire of the empty-headedness of certain well-born youths around Florence. I don't think James should even be considered when it comes to that story, though the internal narrative of *Knights and Dragons* certainly seems, on rereading it, as I did the other day, to owe a good deal to his method.

PHILLIPS. There are other relations between those two novels.

SPENCER. Oh, yes. *Knights and Dragons* was a kind of dark companion to *The Light in the Piazza*—someone with problems back home working free of them in Italy.

PHILLIPS. Both have mature women wrestling with heavy problems.

SPENCER. Yes. Many of my women characters crack up under the strain of bad fortune or psychic miseries they cannot sustain. Margaret Johnson, the mother in *The Light in the Piazza,* had had a psychic break of sorts before the time of the story. Martha Ingram, in *Knights and Dragons,* thought herself tormented and pursued until she actually was mad for a time, I think, though she managed to surface. All that story is like an image seen wavering from underwater. I wish I could have let it all play itself out in Venice, where it first occurred to me. When I got to Catherine Sasser in *No Place for an Angel,* I was able to see better what these overstrained psyches were suffering from. Catherine taught me a lot. But she got nothing except love in a pure state, which amounts to resignation. I didn't think that was enough, either, though to some lucky souls it may be. I've had trouble finding fictional women—different from the search for real people—who could take, or accept, what they had to be, and find their way. Some of my stories seem to be testing out characters, especially women, along those lines. When I finally got to Julia Garrett, the central character in *The Snare,* I felt satisfied. Her path led her right through the human jungle, but she came out sane. Maybe not safe and sound, but anyhow, at the story's end, coping, and on a human level, too.

PHILLIPS. Did you intend the knights of that title to be the men in Martha's life, and the dragons to be mental illness?

SPENCER. Women often dramatize the men in their lives; they assign them roles. Maybe I've done that, too—once in a while. When women friends confide in me, I often notice this theme. When I wrote the story, I was going through a long phase of finding myth-themes for stories centering on women. But I think the dragon for Martha was clearly set out from the beginning as her ex-husband. And Jim Wilbourne, the knight (remember all those old paintings?) who perceived her plight and should have liberated her, turned out to be rather dragonlike, too. So there's the irony.

PHILLIPS. Martha seems to feel so exiled that she suffers paranoia. Was this a trait you saw among numerous Americans in Italy? Did you share any such feelings?

SPENCER. People abroad *do* experience the pangs of separation, which is something like that graver word, "exile." They want to be thought of, not forgotten, but thought of with understanding at least, not condemned. Any evidence that this is not possible . . . well, they feel afflicted, and lacking other news, exaggerate it. People—Americans, for example—who stay abroad too long do feel a sense of guilt. I've heard this expression many times.

PHILLIPS. We were talking about other American writers you admired.

SPENCER. I recently discovered Dreiser, whom I had tried several times but simply couldn't read. Now I'm hooked. Partly due to Robert Penn Warren's fine study *Homage to Theodore Dreiser,* but also because of something that happened. I was driving with my husband through a desolate area of upper New York State. There were lakes with dead trees standing in them, lonely, twisting mountain roads, ratty small towns with maybe one streetlight, a remote feeling. I thought about the murder which happened near there in *An American Tragedy*—Clyde and Roberta, and the bird calls (was it a *weir-weir*?)—it suddenly all grew unbearably real. So real it frightened me. It seemed all to have happened, just the way he said. This is the breakdown of that reality line that fiction can make.

PHILLIPS. Your first collection of stories is dedicated to Eudora Welty. I take it you admire the work, or the lady, or both.

SPENCER. Eudora Welty is a perennial favorite. My discovery of what she was doing with the old home landscape held as much delight as what Faulkner was doing, and I especially mean *The Golden Apples,* though many others are great. I once threatened to give *The Golden Apples* to a new acquaintance, and if she didn't like it, I doubted we'd have much in common. Eudora Welty I first met, personally, partly by the coincidence of having gone to a college, Belhaven, which was just across the street from her house in Jackson, Mississippi. Some of us in a little literary society wanted her to come over and be our guest soon after her first book appeared. She came and we chatted later, and she did not forget the occasion—nor, certainly, did I. She was not so well or widely known back then as she deserved to be and later was. It was easier to see her occasionally, both in New York and Mississippi. I certainly admired her work and do still, but we have such a difference of approach, don't you think? I can't compare things like this when I am involved. The same for Faulkner. If my material seems like his, as I say, it must be that we are both looking at the same society. For instance, there is a Yocona River in North Mississippi; the family in *This Crooked Way* comes from Yocona, which I knew about all my life. People used to say "Yocony." Only long after the book was published did I realize that Faulkner's Yoknapatawpha probably had the same origin.

PHILLIPS. What is the story in the publication of your first novel? Did you have help from anyone in placing it?

SPENCER. I had written and sent off a number of short stories, and had had encouragement but no results. I started a novel based on some of these stories. I had been fortunate before that, though, in landing a graduate fellowship to Vanderbilt—ideal then, perhaps still, for anyone interested in creative study. The ghosts of the great—Ransom, Warren, and Tate—were still around, not that they were anything but alive then, but simply elsewhere. And one of the original members of the Agrarian group was still there, Donald Davidson, a superb teacher, one of the great minds I've known. I wandered away from Nashville, taught, returned to a job there, then worked on a newspaper as I said, then quit to work on my novel. Davidson knew I was working on it, and when David Clay (a New York editor with Dodd, Mead, who had gone to Vanderbilt) came through, he brought us together. So within a short time of showing Clay the unfinished manuscript, I had my first contract.

PHILLIPS. Did you, or do you, keep a journal?

SPENCER. I wish I had time to keep one. Sometimes I do; lots of good material comes along, just factual stuff, that I like to think about and make use of, but I forget if I don't write it down. There will never be a shortage, however, of one inexhaustible thing—plain old life.

PHILLIPS. Were you conscious of writing autobiographically in your first two novels? Those families seemed so well realized, it is difficult to think of them as fictional . . .

SPENCER. There is no autobiography in my early novels, or in any of my novels. Some of the stories, yes, but I can't find myself at all in the novels. I got into trouble, though, because people in our town all know each other, and have known about each other for generations, and because I had to draw on the locale, I found myself writing about people like them, though they weren't meant at all to be those people. But I've learned you can never tell anybody that what they want to believe isn't true. So no matter what I said, they still knew better, and I finally just gave up and didn't say anything. In *Fire in the Morning,* the portrait of my grandfather—a man I much admired—was deliberate, but all the events were fictional. Of course, there is a terrifying thing which may occur: *one sometimes invents what has actually happened.* This won't bear too much looking into.

PHILLIPS. Your family was upset with you over the Mississippi novels?

SPENCER. My family was upset with me-as-novelist, especially my mother, because she couldn't make the jump to modern writing or to any published writing at all being done by anyone she *knew.* It was supposed to be done somewhere else by unknown hands. However, I could always "go home again," if that's what you mean. I live in Canada with my husband. Nobody is keeping me away. Mercy, they've got more to think about than just me.

PHILLIPS. Whether you could "go home again" or not, you left the South for Italy, and then you left Italy for Canada. Why?

SPENCER. I got married in Italy to an Englishman, and lived there a couple years more, but my husband thought he could make a better go of things in Canada. His sister was in Montreal and wrote some good things about it, and about Canada generally. His mother's family had been Canadian in origin.

PHILLIPS. You didn't consider moving to the South?

SPENCER. No, John found the South impossibly hot and overcrowded with my relatives, so we set out to try our luck in a place I never dreamed of visiting, let alone settling down in! It was really the best compromise I could make, so I accepted it. I've grown to admire Canadians and to love Quebec, especially Montreal.

PHILLIPS. Would you say that you are well adjusted to Canada?

SPENCER. Oh, no, I can never "adjust" to losing anything I really love. I still miss the South; to a lesser degree, I will miss Italy. There's some argument for being able to stay in one region all your life, especially if your roots are there. Whether you write or not, there's a powerful element of feeling involved, and once uprooted, those feelings weaken. I don't think I've ever really cut the root; I never wanted to. But there's a loss of immediacy in one's experience. You have to count on memory more and daily rhythms less. But memory is a Muse, after all, a girl with a vital life of her own.

PHILLIPS. What is the function of locale in your work?

SPENCER. Some of my suburban or city-apartment stories could occur just anywhere, but these go only for a few pages. Generally, I think of fiction through people in a place. They are particular people in a particular place. "Who" and "where" is then quickly followed by "when" and "what" and "how." "Why" relates to ideas. I think Southerners are strong on ideas, but in a different way from writers elsewhere. I must be careful not to make a silly generalization, but my feeling is that Southern writers (Southerners generally) do not perceive any idea as abstract. We move toward an idea gingerly. Once formed, it is powerful and may eat you up. It's better to keep it young and playful as long as possible. But the way the Southern mind seems to work is through particulars, through felt character, experienced atmosphere. Isn't life like that? We live it, only half-knowing what it is, aware of possibilities all along, but often mistaken as to their full meaning. Then time may change it all, throw it in a new perspective. A strongly felt locale and a strongly felt character in it—these are usually the starting places of my work. I can see both—characters and place—in my head. A person, or persons, in a place, something on their minds, a confrontation, an event, a fragment of memory, an action, something to start you watching it, your mind following it . . .

PHILLIPS. Once you have your locale, and your characters, how rigidly do you plan your novels? They seem extremely well made.

SPENCER. I plan most novels ahead—they don't just happen. I think all the characters in them live in them, as though the form were a house and they were the people, and none other, who resided there. Some characters have come to the novels out of stories, and some have migrated from one novel to another. I do not plan so far ahead for stories; it does seem that a story is a more spontaneous creative act. I sometimes just drop down and write a story. I could never ever do a novel like that. Both *The Light in the Piazza* and *Knights and Dragons* started as stories, but there came a moment when I had to see them as longer works, to stop and consider.

PHILLIPS. Many of your characters seem to be "loners." Why would you choose this type of character above all others?

SPENCER. I guess I'm a mixture of sometimes wanting to be off alone somewhere strange, and sometimes liking people, desiring company. But "loner" characters are good to have in a work of fiction. They have perspective, are less easily involved in an action; they can comment, are apt to be ironic, compassionate, witty, perceptive.

PHILLIPS. Is all your travel helpful to your work?

SPENCER. I don't feel that I travel all that much. The trip to Greece in 1977 was my first in a long time, and my first ever to Greece. I was thrilled with Greece—a place I'd always wanted to go. I visited a Canadian writer, Audrey Thomas, for a time. She had part of a house in a fishing village on the south coast of Crete, Aghia Gallani. I loved the life. We swam twice a day. I used to go down early and see them bring the catch off the fishing boats. And the farmers coming into the square with loads of fresh melons used to whack them open and give me sample slices to eat. The whole town knew everybody. The woman who owned the house had a loom in the parlor. I watched her weave. Every morning about a hundred donkeys began to go *hee-haw . . . hee-haw . . . heeee-haw . . .* just like in Mississippi. Greece inspired the South somewhere along the line. I love the whole Mediterranean world. I think most people do. Maybe it's a buried racial memory, and we all came from there.

PHILLIPS. What differences have you perceived between American and Canadian literature?

SPENCER. That's an interesting question. Canadian literature has made a worthy, self-conscious effort to be itself just in the last ten years or so. Which is to say there is some needed walling-out of American influences. Still, many have noticed comparisons. Alice Munro's studies of small-town Western life owe much to her reading of the Southern writers; I think she told me that herself. Think of Margaret Laurence and Willa Cather. Parallels abound between French Canada and the South—a conquered society with different customs having to exist in terms of a larger, controlling nation, for instance. The French here have their own language, to give them unity, centrality. But it, of course, restricts their audience. Still, Marie-Claire Blais is widely translated, as is Anne Hébert. Less well known are such good novelists as André Langevin and Hubert Aquin. There are similarities between Blais and Carson McCullers; and Hébert has a historical sense of French Canada—one looks to the Southern writers like Andrew Lytle for comparison. Novels that, to my mind, are *just* Canadian, without any possible reference to another society, are Margaret Atwood's *Surfacing* and Timothy Findlay's *The Wars*. I admire Robertson Davies, his *Fifth Business* especially. But it is rather a special case.

PHILLIPS. Are you at all conscious of being a woman writer? That is, a woman who writes fiction?

SPENCER. At the start, I felt put off by sensitive women writers whom I'd read but did not want to be like, even though I'd started by admiring them. I mean someone like Katherine Mansfield, then later, Virginia Woolf. I thought both were overlyrical, not nearly tough enough. So I tried to get a natural bent to lyricism (I had started out in college writing poetry) out of my style, to develop a plainly stated, hearty style—hospitable to sensitivity but not dependent on it.

PHILLIPS. Do you mind the term "woman writer"?

SPENCER. Would you mind the term "man writer"? "Woman

writer" is just next door to "lady writer." I wanted to be firm and even tough-minded—if not "tough" in the Hemingway sense—a novelist only, as distinct from a woman novelist. That was my early reaction—it had nothing to do with women's lib, of course—but for me it was the right beginning. Even in *Fire in the Morning*, my first book, I originally wrote long, lyrical, girlish passages about the young woman who came to that town from a past outside it and married the central character. I had looked on it at first as primarily her story, as it might indeed have been if I could have got my prose to measure up. I think I was too girlish then myself to write well about her various sensitivities, hesitations, et cetera. My first editor urged me to cut all that out, so little of it remains, enough I guess to see what the rest might be like; and the weight of the book fell on the men and some of the older women who were part of the town, and they held it up.

PHILLIPS. How do you determine from what point of view to tell a story? *This Crooked Way,* for instance, has four parts in the first person, only one part in the third person. Why not all five in the first person?

SPENCER. Point of view usually comes with the story in my mind and can't be changed very fundamentally afterwards. I know that "trying from a different point of view" is a recommendation in creative writing workshops, but I could never do it; the whole integrates at once in one way, and there's just no disintegrating it. In the novel you ask about, I had the problem with point of view toward a central character, who was primarily obsessed—a God-driven person. I had some straining to do, but I felt I had to arrange significant points of view around this figure. How could he be able to assess his own story and have the reader believe that his assessment could be reliable? So I balanced around him certain voices—a former best friend, a niece, then with deeper significance, his wife, then back to him again for the finale. This was experiment, if you like, but I think it had to be done that way to get the total picture.

PHILLIPS. And why was one part, the beginning, in the third person?

SPENCER. It was my way of coming in from the outside, to lead both myself and the reader into the story. The third person is admirable for its power to move inward, then enclose.

PHILLIPS. What are your feelings about "experimental prose"?

SPENCER. Writing is always an experiment. But, on the whole, I guess I am anxious to be understood, to be clear. That leaves out the "experimental," to put it in its usual meaning. Flannery O'Connor once said, "If it looks funny on the page, I don't read it."

PHILLIPS. Do you consider yourself a religious person? *This Crooked Way* is really about religion.

SPENCER. I was brought up to be very religious and sent to a Presbyterian school, so at various periods of my life I have felt close to that sort of thing. I think I have a feeling for the Protestant Southern experience just from seeing so much of it, as well as from some personal participation when I was growing up. There's a lot of variety in it, but it's mainly Bible-based. In 1975, when my father was in his late eighties, I was home to see about him, and saw he had brought in some large pieces of petrified wood from a small cattle place he had near town. He said, "I reckon those things have been there since the Flood." I said, "What flood?" He said, "*The* Flood!" Well, the Mississippi River had been known to break out in notable floods, but I never knew the high water to get up to our town, which is in the hill section. I pursued: "You mean 1927?" He got angry: "I mean the Flood in the Bible!" That one, of course, covered the whole earth, involved Noah's Ark, and presumably left petrified wood outside of Carrollton, Mississippi!

PHILLIPS. Your mother was just as religious?

SPENCER. She saw the Hand of the Lord everywhere. I remember when the British army retreated from the Continent at Dunkirk, she remarked that the Lord had sent a fog to cover them. Being a Presbyterian, she got upset when people made fun of "predestination," but hoped to retreat with dignity by saying it was clearly set forth in the Bible. She took it for granted that everybody believed in the Bible, or that if they didn't, they knew they ought to.

PHILLIPS. Is there such a thing as an ideal reader you write for?

SPENCER. I never think of any one reader. But I do hope to be a source of interest and delight to those who want to follow me, which excludes, I guess, certain kinds of readership. It would mainly exclude, I hope, people who want to see life only from one aspect—sex, religion, politics, even "Southern-ness." I doubt if those who have special interests find my work offers great satisfaction. I'm a questioner, a searcher. . . . I'd like to interest people who are that, too.

PHILLIPS. Your books all have beautiful titles. How do you find them?

SPENCER. I like to choose around until I find the right one. There's always an original impulse toward writing a work which has not yet been formed. When I look for a title, I go back to that. *The Voice at the Back Door* . . . when I thought of the South and race, the blacks, I first remember how black servants of ours, or blacks we knew, would come to our back door when they were in trouble. They would stand and call out of the night. It was further considered a breach of custom for a black—or Negro, as we called them then—to come to the front door. In our whole town, I think, only our old nurse, Aunt Luce Breckinridge, was permitted that. She was born a slave. In a recent program on William Faulkner, photographed at Oxford, a black man told about the old family nurse doing the same thing, going in through the Faulkner's front door. I doubt anyone not born down here would know the significance. So I went back to that germinal thing, that small but significant custom, for that title.

PHILLIPS. What about the title, *The Light in the Piazza*?

SPENCER. You like that title?

PHILLIPS. Yes.

SPENCER. At the publisher, they jokingly referred to it as "The Light in the Pizza"! Oh well. As a title, I hope it functions several ways. There is the duality of the word "light"—the real light in Italy, so beautiful and strong that one feels one can see everything. Then there's the symbolic meaning, which is pointed up a number of times in the book—light and enlightenment, I suppose. And of course Clara's name itself—her name means light. I was also playing up comic aspects of the novel in the title, but most people missed that. I once said, in an interview in *Mississippi Quarterly* where the same thing came up, that just when you think you can see everything, the motives of these characters, and what they are actually doing, and why they are doing them, are all opaque. The poor girl's mother stayed in a state of confusion all the way through.

PHILLIPS. I'm glad you mentioned the significance of Clara's name.

Many of your characters' names seem to be tip-offs to their function or meaning, such as Jimmy *Tallant*, Jerry *Sasser*, Beckwith *Dozer* . . .

SPENCER. I generally name my characters the way I do because that is their name. Sasser I see no significance in; Sasser is a fairly common name in the South. Clara did, of course, have the tie-in to light.

PHILLIPS. What about symbols, then? Are there any that you consciously utilize? There seem to be a lot of horses in your novels and stories, horses used in the Lawrentian sense of sensual power . . .

SPENCER. There are certain recurrent figures in my work, I know. I guess I am drawn to write over and over about horses because of a fascination I feel for them. One of my stories is called "The Girl Who Loved Horses." I was brought up around animals, and for riding I had first a donkey, then ponies, then horses. We lived on the outskirts of a little town, had a big property with a barn, kept mules and cows. It was no trouble to feed ponies and later a couple of riding horses, nothing fine, though. I was lonely in the winters when none of my cousins were around and outdoor sports were practically impossible. So I used to ride a lot, alone. Then, on my uncle's plantation, I would ride with him some summers almost every day. In those days, you had to ride a horse around a plantation to see what was going on. I rode at school, too, and wherever I happened to be. At Oxford, at the University of Mississippi, when I was teaching there, I kept a horse the whole time. So horses crop up in my stories—pun not intended. I think I love them aesthetically; actually I'm a little afraid of them, of the spirited ones; part of riding excitement is in the tension. I've been run away with, thrown, bitten, and kicked, though not in the head, I'll have you know!

PHILLIPS. Are you conscious of any other symbols?

SPENCER. Storms show up in my work a lot, too, for much the same reason; they were fierce, dangerous, sometimes awesome around where I lived. Listen, if you want to find a symbol, there's nothing stopping you. Symbols should be like that in stories—not hauled in, but rising out of the possible, in feeling and event.

PHILLIPS. Some of the events in your later fiction seem improbable, like Arnie in *The Salt Line* mounting the large sea turtle he meets while swimming, and proclaiming, "Take me to the deep." Such events give your work a dreamlike quality. Any comment?

SPENCER. It may be that most of these actually happened. The South is semitropical, near the Gulf Coast especially, and many events partake of the strange natural phenomena in the area. South American fiction often sounds fantastic, but I bet a lot of it is to be thought of as the actual. The sea turtle episode was related to me and my father. He used to go with a group on a charter boat to fish in the Gulf. They once went ashore on a small island, and there in the shallows one of them discovered a giant turtle, which he rode out to sea for a distance. My usual theory is not to invent very much, only uncover what happens anyway, "strange as it seems."

PHILLIPS. I've been wanting to ask you: Is *The Light in the Piazza* your glory or your albatross? Its fame, I mean.

SPENCER. It's my albatross. I think that it has great charm, and it probably is the real thing, a work written under great compulsion, while I was under the spell of Italy. But it only took me, all told, about a month to write, whereas some of my other novels—the longer ones—took years. So to have people come up to me, as they do, and gush about *The Light in the Piazza,* and be totally ignorant that I ever turned a hand at anything else, is . . . upsetting. I suppose I should be grateful they've read that. You know, I always thought it was so nice of President Kennedy to have said when he met Norman Mailer at the White House, "I've read *The Deer Park* . . . and the others." The fact that Kennedy didn't come out with *The Naked and the Dead* must have been gratifying to Mailer.

PHILLIPS. The character Elinor appears in both your first and second novels, *Fire in the Morning* (1948) and *This Crooked Way* (1952). I feel she represents certain aspects of your own personality. How do you feel about that?

SPENCER. I saw her objectively, not as myself. However, several people said the same thing you did. I wanted at first in the second book to give her a new life, a better marriage, etc. But her family's story fascinated me. I felt I knew it already, so I wrote that. Actually, I was intrigued by a story of her own family that she (an outsider) came out with at the Gerrard dinner table. About how her father got his plantation, and who her mother had been, and so forth. She told it to "put down" a rather slick Yankee type who was talking of the South in stereotype, *Gone With the Wind* terms. When casting about for a subject, I thought I would follow that, explore it, see where it led me. My own family had always been in the hills, but close to the Delta, and I knew a lot of stories, a lot of lives.

PHILLIPS. The town of Tarsus in the one novel and the town of Lacey in the other seem the same.

SPENCER. Hmmmm. . . . The geographical layout of both is close to that of Carrollton, Mississippi, my hometown, it's true. I intended just about everybody as fictional. But some maps get engraved on your soul.

PHILLIPS. I've always felt that your novel *The Voice at the Back Door* (1956) would have concluded perfectly with the words "You just can't tell" in the last chapter, before the "Epilogue." That ends on just the right note of hope for improvement in racial relations. Isn't the "Epilogue" anticlimactic?

SPENCER. Well, no. . . . I still see it as a necessary part of the book. Maybe it goes on a little too long? The book was about *all* of them, you see: Duncan was no more its main character than Jimmy Tallant or Beck, Tinker no more than Marcia May or Lucy. They had all been affected by the events they lived through, and had to be seen as coping in the future with what was now their past. I also had to have the part about Cissie's being fully conscious of what she had done and not giving a damn. Cissie is the "Southern Bitch," totally self-confident, entirely self-assured. Someone else, however, also told me the book should have ended just where you said. But to me it is right.

PHILLIPS. Wasn't William Goyen your editor for *No Place for an Angel* (1967) and *The Snare* (1972)?

SPENCER. Yes. It was a wonderful surprise when Bill came to Mc-Graw-Hill as editor. I had been stuck for somebody to work with, as there had been certain departures. Yet they wanted to continue to bring out my work. Bill was a fine writer, as you know—I admire *The House of Breath* enormously—and he helped me get going again after some personal upsets, hang-ups, whatever. He got enthusiastic about *No Place for an Angel* and really worked on it with me. Our only trouble was that, both being writers, we would go into spasms of fictional excitement at the same time. Bill's wife, the actress Doris Roberts, is a level-headed girl, and she had a wonderful knack for bringing us both back to earth. Bill also helped get the story collection *Ship Island* together. I had a very happy time working with him. He also read one early version of *The Snare,* but he left publishing to do his own writing full-time before it was completed. He did, I think, make some valuable suggestions. It's probably my most underrated book.

PHILLIPS. Both *The Snare* and *The Salt Line* (1984) seem built upon a fascination with the underworld—criminals and countercultures not found elsewhere in your work.

SPENCER. Actually, as far back as *The Voice at the Back Door,* I had a group of crooks running a gambling syndicate come up to put some capital in a small-time highway operation. I had fun writing about these people, who seem—in addition to everything wrong and shady— rather funny. In *The Snare,* the sinister gang is much worse. They are perverted, dirty, depraved, and altogether despicable. I don't try to point out morals, but I think here that it wasn't necessary. Marnie and Wilma were simply ghastly examples of humanity. They were not even clever or amusing.

In *The Salt Line,* Frank Matteo started out originally to be a little like this, but I saw as he came to life for me that he wasn't all that low. About this time, I had access to a lot of material given to me by a friend who is a reporter and had done extensive interviews with certain Mafia types. This gave me ground to move in, as I could see the wide spectrum of types, each with an individual story, the good within the bad— which, of all things, strikes me as most touching, as though the good struggles to live and is always being slapped down. Frank had something of this struggle internally, and though the book is not his story, at least that good is not extinguished in the end.

PHILLIPS. That whole novel seems to be about crossing certain borders and boundaries.

SPENCER. The idea occurs and recurs. First, the beginning idea is in the title, but before that it was in my experience. The salt line is a liberating point between the restrictive side of living in small-town Protestant

Mississippi, and the tolerant attitudes of the Coast. In the novel, however, Arnie comes there to cut himself off from the wounding experience of being turned out of his university, to start a new life. And Lex, his nemesis, comes there to score in a materialistic sense, to set himself up in the world. A doom waits for both, but Arnie accepts and converts his doom into a continuance, a life acceptance, and Lex . . . well, it's all in the novel. There is also the crossing to the island, which represents a mystical stepping-up of the Coast experience. There are other ramifications.

PHILLIPS. This novel marks a departure for you, doesn't it, in that the two protagonists are men? Your recent novels seem to be about women.

SPENCER. I found it very difficult to write a story mainly involving men. The central character, I saw early on, would have to be male, but I had envisaged him as mainly relating to a number of women. Actually he does, if you notice. There are more women than men, or at least as many, in *The Salt Line*: Evelyn, Mavis, Dorothy, Lucinda, Barbra-K. But for some reason, the males do dominate the story. One person I didn't particularly welcome in the book was Lex. But once he got into it, I couldn't get rid of him, so I had to make the best of him. My idea is that stories are found, not invented. Having found this story, I had to write it the best I could. Maybe it should have been found by someone else, by a man, rather than a woman. But it wasn't.

PHILLIPS. Is this novel a glorification of past events, of the Old South?

SPENCER. One title I thought of for the book was *After the Storm,* or *Wake of the Storm.* Central to my idea was a very American syndrome, the passing of the days of glory. American society does throw people at times into great heroic relief: then events move on and they are dropped, forgotten. They are bound to remember. Memory could become a sort of life in itself, but Arnie knows you have to move on. Evelyn is in counterpoint to this theme, for though she has crossed a boundary— she died—she too is not confined to the past; when she appears it is not to take life back, but to urge it forward. The notion is that the dead continue, not as the past, but continue to live.

I question your phrase, the "Old South." Arnie is not trying to renew the Old South in the meaning it always gives to Confederate ideals. The feeling of life along the Coast was never that—the Coast as I see it related to the Gulf, the Caribbean, Mexico, and New Orleans. It does not turn inward, though wars and histories always turn up in its experience. A certain atmosphere, built up through the years, relating to its flora and fauna, traditions and architecture, made it the unique place that it was. This uniqueness is not "Old South" so much as personal. Arnie does not want this entirely obliterated in the storm's wake by new building on the current order. He has, I think, the admirable, correct idea that renewing himself can't be done directly—only indirectly, by giving himself to something he can believe in. The novel is about personal renewal, but with that realization central to it.

PHILLIPS. Did you have Shakespeare's *The Tempest* in mind when you wrote *The Salt Line*? There seem to be parallels.

SPENCER. Oh, yes, *The Tempest*! There are certainly enough feelings about that floating around. The island has a mystical sense to it, and visions there are possible. It is more in feeling than in literal parallels that it gets through. Arnie is in a way a benevolent spirit, like you might think of in connection with Prospero. I think he possibly has some mystical powers. A good deal of that feeling also came from the logs of an artist—a very fine one—called Walter Anderson, who lived on the Coast and constantly went out alone to paint nature on Horn Island. His vision was directed toward the actual natural life he found, yet he was profoundly mystical, as his work shows. There are a lot of moon references, too—in relation to the women— but it is not all worked out as some might have done.

PHILLIPS. Let's talk about your latest book, *Jack of Diamonds* (1988). It seems to me the themes of the stories are very interrelated. Taken as a whole, it is one of your strongest books. Were you consciously writing variations on a theme?

SPENCER. The stories were written over a period of about seven years, and I worked on other projects during that time, too. I wasn't conscious of a common theme while I was writing them; they're not interrelated as to character and setting. But when I look back, I see there is a related theme. Perhaps it is mystery in close relationships. All the main

characters in these five long stories are women, and each has a relationship in which important matters are concealed.

I don't think this is an unusual preoccupation. It only means that in
every real—or intense and highly important—relationship, complete
openness cannot exist. There is always something mysterious and illusive
about "the other." I have dramatized this in various ways in the stories,
without consciously trying to do so. Only in the last one, "The Skater," is
the search a different thing. I think there the main character, Sarah, seems
to be searching for a hidden truth, first in her lover, then in the young
man Goss, but she is really searching for the true nature of herself.

PHILLIPS. In "Jean-Pierre," on one level, the story seems to be
about what the French went through in Montreal, in the quest for assimilation. But on another, it seems to be about one's inability to understand
others. Callie's husband seems especially inscrutable and mysterious. Did
your own marriage to a citizen of another country [Englishman John
Rusher] in any way help formulate the theme of this story? Or was it all
those years you lived in Montreal among the French Canadians?

SPENCER. This story really is about mystery compounded by the deliberate effort of French Canadians to insist on their separateness. They
did not seek, but resisted, assimilation. Callie and Jean-Pierre relate on
the level of passion, but he seems from all indications to be in mortal fear
of the judgment of the English business community. His side of the
story—why he left so strangely—would be very different, I think, from
hers. The strain this places upon her is what makes the story work.

As for my husband being English, this does at times present interesting points of contrast in our ways of doing things, our attitudes, and so
forth. But the real source of this story was the Québecois.

PHILLIPS. In "The Business Venture," Nelle seems under the impression that she can lead her own life the way she wants to in this day
and age. But given the social milieu of her Southern town, can she?

SPENCER. Nelle had reached the point of seeing her own life as her
"crowd," with whom she had been identified for so long. She knew she
had to be practical, and following along from one practical point to another, in order to make the business go, she stepped over a lot of lines. But
she was superior—of a better family socially than the rest—and perhaps,

too, she had the confidence of the innocent. It's really Eileen's story, not Nelle's—the mystery of Charlie that Nelle is able (all so innocently, just by being there) to make plain. Once the mystery is gone, Eileen sees the plain truth, and her illusion about him goes, too.

PHILLIPS. In this story, the outsiders are not the French among the Canadians, but rather the blacks, pro-blacks, and nonsociety figures in the New South. It is the minds of the blacks whom the whites cannot comprehend, despite their apparent "loyalty."

SPENCER. This is a very old state of affairs. It does figure into this story, because Nelle has evidently been successful in uniting herself to black "loyalty," while the others are uncertain outsiders to it.

PHILLIPS. Again, in the title story, "Jack of Diamonds," the daughter discovers that she hasn't understood the nature of her parents' marriage, or her father; and in "The Cousins," there is an ambiguity of emotions between the cousins, and Ella Mason's inability to decipher the true nature of Eric.

SPENCER. I don't doubt the cousins all loved each other, in a family-related sort of way. But thrown into more intimate relationship when they were on their journey abroad, they began to run into mysteries. I look on the triad of Ben-Ella Mason-Eric as being the essential one. She seems to love them equally, until she and Eric are thrown together, while Eric is in a long suspension of both trying to be like Ben and to be separate from him. When Ben throws the burden of Eric's departure squarely on Ella Mason, she feels she has to go and find him. This was a breakthrough of sorts, but very late, possibly too late, to recover what was there for them both.

Incidentally, everywhere I go, people tell me they love "The Cousins." I don't know why—maybe it's because all families have this sort of mystery hanging about them?

As for "Jack of Diamonds," the girl really had all the materials at hand to know that her mother's state of mind must have contributed to her fatal accident, but she hid it from herself. It was again her love that made her not want to face the truth in things. But the discovery of her father's former relationship with Eva made her inner evasion no longer possible.

PHILLIPS. The final story, "The Skater," seems to be about attachments—to children, mates, lovers, the past. Yet the heroine seems at a loss without her children, who are grown, and her husband, who has grown distant. Would you say the young man, Goss, is a son figure more than a potential lover?

SPENCER. Sarah seems to be seeking her own nature in her relationships with Goss and Karl. Many threads tie her to Goss, among them, their both being Canadian, both having residence in Westmount. They also both have Ted, her husband, in common, and have tried together to figure out the old father figure. Goss wants to be adopted—she wants to adopt. She will skate in wider circles now, with more confidence.

PHILLIPS. *The Light in the Piazza* has been the public's favorite book of yours. Do you have a personal favorite?

SPENCER. I often think *This Crooked Way* is my favorite book, though the writing is not so mature or sustained as in others, like, say, *The Voice at the Back Door.* It did have original, deeply felt ground to explore. It was something I don't think Faulkner—giving his awesome genius every due—ever touched on, and when Flannery O'Connor came along, her strict Roman Catholic point of view prevented her seeing it, to my mind, as it was. But this was before she started publishing. The religious fervor of the willful, ego-centered man, his sense of a personal God-mission, the way he took to express it, the way it took him, the myth of it, and the ritualistic resolution . . . this all holds me still as being rendered in an accurate way, despite stylistic flaws.

PHILLIPS. And your favorite of your own stories?

SPENCER. I don't know. I like "Ship Island" very much. It was misunderstood by a lot of people, the way *Knights and Dragons* and *No Place for an Angel* were misunderstood. But it still stays with me for some reason—I'm not sure I know why. Perhaps because I always gravitated toward the Gulf Coast. I also like "The Finder," "Indian Summer," "Prelude to a Parking Lot," and "The Girl Who Loved Horses"—four long stories which I consider to be among my best.

PHILLIPS. Who among your contemporaries do you enjoy reading?

SPENCER. Well, Eudora Welty, and Katherine Anne Porter—I guess she's still "contemporary"—I love *Pale Horse, Pale Rider.* Then there are John Cheever's stories, Walker Percy's *The Last Gentleman,* and Joyce

Carol Oates's stories—I haven't read them all, but want to. And on and on . . .

PHILLIPS. You recently moved from Montreal to North Carolina. Has that move affected your writing in any tangible way?

SPENCER. I moved in June 1986. Nothing so far to report. Currently, I'm finishing a novel called *The Night Travellers*. It's partly set in Canada, during the exile of American draft defectors there, during the Vietnam mess. In the Jamesian sense, I guess it's an "international novel." It's now about finished, except for some final revisions, and should be out next year.

PHILLIPS. How do you feel about money, in relation to serious writing? Would you write better if you had more or less of it?

SPENCER. It's nice to have it. It's ideal not to have money worries. However, writers have always proved their work can exist in extreme poverty or extreme wealth. . . . Personally, I just like to be well enough off. I've written under very poor circumstances, and made do on a daily basis only by counting pennies, and sometimes even dropping in on church suppers to cease from a diet of peanut butter sandwiches. I don't know if I wrote better then; it just seemed a nuisance.

PHILLIPS. Have there ever been long periods when you could not write?

SPENCER. During the last decade, when my parents were in a long decline—they have since died—I was needed to help them out a good bit, and I was disturbed by their aging, the whole implacable process of it. I did mainly short things during this time, and found that any longer thing I attempted was broken up by recurrent problems. Otherwise, I am sometimes stopped in my work by a normal course of having finished up one crop and having to put in a whole new planting. This is gradual, almost a natural process of replenishment, and I get impatient while it's happening, and think the whole thing's over, I'll never write again. Then I do.

PHILLIPS. Do you reread your own books?

SPENCER. I often have to, to get together readings or comments. But not all of anything, I think. I feel I've heard it all already. I'm sometimes surprised that I let such awkward parts get by, and occasionally that I could have possibly written anything good.

PHILLIPS. Have your sensibilities changed over the years?

SPENCER. There were many things I couldn't see clearly when I was younger, and I was inclined to make judgments about them out of ignorance. I don't know if there has been a change or a deepening of sensibility. If either, I hope my work reflects it!

PHILLIPS. How much of writing has to be firsthand experience?

SPENCER. That's an old question. My feeling about using such things is that anyone has got to be aware of the dark side of life; it gets into all human relationships, be they ever so joyful, balanced, and wise. No way around it. At a certain swivel of circumstances, the saint may turn into a devil— frightening but true. So when one brings on the scene the admitted crook or outcast or underworld figure, one is really just dramatizing what is latent in the nice little boy next door, or in one's old Sunday School teacher, the high-school principal, or the U.S. president, and the next is—guess who?—one's self.

PHILLIPS. Given thinking like that, does being a writer make relationships more difficult?

SPENCER. I've found there are many different temperaments among writers. I am personally often distracted, absent-minded, fractious, and anxious. I guess this makes me difficult at times. It's nice to be able to say, "Well, you see, I'm a writer," especially if it saves you from losing a friendship or getting kicked in the behind.

PHILLIPS. Do you think you would have been as happy, or less happy, if you hadn't become a writer?

SPENCER. I think I would be far less happy without a creative outlet. Everybody needs one in some form, to some extent. I'm just glad I found mine in writing, and early on.

PHILLIPS. Finally, do you have any advice to give to young writers?

SPENCER. Writing is hard work and guarantees no security, no rewards or pensions—it can't promise you anything. Bearing that in mind, you go ahead with it because you love it. Any art has the aspects of a love affair, lifelong.

(1989–1991)

William Jay Smith

Photograph by Rollie McKenna

William Jay Smith

William Jay Smith—whose latest collection at the time of this interview,
The World Below The Window: Poems 1937–1997, *was published by the*
Johns Hopkins University Press *on April 22, 1998, his eightieth birthday—is the author of more than fifty books of poetry, children's verse, literary criticism, translation, and memoirs. He is also the editor of several influential anthologies. Smith served as Consultant in Poetry to the Library of Congress (a position now called Poet Laureate) from 1968 to 1970. His memoir,* Army Brat *(1980), was praised by Eudora Welty, Ralph Ellison, and others, and his translations have won him awards from the Swedish Academy, the French Academy, and the Hungarian government. Two of his collections of poetry were final contenders for the National Book Award. His prizewinning children's verse is collected in* Laughing Time: Collected Nonsense *(1990), and his criticism in* The Streaks of the Tulip: Collected Criticism *(1972). Poet-in-residence at Williams College from 1951 to 1961, and chairman of the Writing Division of the School of the Arts at Columbia University from 1973 to 1975, he is professor emeritus of English at Hollins College. A member of the American Academy of Arts and Letters since 1975, and its former vice president for Literature, Smith maintains two residences—one, an apartment in the fifteenth arrondissement in Paris, the other, a house called Bryant Cottage in Cummington, Massachusetts. This interview took place in the upstairs den of the latter, on a hilltop in the Berkshires.*

Built in 1801 as a wing of the William Cullen Bryant homestead, the Bryant Cottage was dismantled and sold in the middle of the last century, and then moved to another part of town. In 1910, the house was purchased by Mrs. William Vaughan Moody, the wife of the Chicago poet, who christened it "The Thanatopsis Cottage," in the mistaken belief that Bryant had written his famous poem there. She moved it to another part of the mountain and restored it as a literary retreat. Padraic Colum, Robert Frost, Edwin Arlington Robinson, and others came there in the summer to write. (The house was once offered permanently to Frost, but he declined, saying that he needed something closer to a school for his children.) In the summer of 1921, Glenway Wescott wrote his first novel there. Smith bought the house in 1966, shortly before his second marriage, totally unaware of its history. In recent years, the Smiths have doubled its size, adding a new wing designed and built by Smith's stepson.

To reach the overhead den, one must climb a steep and narrow circular staircase, which to a stranger seems precarious. But Smith, a large man, ascends with ease. When he does, he says he feels like he's on shipboard, a feeling familiar to him, since during World War II he served for almost two years as liaison officer aboard a French war vessel in both the Atlantic and the Pacific. There are two rooms upstairs, each filled with books. The first room contains a bed, the second, Smith's desk, manuscripts, bookshelves, and files. Windows overlook the mountains, fields of loosestrife and goldenrod, and a metal lawn sculpture by Smith's son, Gregory. Smith proudly announces that he has just cleaned up the clutter for the occasion.

The interview took place over a weekend in October 1997, and was updated in 1998. Smith was at ease, speaking slowly and thoughtfully. He remained seated at his desk for the duration of each session, reaching from time to time for a book to illustrate a point. When he quoted verse, however, it was from memory. At the conclusion of each session, he and I were treated to an epicurean meal prepared by Smith's French-born wife, the translator Sonja Haussmann, whose translation of a selection of her husband's poems, L'Arbre du voyageur, was published in France in 1990.

⋅   ⋅   ⋅

PHILLIPS. How do you feel now that this large selection of your life's work, *The World Below the Window,* is being published? Are you happy with it, and do you think you've done all that you set out to do as a poet?

SMITH. Since I came from so unlikely a background, having grown up on an army post as the son of a professional soldier, I think that my literary aspirations were somewhat limited in the beginning. I'm happy that a few of my poems have found a wide audience. It would be nice to think that they might be around for some time. But then, as Louise Bogan put it, being a successful poet is like being a successful mushroom. A poet springs up and is what he is—shaped by whatever talent he has—and that is that. I hope that I have been true to what talent I have.

I'm really astonished that I have survived this long. I can't believe that I've been at it for all these years. I still like to think that I have something worthwhile left to say.

PHILLIPS. An army post does seem an unlikely starting place for a poet. How did you become interested in poetry?

SMITH. I was born in Louisiana, but brought up in Missouri, on the edge of the South. Both my parents were Southerners and great talkers. As a child, I listened endlessly to them telling stories. They talked so much that I sometimes think that I had to become a writer in order to get a word in. It was the pattern of their speech, the rhythm of the words and sentences that delighted me. I like to feel that my poetry is part of the oral tradition that is very much alive in Southern literature. Poems like John Crowe Ransom's "Captain Carpenter," and the stories of Eudora Welty, have to be *heard* to be appreciated. Eudora Welty once said that her ears just opened out like morning glories when she was growing up, and the same thing was true for me. I loved to listen, and talk was so important because it constituted really all the entertainment that there was. Then when I went to Sunday School and church, what I heard was the King James version of the Bible, and there was no better training than that for a poet's ear.

I was fortunate in having excellent teachers who were passionate about poetry. Every morning, one of them read to us a lyric from Palgrave's *Golden Treasury* and another from Robert Herrick. And then, as I have described in detail in my memoir, *Army Brat,* just as I was beginning high school, an elocution teacher—or "expression teacher," as she called herself—came along and took me under her wing. She wanted to prepare me for a career on the stage, and had me memorize long passages of poetry, and for that I have always been grateful.

Many of my poems have first been written completely in my head before I have put pen to paper. When I was in the navy, I'd be working on the deck of a ship with no pencil or paper before me. I would say the poems aloud, over and over to myself, until they seemed right. I still do that.

It is ironic that now, when there is a constant proliferation of poetry readings, so much of what is read simply doesn't come off the page, because it was written more for the eye than for the ear in the first place.

PHILLIPS. Do you think these early memorizations of your work account for its formal nature? Rhyme is a great aid to memorization, isn't it?

SMITH. No question that rhyme helps to keep it all in your head. The fact that I read my poems aloud constantly while composing them may well account for their formal nature. They move from the lips to the ear—as poetry did in ancient times, and as it should today.

PHILLIPS. Why don't you say more about your navy experience?

SMITH. In June of 1942 I was sent to Pearl Harbor, then on to Palmyra Island, which is a thousand miles southwest of Honolulu, six degrees above the equator. I was personnel officer of the air base there for ten months. The yeoman who worked with me pointed out that naval officers were supposed to report regularly on any language capabilities that they had. So I wrote a letter to Washington outlining my background in French, Spanish, and Italian. I sent it off thinking that that would be the end of it. But about five months later, I was ordered to North Africa. I spent several months in Casablanca, and then was named liaison officer on board an Aviso Colonial, *La Grandière,* a French gunboat that was sent to Norfolk, Virginia, to be remodeled and then out to join the American South Pacific Fleet. I was the first American officer to serve on board a French ship during World War II. No one knew what to tell me to do; I had to create my own job. I had a signalman and two radiomen, French-speaking, of French Canadian descent, and we were responsible for all the ship's communications. We spent a year and a half in the South Pacific, calling during that time at most of the French possessions, the Marquesas, Tahiti, New Caledonia, and the New Hebrides. We were an escort ship with big five-inch guns, but no speed, and so we were usually left behind the main line as a station ship.

There was a good library aboard, and I had a lot of free time. That's when I started writing poetry in earnest. On shipboard, I completed poems like "The Massacre of the Innocents" and "Of Islands." I sent a number of poems to *Poetry* and they received a prize. Then Oscar Williams asked me for work for his anthology *The War Poets*. Those war years were extremely important for the formulation of my work.

After I left the ship in Panama in 1945, I volunteered for the Navy Language School in Boulder, Colorado, and went there to study Russian. Although I left before the end of the course, having completed four years in the navy, I'm glad to have had those several months of total immersion in Russian. They've been invaluable to me.

PHILLIPS. What about your subsequent work as a translator, which has been extensive? Has that helped or hindered your own poetry?

SMITH. It's not possible to write poetry all the time. When I'm not able to compose something of my own, I like to keep my hand in language, and that I've done with translation. And I've learned a lot from the poets I've translated.

PHILLIPS. Were the French Symbolists a conscious influence?

SMITH. I came to them quite naturally. I had read Laforgue, who influenced T. S. Eliot, before I read Eliot and his paraphrases of Laforgue. So in a sense, I went directly to the same school as Eliot, and discovered many of the same things he did. I wrote a master's thesis on an old French epic fragment of the thirteenth century, *Ami et Ami*. Work on that influenced my early poetry, also. I've kept up an interest in French poetry and prose. In the 1950s, I brought out *Selected Writings of Jules Laforgue,* the first extensive selection of his work in English. I later translated his *Moral Tales.*

PHILLIPS. How would you define the translator's responsibility to the original?

SMITH. One thing is certain: no poet should undertake the translation of the work of a foreign poet for whom he feels no affinity. Not everyone is capable of translating everybody else. This affinity may be difficult to gauge, because one is perhaps drawn to a writer who represents something one lacks, or wishes to fortify, in one's own work. Then, of course—and this is often totally forgotten—the translator must have absolute control of his own language, the language into which he is translating. Today, since the study of foreign languages has gone out, we find young poets translating from languages they do not know into others they do not know, namely their own.

The translator's chief responsibility is to convey in another language the meaning of the original. You can, of course, do an imitation, as Robert Lowell did, and as others before him have done. But it's interesting to go back and check the great poetic translations: Chaucer's and Wyatt's translations of Petrarch are very close to the originals in both form and content, and brilliant. It's a mistake to think, as Lowell apparently did, that you can do better than your original. His arrogance made for inaccuracy in translation and inadequacy in poetic quality.

PHILLIPS. How does translating languages you know well, such as French and Italian, differ from translating languages you know less well, such as Russian and Romanian?

SMITH. My background is in the Romance languages, along with Latin and Vulgar Latin, which I studied intensely. My Russian is not good, and I've always collaborated with a native speaker, usually with Vera Dunham. But I've worked so closely over the years with Andrei Voznesensky that several of his poems in *An Arrow in the Wall,* which I edited with Frank Reeve, I translated entirely on my own. I don't feel as confident in the beginning working with Russian as I do with French. But sometimes it makes it easier to take liberties if you don't know the language so well; you're less constrained. In the case of Romanian, I've worked on her own poems with Nina Cassian, who is fluent in both French and English. And in Swedish and Hungarian, which I know only slightly, I've collaborated with informants such as Leif Sjöberg and Miklós Vajda, both magnificent linguists, and we've checked out every word in other languages that I know better.

PHILLIPS. From Jefferson Barracks you went to Washington University in St. Louis, right? And it was there that you met Tennessee Williams?

SMITH. Yes, he came there after he'd been to the University of Missouri, and after he'd worked for a while for his father in a shoe factory— as a senior when I was a freshman. I seem to be the only person left who knew him before he became Tennessee Williams—when he was still Thomas Lanier Williams. I'm now writing a piece about our years together in St. Louis.

Clark Mills McBurney and Tom and I organized a chapter of the College Poetry Society. We met regularly at Tom's house and severely criticized one another's work. Tom was then writing mainly poetry and was just beginning to write plays. We later organized what we called the St. Louis Poets Workshop. We had some stationary printed up and sent our poems out to magazines, with a covering letter claiming that this work was but a sampling of the renaissance in poetry that was then taking place in St. Louis. The poems all came back, with the exception of one that I placed in the *American Mercury,* and others which appeared regularly in *College Verse,* where we all won prizes.

PHILLIPS. What were the circumstances behind placing your first book—called simply *Poems* and published exactly fifty years ago?

SMITH. Sheer luck. There weren't many small publishers or even many little magazines in the 1940s. Claude Fredericks and Milton Saul, who ran the Banyan Press, were just beginning. They'd published only one title and were casting about for another. They came to me and asked if I had a book. I didn't at the time, but said, "Yes," right off, then went home to put one together. Dylan Thomas had come out not long before with his *21 Poems,* and twenty-one seemed to me the right number. I'd written many more, but narrowed the choice to twenty-one, hoping that they would elicit the same kind of enthusiastic response that Dylan Thomas's twenty-one had.

While the book was being printed, Marianne Moore wrote to the editors of *Furioso* about a poem of mine, "Cupidon," which she called "a permanence, a rare felicity." The book had no dust jacket, but the publishers put a little band around it with Marianne Moore's quote. With that endorsement, the book was reviewed everywhere—so Marianne Moore really launched my career.

She knew "Cupidon" by heart, and whenever I saw her, she would recite it to me. She told me that she had sent it to T. S. Eliot, who replied, "It's very nice, but what are those blankets doing there?" He was referring to the stanza:

> To love is to give. His words like wire
> Dragged the ocean floor.
> Throw ten of your blankets on the fire,
> Then throw ten thousand more.

In the poem, an old man is stating that one should give up everything for love, while in actuality closing the door and taking everything in. I was thinking of the ceremony of potlatch in which the Northwest Indians, in order to show their power in the tribe, throw as many blankets as possible on the fire. The one who divests himself of the most blankets gains the greatest power. The blankets demonstrate the sacrifice of all that is warm and protective, but the irony is that they can also extinguish the fire. I thought that in the context of the poem this was all very clear. And it seemed odd of Mr. Eliot to object to my blankets, when he had so many truly obscure images in his own poems.

PHILLIPS. When you read through your poems, are you aware of a William Jay Smith style? If so, what characterizes it and when did it gel?

SMITH. That's for other people to judge. As Frost said, it's up to other people to say whether or not you're a poet, not you. And they can also probably best characterize your style. I do think I had a recognizable approach from the very beginning, which is why I could reprint several early poems in this new collection. A poem like "Quail in Autumn" was written sixty years ago, when I was an undergraduate.

PHILLIPS. You had apparently established yourself as a master of the short formal lyric. But around 1966, you made a shift to a more relaxed, long poem. I'm thinking of "The Tin Can," "Northern Lights," and "Morels." Were you influenced by any poets at that time, or did this come about by different demands you were making on yourself or on the poem? I wondered if you had been reading Whitman.

SMITH. Early on, I was not a great reader of Whitman; I have been since. But I wasn't thinking of Whitman then. Right now, I'm doing a final version of the last poems (*Les Derniers Vers*) of Jules Laforgue. And what he did, I did. He first wrote very tight lyrics, then broke them all up. He said, "I must break up everything." And in the 1950s I translated Valery Larbaud. In his *Poems of a Multimillionaire*, he had been influenced by Whitman but was a very witty and sophisticated writer in a way not at all Whitmanesque. Laforgue and Larbaud were the writers who really influenced me.

Some critics said at the time that I had been influenced by the Beats—Ginsberg, Corso, and the others. That's not true. I had my own interest in free verse quite independent of theirs.

PHILLIPS. You were a strong opponent of the Beats in the sixties.

SMITH. Yes, I objected to the carelessness, the sloppiness, of much of their work. I thought then—and I think now—that free verse ought to be just as carefully written as formal metrical verse.

Today, it's nice to have the so-called New Formalists reviving form, but I don't think that form ever went out. But let us not forget that a poem written in strict form can be just as boring as one written loosely in free verse. It's a question of the skill with which it's handled, the way thought and feeling are communicated. A rigid form in itself does not necessarily assure one of memorable poetry.

PHILLIPS. How do you decide what form a poem will take?

SMITH. The poem decides. You can think beforehand it will be this or that, but in the course of writing, the poem takes on a shape of its own. Age-old forms give a certain timelessness to poetry, and a timeless quality is what I most admire and what I constantly strive for. Within ancient formal patterns, language can be unmistakably contemporary. As in Charles Causley's ballad "Nursery Rhyme of Innocence and Experience." Causley, in that poem, refers to a man who has sailed off to Algeria. That's a modern reference. And coming in the midst of this ancient ballad form, it cuts through and makes for a certain memorable tension.

PHILLIPS. Do you ever rewrite published work?

SMITH. In the new collection, I did change a few lines in some of the early poems, and deleted a stanza here and there. But I did no *major* rewriting. I tried not to do what Ransom and Auden and Marianne Moore had done by rewriting entire poems. They were, of course, changing what they thought about a subject or event, but my poems are not so much poems of ideas as they are poems of feeling. You're not violating a feeling if you change a line, but you can be violating a thought by such a change.

PHILLIPS. You never write a "confessional" poem?

SMITH. I've deliberately left myself out of my poems, but even if I have objectified my feeling, I'm still there. The poet is always in the poem. James Fenton has written about the heartlessness of form in my poem "American Primitive," where the story of a man who has hanged himself is compressed into a few lines. Fenton points out that there was material here for a short story. If you read my memoir, *Army Brat,* you see what that poem is based on. But to objectify the experience, I set it back a hundred years, which accounts for the way the man is dressed—the high-top shoes and the stovepipe hat.

When I wrote it, I was not aware that I was going back to a childhood experience. I went that deeply into my psyche. As Fenton points out, it's what is left out of this poem that's important. Of course, it took a lot of doing to know what to leave out. A lifetime of writing, really.

I've always thought of poetry as an art of distillation—of setting down as much as one can in as few words as possible, and of saying it as simply as possible. The real complexity lies underneath. The greatest artist doesn't show that he is being difficult, that he is saying something complicated. It's when the reader goes back and rereads the poem for the second or third time that he realizes there's a lot more there than he originally thought. He is discovering that the poem has resonance, that it gives off what García Lorca refers to as *sonidos negros,* "dark sounds." Resonance is one of the most important elements in poetry, and one lacking in much of contemporary poetry.

PHILLIPS. In addition to your large body of translations, you've also produced a considerable body of children's verse and nonsense verse. How do you see those within your oeuvre?

SMITH. Writing for both adults and children makes me feel at times rather schizophrenic. I've discovered that there are some readers who know me *only* as a writer for children, while others know nothing of my children's books. But I don't know why those worlds should be so separate. I hadn't thought of writing for children until I had children of my own, when my son David was four years old, and then it just happened. And I was delighted that I did. Now I'm writing for my grandchildren. I've had college students come up to me, suddenly realizing that I was the author of poems they'd read and enjoyed as children. "You wrote 'The Toaster'?" they ask, still unconvinced. Then they recite:

> A silver-scaled Dragon with jaws flaming red
> Sits at my elbow and toasts my bread.
> I hand him fat slices, and then one by one,
> He hands them back when he sees they are done.

That poem has been illustrated many times, but the illustration I prefer is one that was sent to me by a small boy. He had copied out the poem and drawn a fierce dragon with flames shooting from his mouth, and right in the middle of the flames, he had pasted a real piece of toast. I keep that drawing here in my office to remind me of the kind of response one would like to have from a reader.

One nice aspect about writing for children is that the poems just go on and on—what is good for one generation is good for another. Of course, that's true of all poetry—the best poetry. I've been fortunate in that some of my children's poems are reprinted regularly in anthologies and textbooks throughout the English-speaking world, and have provided me with a certain income that has remained steady for many years. In Russia, my children's books are best sellers. In the translations by Boris Zakhoder, the translator of *Winnie the Pooh* and *Alice in Wonderland,* they have sold hundreds of thousands of copies. But because they were printed before Russia signed the copyright agreement, they have not brought me a cent. I'm delighted all the same that they have given pleasure to so many children. Kathryn Crosby (Mrs. Bing Crosby) called me when she returned two years ago from Novosibirsk, in Siberia, where she had been performing Chekhov, to tell me that in the Red Torch Theatre there, a musical based on my children's poems was playing to packed houses.

I am not the first to say that, in the deepest sense, childhood is a poet's greatest resource, the gold mine to which he returns throughout a lifetime. I've always admired Klee's statement that he wanted to paint like a child, but like a wise child. And that is what I have wanted to do in poetry.

Unfortunately, there seems to be a general feeling in this country that anyone who writes for children is lightweight, not to be taken seriously. This was not true of W. H. Auden, who encouraged me in my work for children. For him, Beatrix Potter was one of the finest prose stylists in English, and he had great respect for Lear and Carroll. And for Walter de la Mare, who has always been highly thought of in England. In this country, his work appears in almost any anthology you open, but he is not much appreciated by poets. But I can remember standing between Dylan Thomas and John Betjeman in a pub in Oxford, listening for a good half-hour to their praise of Walter de la Mare, as they cited individual poems and stories back and forth. That just would not happen here. And it's too bad.

PHILLIPS. In his autobiography, Karl Shapiro says that the surest way for him to stop writing is to travel abroad. But travel seems to have nourished your work. Is that true?

SMITH. Very much so. Europe stimulated my imagination, I suppose because of my background in languages. But I remember Elizabeth Bishop commenting on some of Barbara Howes's poems about Italy. Elizabeth said that she didn't respond to Italy imaginatively the way she did to South America. So it's all probably a matter of personal chemistry.

PHILLIPS. Is the role of the poet today different in America than in other countries?

SMITH. Yes, indeed. The poet does not have the role of intellectual spokesman here that he has in Europe, particularly in Eastern Europe. In Russia, the poet has always been the voice of the people's deepest feelings, its conscience, and consequently he or she has played an important part politically and historically in the country. The poet has always been looked up to—still is today. When I was a Fulbright lecturer in Moscow in 1981, I was treated like a rock star. If I mentioned to a taxi driver that I was a poet, he would drive me all over the city free of charge. And poets have been respected and even revered in France. One can't imagine Americans arranging a public funeral for Robert Frost as the French did for Paul Valéry in Paris. Valéry's funeral was truly a national event of importance. In many South American countries, poets have held high governmental and diplomatic posts. Here it became a media event to have

Robert Frost read at President Kennedy's inauguration. But most of the time poets are scarcely noticed at all.

PHILLIPS. Is there a discernible lifestyle among American poets today?

SMITH. Most poets now are teachers and live on or near college campuses. In the generation preceding mine, with poets like Wallace Stevens, who was an insurance man, and William Carlos Williams, who was a doctor, and T. S. Eliot, who was a bank employee and then a publisher, there was a greater variety of professions and backgrounds. It was only in the 1950s that the teaching of writing at universities became so widespread.

Robert Frost made the poet acceptable in academia, but he was careful never to get involved in the teaching of writing. Poets today in the universities can seldom avoid it. And such teaching is not always beneficial to the poet and his poetry. When you teach, you use your critical as well as your creative faculty, and it is not always easy to keep those faculties separate. To my mind, it is important for a poet to do something completely unrelated to writing, if at all possible. In England, until recently, poets have had to make a living in some other way—in journalism, government positions, what have you. I think that has been better for their poetry.

PHILLIPS. You met a great many writers during your four years abroad; did you ever meet Ezra Pound?

SMITH. No, I'm sorry that I didn't. I was shy when I was young. When Cyril Connolly first published a poem of mine in *Horizon,* he asked me if there were anyone in London I wanted to meet. There were many people I was dying to meet, of course, but I was too shy to mention anyone. I didn't go on literary pilgrimages in the early days. In Florence, I lived near the Sitwells and Sir Max Beerbohm. I could have gone to see them, but I didn't. I did see writers who passed through Florence— Stephen Spender, Sinclair Lewis, and Harold Acton, who lived there. Spender and Acton became close friends. I helped Sinclair Lewis pick out the house he rented in Pian' dei Giulleri, above Florence, and which he occupied the year before he died.

PHILLIPS. You did meet Dylan Thomas?

SMITH. Yes, I saw him repeatedly in 1947–48, when he lived near Oxford. On Saturday nights, Barbara Howes and I would join him and his wife Caitlin and a small group in a series of pubs. He was very amusing, a wonderful storyteller, and we spent many happy hours together. Without my asking, he took an interest in my work. Without ever saying a word to me, he passed some of my poems on to the editor of *Life and Letters* in Wales, where they appeared. Even then, it was clear that, for all his brilliance, there was in him a self-destructive element that was taking over. And when we returned to New York in the early fifties, it was exactly at the time that he was dying in St. Vincent's Hospital, just across from our apartment on Perry Street.

PHILLIPS. Did you suffer as an expatriate, living abroad for so long a time?

SMITH. Living abroad made me feel more American than ever. Like Henry James, I came to examine what it truly means to be American. And of course, the European experience worked its way into many of my poems, like "Morning at Arnhem" and "The Park in Milan."

PHILLIPS. Stephen Spender, who has praised your poetry, has spoken of its "painterly qualities." Would you comment on that?

SMITH. I had never thought of that until reviewers like Spender pointed it out. But then I realized that I had always wanted to be a painter, and that my imagination is definitely a visual one. In Florence in the 1950s, I started to paint, and most of the small landscapes I did then—watercolors and oils—I gave away. As Elizabeth Bishop said of hers, they were definitely "not art." But they were interesting documentation. I wish I had kept more of them—I have only one or two left. I was very pleased not long ago when my son Gregory, who is a talented sculptor who works in welded steel, said that he thought highly of one of the Florentine watercolors, and that it ought to be reproduced on the dust jacket of one of my books.

PHILLIPS. How important is it to your work that, on your mother's side, you are of Choctaw descent?

SMITH. All in all, I'm genetically a combination of many strains—English, Irish, and French, as well as Choctaw. My Choctaw blood, limited though it is (I am one-eighth, I believe), has perhaps not overtly found its way into my work. But in underlying ways it may have. A close relation to the natural scene, a reverence for nature—I hope that my poems reflect these qualities of the Native American sensibility. I would like to think also that the visual element in my work owes something to my genes. When I started to do my typewriter poems—concrete poems composed on the typewriter in which the letters make pictures—someone said that they looked like Indian pictographs. And perhaps they do. I was using the letters on the typewriter the way the Indians used pictorial symbols.

In any case, my exploration of family history has led me to a permanent interest in the removal of the Southern Indians to west of the Mississippi, and to my writing the long poem "The Cherokee Lottery," which concludes my new collection.

PHILLIPS. You were Consultant in Poetry to the Library of Congress from 1968 to 1970. Was it a good experience?

SMITH. It was baffling at first because, as in my liaison job on board the French ship, there were no guidelines. William Maguire, in his history of the consultantship, *The Poet in the Catbird Seat,* points out that I traveled more than any other consultant. I went first in 1969 to Japan and East Asia—Korea, Indonesia, and then in 1970 to the Soviet Union, where I traveled to Georgia and Siberia. Then afterward to Poland, Romania, and Hungary, Cypress, Israel, and Turkey. In Romania, my meeting with Nina Cassian resulted—two decades later—in my editing and introducing in this country the volume of translations of her selected poems, *Life Sentence.* I went back many times to the Soviet Union, and several times to Eastern Europe, to Hungary especially. At the Library of Congress, I organized the first International Poetry Festival. I had eight poets from different countries around the world—among them Yehuda Amichai from Israel, Vasko Popa from Yugoslavia, Francis Ponge from France, and Nicanor Parra from Chile. It was a fascinating group, and we had a wonderful time together.

PHILLIPS. What was your involvement as poet-in-residence at the Cathedral of St. John the Divine in New York?

SMITH. I followed Daniel Haberman, the first poet-in-residence when the Poets' Corner at the cathedral was established. I served from

1985 to 1988, supervising the election, by the thirteen writer-electors, of two deceased American writers each year to be inducted into the Poets' Corner, and then arranging the program of the induction in the fall of each year.

PHILLIPS. For a time, you were sole poetry reviewer for *Harper's*. What about this experience?

SMITH. At times it was horrible. I found that I made countless enemies. Not because of what I wrote, but because of what I didn't write. Certain poets never forgave me for not having mentioned their books. My piece was an annual roundup. You know how it is when the books arrive and accumulate—you have to make a selection and tie things together. In doing so, you pass over some excellent things. But it was clear in some cases that I just did not approve of some of the poets I omitted. Like Auden, I don't enjoy reviewing bad books, but I've done it on occasion when I thought it necessary to take a stand or make a point.

PHILLIPS. What is the state of literary criticism in America today?

SMITH. It's at its lowest ebb, I think. Almost anybody today can put together a collection of articles and book reviews, and call it criticism, without having any focus whatever. Whole areas of poetry are neglected. It's bizarre. Take Helen Vendler, for example, who has the most powerful critical position, and who has written brilliantly on Wallace Stevens. But in championing some younger figures, she loses all credibility. Dave Smith, who has written good poems, is far from being the demigod she made him out to be. In her espousal of the elaborately baroque, she seems to dismiss any poetry that is immediately accessible, simple, and direct.

When poetry magazines like the *American Poetry Review* and *Poetry Now* came out as tabloids, it was the beginning of the end of serious poetry criticism in this country. How can you present something that's meant to endure in the form of a throwaway newspaper? By its nature, this is not durable criticism. Then the whole commercial scene took over, as well—big photographs of poets and critics, and less and less concern about what they were saying. It all started back in the forties with Oscar Williams and his anthologies. As an advertising man, he chose interesting photographs, and he used advertising techniques to advance his collections. He emphasized the wrong, the less important, aspects of poetry, and moved further and further away from the actual texts. People remembered his wife, Gene Derwood, more for her glamorous portrait than for her poems. We don't really know what Shakespeare looked like, and it doesn't matter. What matters is the poetry.

PHILLIPS. What was your fascination with the *Spectra* hoax? You wrote a whole book about it.

SMITH. I was fascinated to see that so many important people had been misled and taken in by what was trumped-up, inferior work. I thought by examining the hoax that I could show just how bad literary criticism could be, and how unfair and silly critics continue to be. My book had considerable critical attention, but its message was lost. Some of the reviews of it were as badly written as the poetry Bynner and Ficke had put together in their hoax. I was shocked then, as I am now, by the total absence on the critical scene of common sense, and of a sense of humor that goes with it. The situation in poetry today is not unlike the prevailing one in 1916, when *Spectra* made its appearance. It's a boom time. There is less talk of "schools" now than there was then, but only because the word "school" has gone out in favor of the word "generation." Now a new "generation" seems to come in every other month. The Beat Generation replaced the Silent Generation, and the Confessionals replaced the Beats, and so on. Now it's the New Formalists. Tomorrow it will be something else.

PHILLIPS. Why is the critical situation so different today from a generation ago?

SMITH. Critical writing just isn't appreciated in the same way, and fewer poets are writing criticism of real merit. It was always illuminating to read critical pieces by Marianne Moore, for example—odd though they were. They were delightful; she would come up with such unexpected things. I love what she said once about "climax" in poetry. Climax is a pyramid, she observed, but that pyramid can be inverted, as it is by Ludwig Bemelmans, when he says of the twelve little girls in *Madeline*: "They smiled at the good / and frowned at the bad / and sometimes they were very sad."

A total but effective anticlimax. She had wonderful perceptions, and used examples from her wide reading. As did Louise Bogan in her *New*

Yorker pieces, which were beautifully concise, but wide-ranging and res-onant—like her poetry.

PHILLIPS. Tell me about the "competitive" poems that you and Richard Wilbur used to write down at the local grocery store in Cum-mington, Massachusetts.

SMITH. It was Dick who began the game. We both used to reserve copies of the *Sunday New York Times* at the Cummington Family Store (now called the Old Creamery). Our names were put on each paper, so no one else would get it. And whoever arrived at the store first would write a little verse on the other's paper. They were usually little jokes about each other's poetry or person—charming insults, really. Here are some:

> WILBUR: Bill Smith squats down and meditates
> On Illyés, whom he then translates:
> Some think he's brilliant, but to the rest
> He's the pest of Buda and the Buddha of Pest.

> SMITH: What if one day while Wilbur rested
> His fertile brain became infested,
> Would an *InFest*schrift be then designed
> To mark the decay of that noble mind?

I saved some of them in a notebook, and on my sixtieth birthday, Sonja had them privately printed in a limited edition, called *Verses on the Times*. It was actually reviewed in the *New York Times*. Finally, we had to stop our practice because the store changed hands, and the new owner no longer reserved papers by name. But Dick and I still exchange verses by mail from time to time. It's been great fun for us both.

PHILLIPS. Do you share your serious work with Wilbur?

SMITH. Yes. We've been close friends since the fifties, and have lived near each other for thirty years. I greatly value the advice he has given me on many of my poems. And I've seen a number of his most famous poems before anyone else except his wife. Dick is always seeking advice about his poems, although he rarely takes it. But he has on occasion made a few changes that I suggested. I've also sometimes helped him arrange the order of poems in his books.

PHILLIPS. Which other poets do you share your work with?

SMITH. You are one, of course. And two younger poets, Henry Taylor, who was my student at Hollins, and who has since won a Pulitzer Prize, and Dana Gioia. The two of them went over my *Collected Poems 1939–1989* and helped me decide what should be in and what should be out.

PHILLIPS. All those poems, and all those translations—but you wrote only one play. Why?

SMITH. Yes, *The Straw Market,* a satire on Americans in Florence, which I wrote in 1965, when I had a Ford Foundation grant to spend a year at the Arena Stage in Washington. The play was produced the following year at Hollins College, directed by Harold Stone, with New York actors in the lead. And then it was given as a staged reading at the YMHA Poetry Center in New York. But it has never had a full New York production. I suppose that fact discouraged me. But I also did a dramatic version of my memoir, *Army Brat.* It's called "a dramatic narrative for three voices," those of the poet, the mother, and the father. It was presented at the Public Theater in New York and at the Library of Congress, with wonderful actors taking the parts of my mother and father, while I read the part of the poet-narrator. Many people found it quite effective. I've often thought I might turn it into a full dramatic production. I've always loved the theater. But I have to finish some other projects first.

PHILLIPS. You did public speaking of a different order back in the early 1960s, when you were a member of the Vermont House of Representatives for two years. South American and European writers are often actively engaged in politics, but American writers are not. How was that experience?

SMITH. I wrote a piece, collected in *The Streaks of the Tulip,* about how I happened to run for office in the town of Pownal, Vermont. I was asked to run for selectman, and I was flattered to be asked, since I was an outsider, not a born-and-bred Vermonter, and only forty-two at the time. But I realized I didn't know many people in the town, and felt that I should go around and call on them, which I did. They said, "It's wonderful that you're doing this, but you should really be running for the state legislature." I said, "I don't really want to run for anything." In the end, I lost by forty votes, and several people came and said, "Remarkable for a complete outsider," and they talked me into running for the legislature. I was the nominee of both parties and was destined to be a shoo-in. But then the state was to decide whether or not to allow pari-mutuel betting, and our town was to be the site of the first race track in the state. I took a stand against betting, and said that I thought the track would be a disaster, which ultimately it was. A lot of big-city interests started agitating for the track, and I received threatening phone calls late at night, saying that my house would be burned down if I continued to oppose pari-mutuel betting. So I fought to win, and even though betting and the track were voted in, I won by forty votes.

I wrote a number of occasional poems while in the legislature, which I read on the floor of the house, and some of which got published nationally through the wire services. I was named Official Poet of the Legislature. One particular poem that has frequently been reprinted was "A Minor Ode to the Morgan Horse," written when the Morgan horse was voted the official state animal.

It was very enjoyable to be doing something totally unconnected with writing, and stimulating to be associated with a small group of so-called Young Turks of both parties, who were working to change the state, and to elect two years later my seatmate Philip Hoff as the first Democratic governor in 109 years.

If I had been in the legislature of a larger state, it might all have been different. Of course, I knew Robert Frost, and he was delighted that I was in politics. He once said to me, "You hold down the southern part of the state, and I'll hold down the northern part, and we'll try to find someone for the middle." I found in the end that the job was taking all my time. I was part of the longest session in the history of the state, and I could see that if I continued, I would have room for nothing else.

PHILLIPS. Speaking of politics, what do you think of the current controversy revolving about the National Endowment for the Arts? Would you sign such a document as they're asking recipients of grants to sign?

SMITH. No, I wouldn't. There shouldn't be any restriction on subject matter in art, but there *is* such a thing as reticence, which these days is completely forgotten. One is not absolutely fascinated by photographs of fornicating couples, heterosexual or homosexual. Such photographs may shock, but they are not necessarily art. Several people such as Hilton Kramer, who tried to question the merit of Mapplethorpe's photography, were pounced on immediately for siding with the censors, which was ridiculous.

If you read Painter's biography of Proust, you know that Proust led a shocking life. But his experience was filtered and transformed in his work. Today, we don't seem to want anything held back, filtered, or transformed—we want everything raw.

When you get government involved with the arts, you're in for trouble. I remember Katherine Anne Porter predicting that if we had a National Endowment for the Arts, the bureaucrats would get in the middle of it, and she was right. Now you have these panels made up of a writer from one ethnic group, one from another, from every special interest, the thinking being that every side has to be represented. And the result is that many awards go to totally worthless and untalented people. Art is not democratic. On the other hand, it would be a mistake if the whole Endowment went down the drain because of the way things have been mishandled.

PHILLIPS. You seem to have an understanding of politics in Stockholm, as well. Why did Robert Frost never win the Nobel Prize for Literature?

SMITH. Frost doesn't go well in other languages. Except in Russian. In French, he sounds pedestrian—I think that was the reason, really. His stature was just not recognized. Eudora Welty hasn't received it for the same reason. Attempts have been made to translate her work into French, and more recently into Swedish, but the results have not convinced the Swedes. They have some peculiar reasons for denying a writer the prize. One member of the Swedish Academy told me that Graham Greene would never get it, because he should have received it when he was young. He deserved it but never got it. But then, neither did James, Proust, Joyce, Valéry, or Tolstoy. The list of omissions is long.

PHILLIPS. How do you write? Pencil, pen? Have you ever worked on a word processor?

SMITH. A word processor? No, I'm very, very old-fashioned. I just work with pen and paper, certainly for poetry. Then I type it all out and review the typed version. I could never write poetry on a word processor. I can't even think of doing it. For prose, I do work directly on the typewriter, from beginning to end, striking out what doesn't fit afterwards, rather than striking it out on a screen while I'm doing it. A word processor may well be fine for second printouts and the like. But as far as composition from the beginning, I don't see any advantage for me. I even use an old-fashioned manual typewriter—not an electric one. I type quite well. I went to business school after high school because I didn't think I would get to college.

PHILLIPS. Do you keep a notebook or journal? If so, to what purpose?

SMITH. I keep endless notes, which are usually on scraps of paper in folders. I should be more systematic, but I do have folders of unfinished poems and essays. I've kept some for years. Then one day, a few words or lines will complete the work. I never know when that will happen.

PHILLIPS. Do you write on schedule? Or is it a matter of bursts?

SMITH. I try to keep to some sort of schedule, wherever I am. When I settled down to complete *Army Brat,* I wrote most of the book from six in the morning until noon, every day for six months. Now I'm planning another prose book, which I would call an autobiographical novel rather than a memoir. If I can devote some time exclusively to it, I can finish it in six months, too. It's all written in my head and in notes. The same is true of my projected poetry cycle about the Indian removal in the South, "The Cherokee Lottery," a few sections of which appear in my latest collection.

Of course, as one grows older, one doesn't have the same amount of energy. I get up very early, but I need a nap in the afternoon in order to accomplish anything in the evening.

PHILLIPS. Did you ever suffer from writer's block?

SMITH. Certainly. My poem "The Tin Can" is about not being able to write. And "The Tall Poets" plays with the same notion in a lighter vein. Ironically, by writing about it in each case, I managed to break the block. If I'm ever truly blocked, I turn from my own work to translation, as I have said.

PHILLIPS. What was the longest silence you endured?

SMITH. There were several years in the 1960s when I was not writing poems. And in recent years, poems have not come as easily as they formerly did. I have a lot of unfinished work. But now again I feel I'm coming back. But I don't think it's important to have work always pouring out. Look at Valéry. Writing for him was extremely difficult. He makes that clear in everything he wrote. The sculptor Brancusi said, "It's not difficult to work. It's difficult to *begin* to work." Often, I think of a writer like Di Lampedusa, who wrote that wonderful novel *The Leopard*. He carried that book around in his head for a quarter of a century, at least. Then he sat down and created a masterpiece.

PHILLIPS. For whom do you write?

SMITH. I like the answer that Robert Graves gave long ago: "One writes for one's friends." With the hope, of course, that the work will eventually reach a wider audience. You cannot write for an abstract audience. If you first please yourself, then your friends, that's about the most you can do.

PHILLIPS. What specific training would you recommend to one who wants to write poetry?

SMITH. I think it is important for any poet to have sound training in his own language, and a knowledge of at least one foreign language. And also to have a good liberal education. I feel genuinely sorry for young people these days who have no required courses in high school or college. They have no information, no background, to draw from. You can't draw from a well if the well is empty. Kids are willing to spend hours and hours learning all kind of facts. But we haven't been giving them any in school—or not enough to build up any reservoir for the future.

PHILLIPS. Any pet peeves?

SMITH. I object to being dismissed, as I have been by certain critics, as just lightweight. That is a total misunderstanding of what I've tried to do. Dorothy Judd Hall once published an essay called "The Lightness of William Jay Smith." And she made a point that I thought valid: that the surface of my poems displays a lightness and sparkle, but that there is always real depth beneath. That's exactly what I've tried for. I hate a heavy, clumsy touch. Two of my favorite painters are Degas and Monet, in whose work you have something deft and shimmering on the surface, and yet such mystery and depth below.

PHILLIPS. It's ironic that you should be accused of being a "light" poet, when a critic like Josephine Jacobsen writes that your dominant theme is death. How do you reconcile the two views?

SMITH. I don't. It's just that some people don't read, or, if they do, they read only my light verse and assume that's all I do. Why do so many people distrust variety? Is it that they are so attuned to dullness that they can't adjust to anything else? Let us not forget that, before all else, art should be interesting. Life has many facets. And a good poet wants to illuminate as many of those as possible in his lifetime.

PHILLIPS. In your poem "The Tall Poets," you paint a rather bleak picture of the current poetic scene. Do you really see this as such a bad time for poetry?

SMITH. I'm making fun of everything and everybody, including myself, in "The Tall Poets." But I'm making a serious point at the same time, by calling attention to many of the absurd goings-on in the literary world that in the end have little to do with the art of poetry. It is always a bad time for poetry, in the sense that the poet, wanting to cut a new path for himself, must necessarily go counter to what is generally accepted. It seems to me imperative that a poet work against the grain, and be able to stand back and look at the world freshly and objectively. That is what I've been trying to do for a very long time.

(1998)

William Styron
Photograph by Nancy Crampton

William Styron

William Styron is one of the founders of The Paris Review, *and one of America's most honored novelists. He published his first novel,* Lie Down in Darkness, *at the age of twenty-six. It was an immediate best seller, as were later books,* Sophie's Choice *and the memoir* Darkness Visible. *The latter was recently named by a panel of* The Modern Library *as one of the 100 best nonfiction books of the century. Styron is a winner of the Prix de Rome and the William Dean Howells Medal for Fiction, and is a member of the American Academy of Arts and Letters. He divides his time between homes in Roxbury, Connecticut, and Martha's Vineyard, Massachusetts.*

Mr. Styron was interviewed in Houston, Texas, on October 19, 1999. The interview was conducted in two parts. The first took place in the chapel of the Bruce Religion Center at the University of Houston, before an audience composed primarily of writing students and faculty members in the university's creative writing program. The questions were largely about the craft of fiction. Styron was dressed informally, in an open-necked shirt and a khaki safari jacket.

In the evening, Styron delivered a reading in the Margarett Root Brown Series, which is held monthly at the Museum of Fine Arts Houston. People from both the university and the city of Houston attended the event, filling the 350-seat auditorium to capacity (many were even turned away at the door). Styron had changed into a navy blazer, and seemed every bit the Southern gentleman. He also seemed genuinely surprised at the large turnout, and began his reading by observing that Houston obviously cares about writing—something rare in an age of MTV, the sound byte, and the thirty-second commercial.

After reading from his forthcoming novel, The Way of the Warrior, *Styron answered questions first from me, then from the audience. Of the eight interviews in this collection, Styron's is the only one that was conducted in public, and that included questions posed by audience members. Additional questions were answered by phone in February of the following year.*

•   •   •

Part 1: Bruce Religion Center

PHILLIPS. Malcolm Cowley wrote that a generation is no more a matter of dates than it is a matter of ideology. A new generation doesn't appear every thirty years. It appears when writers of the same age join in a common revolt against the populace—and when, in the process of adapting a new lifestyle, they find their own models and their own spokesmen. Your first novel appeared on the same best-seller list as *From Here to Eternity* and *The Catcher in the Rye*. Not a bad list. I wonder if you felt part of a generation, and if you felt the need to revolt. I'd like to add from a personal point of view that compared to others of your generation—Mailer, Salinger, Buechner, Calisher, McCullers—you alone write books which continue to get better.

STYRON. I'm glad you mentioned this. I was very happy to hit the *New York Times* best-seller list. That was in 1951. As you said, two of the other books at the same time were *Catcher in the Rye* and *From Here to Eternity*. I didn't climb as high as either of those books. I think *From Here to Eternity* was number one week after week. Oddly enough, I don't think *Catcher in the Rye* made number one, but it was higher than *Lie Down in Darkness*. I was always tickled because at the end of the year, *Time* magazine (in its usual thoughtless way) did a roundup of the year's books, mentioned those books, and said something like, "This was another dreary year for first-time novelists." That gave me a chuckle, because in those days it was sort of sport to hate *Time* magazine.

But I suppose in generational terms, I felt that our forefathers were Faulkner, Hemingway, and Fitzgerald. They were people we tried to . . . not emulate . . . but for whom, I think, most of us had a great admiration and respect. They were—and indeed, as I mention their names now, still remain—the twentieth-century masters they set out to be. And it was tough coming out from under their shadow. I think Mailer felt a horrendous sense of competition, especially with Hemingway. One of the things that dogged his career was to have been perpetually measuring himself against someone like Hemingway.

To some degree, I could say that my chief influence was Faulkner, but also Fitzgerald. Each of us had amazing role models to look up to, and this was both a blessing and a curse, because it is very hard to be another Faulkner or Hemingway, and at the same time keep your own individual voice. I think Harold Bloom made an interesting comment about the anxiety of influence, about how writers are bedeviled by the idea that these masters are looking down at them. I think there's some truth in that, creating a struggle for each generation, which has to create its own identity in the shadow of these great masters.

PHILLIPS. Many critics have picked up on the influence of Faulkner in your first novel. I wonder if you might discuss that. It seems to me that Robert Penn Warren was a major literary figure in shaping your first book. Is there a possible influence there?

STYRON. Yes, Robert Penn Warren—I got to know him well. We became great friends. He wasn't quite old enough to be in the generation of Hemingway and Faulkner, but he was about twenty years older than I, and I looked up to him, too. I still think *All the King's Men* was one of those remarkable landmark novels—probably the best political novel written in this country. As a matter of fact, that book had a very direct influence on me. The opening passage of *Lie Down in Darkness* is an unabashedly imitative version of the same opening passage in *All the King's Men*. It's where I use the second person "you." (You are riding down on this train through the Tidewater, just as you are in this car with Willie Stark driving through the Louisiana countryside.) He had a strong influence on me as a writer, and an even stronger influence as a friend. He was a great man.

PHILLIPS. You've explained that you never construct a diagram of any sort for your plots. Could you share with us your method of construction?

STYRON. I don't know how I can answer that directly, because there never has been a methodology in my writing. Each work that I've tried to fashion has always had a mystique, a guiding energy, a voice. Each work has some *need* to be written. I think, for example, that *The Confessions of Nat Turner* came out of an enormous need to somehow reflect on the contemporary world of segregation as an offshoot of its predecessor, slavery, and to make sense of the world I was living in—which was a sick, sick world. So I tried to reflect on the world of slavery, and when I heard as a young man about Nat Turner, he represented to me an absolute paradox. How could a single black man, in the year 1831, in this world where white human beings totally held domination in some way, rise up and commit this act of vengeance? It haunted me as a young man, and it stayed with me year after year. I think the final revelation coincided with the coming of the Civil Rights movement, during the summer of 1962, which I remember vividly. By the sheerest coincidence, Faulkner died and I got a call to go to Oxford and write about Faulkner's funeral for *Life* magazine.

And that very week I realized that there was some need to finally express the story that had coalesced within my mind and my heart. Days after I finished writing the Faulkner story, I sat down and wrote the first lines of *The Confessions of Nat Turner*. It seemed to me that this was the moment to do it, or I would never write it at all.

I realized that I wanted to make a statement about the segregated life that we were leading in this country, and to make this statement through the story of Nat. So this is an example of how a book evolved out of necessity. For me, it arose out of a need to show through the narrative of Nat Turner the whole horror of slavery, and at the same time reflect on a kind of bondage that was still in existence throughout the United States. The bondage was of a neoslavery; though African Americans were technically free, they were still in chains. So Nat Turner was born. All hell broke loose when it was published, but I got the story written.

PHILLIPS. I read somewhere that you first read about Nat Turner at a very early age, and that his story might have been the subject of your first novel, but ultimately wasn't. If it were your first novel, in what ways do you think it would have been substantially different from the novel that you later produced?

STYRON. Well, I don't know. I've always been fascinated by the story of Nat Turner and the mythology behind his revolt—this mysterious black revolutionary figure who haunted my childhood and boyhood. And I remember after I had finished *Lie Down in Darkness*, I went to my then editor and mentor, Hiram Haydn, a man I respected very much, and said, "I think I'm going to embark on this novel about Nat Turner." I outlined some of the gory details, and he said, "You're not ready for this book. You're going to turn it into a ghastly melodrama, instead of the book with depth and a sense of history that you can do. I advise you to wait fifteen years." And I did. It was the best advice I ever got, because by that time I had learned a great deal about slavery, and I was able to write a much richer book.

PHILLIPS. Ralph Ellison said that the white man in America doesn't see the black man, but in *Nat Turner,* you actually became one. Your choice of first-person narrative for the novel was, I think, a brave choice, and one that didn't endear you to certain African American critics. Did you ever start that book in the third person? Or think about it in any other way?

STYRON. Well, I think at the very beginning I must have played with various other approaches to the story. But basically, I chose to do the first-person narrative on my own book, but I might add, with the encouragement of my friend Jimmy Baldwin who was living in my guest house during that period when I was putting together the ideas for that book. It was he who encouraged me to really go for broke, and to become Nat Turner. Because he was attempting similar approaches in his own work—to get into the skin of white people. He was saying, "Get into the skin of this black man." I remember discussing this with him and saying, "You mean, write from the first person?" He said, "Why not?" So, it was he who encouraged me to do this.

PHILLIPS. He did much the same thing in his second novel, *Giovanni's Room*, where the main characters are white people in Paris.

STYRON. Yes, exactly. So I never really had any hesitation about my so-called becoming Nat Turner, because I felt that—without being sentimental about this, or extravagant—black people and white people do share a common humanity. And why shouldn't a black man take on the persona of a white man?

PHILLIPS. Well, if Flaubert can become a woman . . .

STYRON. Precisely. I reject the idea that one cannot write about another race or gender. As you say, quite rightly, if Flaubert could become a woman, why can't a white American become a black man?

PHILLIPS. And then, of course, Baldwin wrote about it all in *Another Country.*

STYRON. That's right.

PHILLIPS. It's a fine novel.

STYRON. It's a terrific novel.

PHILLIPS. In *Sophie's Choice,* you once again were an outsider grappling with an experience of which you were not a survivor. Despite the fact that you are not Jewish, this book did not generate such hysterical reaction. Could this be because you wrote Sophie as Catholic? Or did this backfire because you made a non-Jew a victim? Were you accused of attempting to universalize the Holocaust, and of taking away from what was largely a Jewish experience? Could you address that?

STYRON. Well, I have no problem with that. Frankly, I would be betraying the actual Sophie if I changed her ethnic origin. The Sophie I knew identified herself, eventually, as Catholic, and I couldn't legitimately change her into a Jew. In no way would I ever be able to epitomize the magnitude of the Jewish suffering in the book. The focus of the book *is* the destruction of the Jews, yet only an absolutist who believes that Jews have a total claim on suffering would deny the murder of others. The point is that I don't really mind the word "universalize," simply because—once having established the incredible magnitude of the Jewish suffering—one has to factor into the equation the truth that millions of non-Jews suffered from the Nazis, too . . . gypsies, homosexuals, and millions of Catholic Poles and other Slavs, mainly Russians. So this never once gave me a problem while writing the book, and only in one or two instances has the book been criticized on the ground that it denies the brute fact of the Jewish suffering.

PHILLIPS. Would you say that *Sophie's Choice,* in a way, is a continuation of *Nat Turner,* and that both of these books are about slavery?

STYRON. That's a good point. It's one of the things that's overlooked about the Holocaust, as it's become known. I never used the word

"Holocaust" in *Sophie's Choice,* because the word was not current when I wrote the book. But what is often overlooked is the significant fact that, though indeed Auschwitz was primarily dedicated to the extermination of human beings, mostly Jews, it nonetheless was also the first reincarnation in the West of slavery since emancipation in 1862. Much of Auschwitz was dedicated to a slave system where Jews, Gentiles, and others were systematically worked to death. So that is a very important historical truth.

PHILLIPS. When *The Confessions of Nat Turner* was published, it received extremely good press, and the book won the Pulitzer Prize. But then a reaction set in, particularly from African American critics. In fact, it is the only book I can think of about which an entire book of negative criticism was published. Usually, when we put together collections of critical essays, we try to balance, to present all points of view. But those writers were very unhappy. How seriously did you take that? Do you read your critics? Should a writer pay attention to his critics?

STYRON. Writers really shouldn't pay attention to their critics if they can help it—though it's hard not to. But this was, I think, a very special case. *Nat Turner* was not simply a novel that a writer had written, and all of a sudden Christopher Lehmann-Haupt and Michiko Kakutani say that they don't like it. You can shrug that off. This became a social and cultural event in which the entire book, *The Confessions of Nat Turner,* became a symbol of black rage against white human beings' interpretation of black history. As such, it had an extra-literary quality, and I felt that in this particular instance, although I did not respond directly to my critics in print, a lot of other people did. It generated a controversy of a kind that has never been seen before or since in this country—in which a book became a symbol of a minority group's rage.

PHILLIPS. In your essay "This Quiet Dust," you regard East Texas as part of the South. The late William Goyen, who lived in this town and taught at the University of Houston several times, insisted in print that he was not a Southern, but a Southwestern, writer. He said that the Southwest had its own language and feeling and landscape. What do you consider to be the properties of a Southern writer or Southern literature?

STYRON. Certainly there is a geographical aspect to the matter. If you're born south of the Mason-Dixon line, that is, south of the Potomac, I would say you're a Southerner, especially if you're reared there. I would dispute Goyen. I think that anyone born in East Texas is a Southerner by temperament and by culture. And that would include the Confederate states. That pretty much defines it. There are many other factors, but that's the simplest.

PHILLIPS. When someone asked Flannery O'Connor if she had been influenced by William Faulkner, she said, "Any person writing in the South doesn't want to lie down on the railroad tracks and wait for the Dixie Limited to roar down upon you." You met Faulkner at least once, didn't you?

STYRON. I had lunch with him in New York with my publisher. We have the same publisher. In New York, he was wonderfully preoccupied. At lunch, he was very polite and sweet. But I went to the bathroom, and when I came back, he was gone. I asked the editor where he had gone. He said, "He went back to the office to write part of his novel." So he was plainly a man totally preoccupied with his work. He was awfully nice, though. He talked about Truman Capote—he thought Capote was a little flea. He called him a flea.

PHILLIPS. We've barely touched upon your second novel, *Set This House On Fire*. It received a mixed reception here, but the French absolutely loved it. I'm curious to hear your speculation on that. Some compare this to the so-called New Novel, some said you were doing a spoof of detective novels, others said you were writing a detective novel. I think one reason it did so well—and this is not to put down your writing the book—was because you had an absolutely marvelous French translator.

STYRON. As a matter of fact, for that particular book, and several books after that, I had Faulkner's translator, Maurice Edgar Coindreau, who almost single-handedly made Faulkner a household word in France, long before he was such in the United States. A man of extraordinary gifts. He translated my work beautifully. I happen to read French pretty well, and it's a marvel.

AUDIENCE MEMBER. I am struck by how skillfully you incorporate characters' memories into the narrative. You don't necessarily fit them in paragraphs, in some places you don't have whole sentences, and there's often a defect in time when you come back. Could you talk about the method you use on a construction like that? How do you create it: Do you already anticipate the memory, or do you have to dip into a narrative that you already have running alongside of it?

STYRON. I'm going to be specific in answering this question by using *Sophie's Choice*. Early on in the novel, in the very beginning, I had the metaphor which I thought would make the book work—which was obviously "the choice." The woman who is made to chose which one of her children lives or dies, therefore making her the murderer of one of her children, is probably one of the most evil acts a human being has ever tried to inflict upon another. But this is what the Nazis did, even though it wasn't a very common thing. In one book, I read about a gypsy woman having to make this same choice. So I had this choice, and I knew that eventually the book would lead to a description of the actual choice. But in between, there's a lot of material I had to fill out, obviously.

And early on in the narrative, I began to set down Sophie's reminiscence about her childhood. Understand this is early in the book, and I was feeling my way around her past. I knew a great deal about Poland in that period. I'd read a lot about it, and I visited Poland. So I had a fairly good sense of that place in time. A fascinating thing happened as she's telling Stingo, the narrator, in this first-person chapter all done as her monologue. She says that her father was a humanist professor—one of these extraordinary, big-hearted human beings who had risked his life for others' sake. He had sheltered Jews and saved and protected them. He had, indeed, been at the forefront in the protectionist movement. And then an amazing thing happened as I was writing this. I suddenly said to myself, "The girl is a liar." I said, "Sophie is telling a lie. Her father's *not* this big-hearted humanist." We are going to find out that he is a vicious anti-Semite. And that in itself carried a great deal of the burden of this book, and in itself was a revelation to me. It is very hard to describe the process exactly, but I just began to pile on incident after incident based on what I imagined her experience to be in Warsaw during the war. And these things accumulated, to me, in a very logical way. But in writing the book, I do know that I didn't do a draft. I wrote the book as I would construct a brick wall, piling brick on brick, so that each chapter—although there was some minor rewriting—was never anything more than a brick in its place.

AUDIENCE MEMBER. So, if Sophie was a kind of unreliable narrator, and you felt that she was lying to you, did you feel that you needed the Stingo character to then be the center of moral good and truth?

STYRON. Yes, I think Stingo is the moral filter through which the book is told. He is, despite his innocence, candid enough to be able to make judgments. He's always questioning what Sophie's motives are—he's always trying to figure out when she's lying and when she's telling the truth. So it's important to have him as a sort of fulcrum around which the other parts revolve.

PHILLIPS. *Sophie's Choice* was a fine film, and we were moved by Meryl Streep's performance, but it was very different from the book in many ways. I think it lacked all of the humor and most of the sexuality. How did you feel about that?

STYRON. They put very little of the humor into the film, intentionally. For that reason, it is not faithful to the novel. The film, interestingly enough, has survived very well. It's constantly being shown, and it's regarded, I think, as kind of a classic. And there's, of course, a marvelous performance by Meryl Streep, among other things. But there are great flaws in the film. I found the absence—and I say this with the greatest respect for the late Alan Pakula, who died tragically last year—of some of the essential values of the book. I remember that when the movie was released in Paris, I had a press conference and a lot of journalists had read the book and also seen the movie. And one of them asked a very important question. He asked me what about Nathan and Sophie and their relationship? This journalist simply continued this line of argument, saying that—I think justifiably—the movie is absolutely devoid of the sadomasochistic tension that existed between Sophie and Nathan. The rage and a great deal of sensuality. There was a certain primness in Alan Pakula that, as good a director as he was, forbade him from confronting certain scenes. And in fact, Meryl Streep once told me that there was a remarkable scene in which Nathan beats her and stomps on her and throws her down the stairs. That was left on the cutting room floor. Meryl said that it was one of the best scenes she had ever done. That was an outtake

I would like to retrieve some day and take a look at. But things like that were missing.

Also, I think the musical component was missing. One of the things that gives the book a certain resonance is the constant use of classical music. And there's virtually none to speak of in the film. Also, I thought there was a very serious miscasting of Stingo. I think Peter MacNicol is a quite gifted actor in many ways, but he was far too callow, too juvenile. The part needed a man with a little more stamina to fill the strength of that part. So that was pretty much my take on it.

AUDIENCE MEMBER. I saw a show with you and Kurt Vonnegut and Joseph Heller, and you said something to the effect of, "All great novelists must have great themes." Could you could speak about that? Also, some critics think that all great novelists have great moral themes. I wanted to know your take on that. Do you associate that morality with spiritual morality?

STYRON. That's a tough question. I wish I could address myself to it adequately, because I have always been affected by the remarkable statement made by Herman Melville, which is, "To write a mighty book, you must have a mighty theme," and God knows he certainly did. If you replace the work "mighty" with the word "important," or something like that, it would be closer to how I feel. I think the novel or book, consequently, must have some sort of underpinning which gives it a certain significance. It need not try to speak with a great voice of vast things, but I think it must arrest the reader's attention with the position that the writer has something—again I'm risking it with a funny word—"important" to say. Another book about another love affair is not going to have an effect on the reader, unless it is done in a way that gives it importance. The writer, before he or she is done writing, should consider carefully what effect on the reader this is going to have. What kind of resonance is this going to make? So many novels coming out—and some of them very competent—nonetheless leave me saying to myself, "I've read this story before. This might be a new twist on it, but it's not really enough to command my attention." So that's part of the question.

As for the moral underpinning and the moral authority, I think any writer will have a sense of rigorous moral view of the world, and should have an idea of the reader's morals. So that it will make the book a place where we can judge how people are acting, interacting, in a moral sense with each other.

PHILLIPS. Would you describe yourself as a Christian author? I'm reminded of Sophie's last words to Perter about choosing meaning over nothing. Wouldn't that be an expression of Christian thinking?

STYRON. I was brought up in a Presbyterian Sunday school environment in the 1930s. Grade-school Bible study left a residue of Christian thought in my intellectual makeup, and it's been very valuable to me. If I hadn't had it, I could never have written *The Confessions of Nat Turner*. He was a preacher, of course, and I had to understand carefully his various feelings about the Bible. But I'm in no way a Christian writer. If anything, I'm a backslid Presbyterian who's very angry with this Presbyterian God, and very angry with Christianity and the major abuses it has been responsible for in our time.

AUDIENCE MEMBER. In one of our classes, we've recently been talking about the use of autobiographical material in fiction, and how it can lead to the destruction of the original memory in favor of the fictionalized version. I'm curious about your position on that.

STYRON. I'll give you an example, once again, from *Sophie's Choice*. This was a great way for me to write in many ways, because I could reflect very vividly on my own life experience—scenes and episodes that actually happened to me. The best example, of course, is the first chapter, which is set in the rooming house. That's a fairly good replica of my life experience, and that was fun to write. But it was also fun to wonder when my own experience would leave off, where I'd start writing imaginatively. So much of the early part of the book— about Stingo going to the rooming house—is actually what happened to me. And indeed, the most vivid and memorable—and, to me, most titillating—moment is in the early part of the book, when I remembered myself as a lonely, sex-starved twenty-one year old, in the wilds of Brooklyn, hearing this monumental fornication above me, and the shaking of the lampshades. This was a very anxiety-provoking thing, especially in those days when you didn't have the opportunity, like you do now, for those sorts of activities.

Actually, the lover who was making all this noise upstairs was a rather wimpy guy who astonished me when I first saw him. I was wondering how he was so boisterously vigorous up there. At that moment, there came the crossover from autobiography into fiction, because how could that be Nathan? I realized that I couldn't have this wimpy guy be the lover of Sophie. I had to have a true—well, in this case it turned out to be—*nut* . . . but nonetheless a man of extraordinary energy and ability. So how this process takes place I don't know, but I do know that it happens when the imagination suddenly takes flight. You abandon the figment of your autobiographical imagination, and fill it in with something wondrous and exciting.

PHILLIPS. Elizabeth Bowen and others have said that an unhappy childhood seems to be a prerequisite for the making of a successful writer, and in my opinion, *A Tidewater Morning* seems to confirm this. Do you want to talk about Bowen's notion, and did you ever consider expanding those three tales into a full-length novel?

STYRON. To answer your last question first, no. I certainly have not planned to expand anything. They're down for the count, so to speak. As for the question about an unhappy childhood, I'm not entirely sure that's the case. I don't know if there is any way to make a judgment on that, because I think you have to qualify the word "unhappy." Certainly, the death of my mother qualifies as a major unhappiness. But on the other hand, in many ways, I think I was quite happy. I wasn't abused, and even though it was in the Depression years, our own little family was fairly well off, given the fact that the local economy—which was a shipyard-based economy—was rather prosperous compared to the rest of the country. I never suffered any deprivations. I was an only child, and I had loving parents. So, I'm not really sure how . . .

PHILLIPS. You have no axes to grind.

STYRON. Yeah, I mean, I don't know how happy or unhappy I was.

PHILLIPS. We don't think of that much as kids, I think. The death of his mother seems to have been absolutely devastating for William Maxwell, if you know his novels and stories.

STYRON. Yes, I think that my mother's death was. I didn't realize it at the time, but I think it was a cataclysm. And yet I have to qualify that by saying that, aside from that, I think that my childhood was fairly contented. So, I would simply question that premise, that's all.

AUDIENCE MEMBER. What provoked you to write the soliloquies at the end of *Lie Down in Darkness*? And had you anticipated that beforehand, or did that come later?

STYRON. A writer friend says that every novel he's written had a point at the end to which the reader is drawn—like a magnet or like magnetic forces. I think that's true of me, and probably of everything I've read of any quality. As I said about *Sophie's Choice*, the ending, or the choice, was integral to writing the book. And in *Lie Down in Darkness*, the same thing is true. In those days, writing in the stream-of-consciousness mode was a technique that was very much in the air. And I wanted to write one; after all, Molly Bloom had one, why shouldn't I have one? So I did indeed know that towards the end of that book, I would be writing a monologue from her point of view. But it required a very important cover technique, which was *not* to go into her mind at any previous point in the book. If you read the book carefully, you'll see that the minds of all the people around her are penetrated, but Peyton's mind is a tabula rasa—bare except for her dialogue. I felt that once her inner thought processes were withheld, it would increase the intensity of what happened to her at the end.

AUDIENCE MEMBER. In your nonfiction, you've made several references to your personal problems, and I was wondering if I could ask about them? Edgar Allan Poe wrote about the question, "Did the writer come from the madness, or did the madness come from the writer?" I don't think that there's an easy answer to that—but do you have a solution?

STYRON. I don't have any real answers, except to say that the two are intertwined. As some of you know, I wrote a book that Bob Phillips mentioned earlier, *Darkness Visible*, about this nearly lethal malady. I realized, after I wrote the book, that this depression that I had suffered was a time bomb that had been ready to go off in my mind, that it was a disaster ready to happen. And as testimony witness to that, I realized that there had been large clairvoyant moments of this depressive mood in almost everything that I wrote. For instance, speaking of *Lie Down in*

Darkness, I wrote about a young woman, twenty-two years old or so, who killed herself. This must have been a message to myself—a message whereby I was telling myself that I needed to exorcise the mood disorder that was always present in my brain. Possibly, writing *Lie Down in Darkness* was a way of avoiding suicide. I'm not sure, but at least I understand now that the pathology of the mind can often produce a great deal of what we write.

AUDIENCE MEMBER. I just read an article in which you had a quote from Flaubert to the effect of, "Live a moderate, ordinary life so that your life of the mind is wild to create." Is that true, and is that sentiment still there?

STYRON. That's a lovely paraphrase, but I'll tell you exactly what Flaubert says. He said, "Be regular and orderly in your life like a bourgeois, so that you may be violent and original in your work." That's Flaubert's advice to his mistress, Louise Colet. It's not something I take all that seriously, but it's an attempt to quell the idea that one should lead a romantic, hell-raising life—filled with derangement and other admirable aspects of the senses—in order to be a good writer. I did my hell-raising before I was twenty-one, and then got married and lived a bourgeois life so that now I can express the violence I want to express, without going to the hospital. That's the mantra I sort of taped on my wall.

PHILLIPS. You mentioned your marriage. You have been married for many years to a poet, and I wonder if this has presented any particular problems or opportunities. Do you think it's a good idea for a writer to live with or marry another writer, or is it a terrible idea?

STYRON. Well, aside from being a poet, she's also a very tolerant woman who has put up with a lot of my misdemeanors and felonies with minimal frustration. So that's part of it. She's a poet also, and a very good poet. I think it has to do with being incredibly patient, because I know that I couldn't deal with myself. So that might give you a sort of angle.

PHILLIPS. In one interview, you called Flaubert your master. Could you comment on what you learned from Flaubert?

STYRON. I think that he is one of my masters, certainly.

PHILLIPS. Conrad, Melville, Fitzgerald?

STYRON. Yes, there is a bunch of them. But I would say that as a single novel, *Madame Bovary* is one of the truly remarkable achievements in Western literature. It creates a world. It is absolutely precise in its examination of the middle-class, provincial world in which this tormented woman has grown up. It is a reverberant book. It is about a woman, but it is also about a society. It creates a wonderful effect. I've always said that the ruthless examination of this woman by the author—the tribute is to this ruthless examination—is that though she is a thoroughly disagreeable woman, when she dies, you want to weep. That is one of the highest tributes you can pay to a writer—that he can create a thoroughly unattractive person, and yet make your heart break when she dies.

PHILLIPS. I am also very moved by *A Simple Heart*. The servant Félicité dies, but she is an attractive person.

STYRON. I have often felt a sympathy with Flaubert, if I may be so presumptuous to compare our careers, because we've confined ourselves to a few novels, a few short works, and I think this is one of the reasons why I admire Flaubert: that he made up in intensity what he lacked in prolific output.

PHILLIPS. Well, you've been pretty prolific.

STYRON. I've been reasonably prolific. I've always felt that one of the reasons that Flaubert was my master was that he restricted himself to these intense examinations of life through a relatively small group of works of fiction. That is one of the reasons I feel a kind of, as I say, sympathy with Flaubert.

PHILLIPS. Early in your career, you published what I think is a brilliant novella, *The Long March*. But you have published very few novellas or short stories, and some that you did were parts of novels. Isn't the form congenial to you? Is there a reason?

STYRON. The fact that I haven't done many novellas or short stories makes it fairly apparent that I don't feel committed to these forms. The novel is the place where I feel the most comfortable saying what I have to say.

PHILLIPS. Did you find the experience of writing your one play, *In the Clap Shack*, radically different from writing a novel, or did it come fairly easily?

STYRON. I did that as a kind of exercise rather than anything else. My friend Bob Brustein, who is one of the great entrepreneurs in the theater, was then the head of the Yale Repertory Theater. He encouraged me to do that—saying, almost as a challenge, "Can you try to write a play?" And I did. I didn't put my heart and soul into it the same way I do in my prose writing. At the same time, it was a challenge, and I wanted to see if I could do it and keep the narrative rolling. I think I did.

PHILLIPS. You did, and I also think it's probably your funniest work. The black humor in there is outstanding. There's also a lot of humor in *Sophie's Choice*. Of course, nobody ever died laughing reading *The Confessions of Nat Turner,* but you can be very funny when you want to.

STYRON. I always felt that when I wanted to be funny, I could be. There is something about the situation of a young man in a venereal ward being falsely accused of having syphilis. Despite the somber overtones, it has a humorous effect.

PHILLIPS. Didn't Brustein also get Joseph Heller to write *We Bombed in New Haven*?

STYRON. Yes, he did. Both Joe and I were prompted into these things by Bob Brustein. I might add, speaking of humor in general, that I was always impressed by an assessment of *Sophie's Choice* by John Gardner. When he reviewed the book, he said that—like Shakespeare—I knew how to cut away from the somberness of my subject to humor, in order to alleviate the prevailing darkness.

PHILLIPS. It's not a bad comparison. (laughs)

STYRON. I do think that without humor, *Sophie's Choice* would be an entirely different, and lesser, book. I think that the story required many moments of levity in order to lighten the darkness.

PHILLIPS. I recently read in the *New Yorker* that there is some renewed interest in filming *Nat Turner*. Is that coming along?

STYRON. There is nothing in terms of a Hollywood-type movie. There is a fascinating documentary being made, even as we speak, on Nat Turner—the entire subject of Nat Turner—done by a team of black and white cinema people and historians.

Part 2: Museum of Fine Art

PHILLIPS. Having just heard you read part of your new World War II novel *(The Way of the Warrior)*, if I were Norman Mailer, I would be very nervous right now. I'm curious about the history of this novel. I believe you were writing it, then suspended it for *Sophie's Choice*. Can you tell us a bit about the process?

STYRON. It is nothing very mysterious—I just ran out of steam. I was writing a novel about marines in the Korean War, which I had the misfortune to be in. And it just never got off the ground. So one morning in the early seventies, struggling with this novel which always threatened itself to be aborted, I woke up with an entirely different concept. It had to do with the fact that I saw this . . . I don't mean to sound metaphysical . . . but I saw this, almost like a vision, this woman named Sophie, whom I had known many years before. And I decided that I'd abandon the Marine Corps novel and plunge into *Sophie's Choice*.

PHILLIPS. You're perhaps the last of your generation to write your war novel, following Mailer, Jones, Shaw, John Horn Burns, and Heller. Is there any reason for that? Perhaps your close friendship to Mailer and Jones made it a sticky wicket?

STYRON. No, it is just that I am gradually getting around to it. It's not going to be a long or elaborate novel. It is just a reflection, really, on the occasion of the dropping of the bomb, and how it affected the lives of the young men like myself who were destined to be in the invasion of Japan. And the moral implications of that. So I don't think that there is any particular reason for me to have taken this long. I don't think it has anything to do with my relationship with the other writers at all.

PHILLIPS. How do you compare the achievement of *The Naked and the Dead* with, say, *From Here to Eternity*? Do you think one book holds up better than the other?

STYRON. Well, I think it's like apples and oranges. They're two remarkably fine books, but they're dealing with two different aspects of warfare. Jim Jones's book is almost—in the best sense of the word—a sociological treatise about the peacetime army. That's what gives it its impact: its extraordinary description of the grungy underside of soldiering.

Further Reading

Philip Larkin (1922–1985)

POETRY

> *The North Ship* (1945)
> *The Less Deceived* (1955)
> *The Whitsun Weddings* (1964)
> *High Windows* (1974)
> *Collected Poems* (1989)

FICTION

> *Jill: A Novel* (1946)
> *A Girl in Winter* (1947)

NONFICTION

> *Required Writing* (1983)
> *All What Jazz?* (1985)
> *Selected Letters of Philip Larkin: 1940–1985* (1992)

WORKS EDITED BY

> *The Oxford Book of Twentieth-Century English Poetry* (1973)

Joyce Carol Oates (1938–)

FICTION

> *By the North Gate* (1963)
> *With Shuddering Fall* (1964)
> *Upon the Sweeping Flood* (1966)

A Garden of Earthly Delights (1967)

Expensive People (1968)

them (1969)

The Wheel of Love (1970)

Wonderland (1971)

Marriages and Infidelities (1972)

Do With Me What You Will (1973)

The Goddess and Other Women (1974)

The Hungry Ghosts (1974)

Where are You Going, Where Have You Been? Stories of Young America
      (1974)

The Poisoned Kiss (1975)

The Assassins (1975)

The Seduction and Other Stories (1975)

Childwold (1976)

Crossing the Border (1976)

Triumph of the Spider Monkey (1976)

Night-Side (1977)

A Sentimental Education (1978)

Son of the Morning (1978)

All the Good People I've Left Behind (1979)

Cybele (1979)

Unholy Loves (1979)

Bellefleur (1980)

Angel of Light (1981)

A Bloodsmoor Romance (1982)

Last Days (1984)

Mysteries of Winterthurn (1984)

Solstice (1985)

Marya: A Life (1986)

Raven's Wing (1986)

You Must Remember This (1987)

The Assignation (1988)

American Appetites (1989)

Because It Is Bitter and Because It Is My Heart (1990)

I Lock My Door Upon Myself (1990)

The Rise of Life on Earth (1991)

Heat and Other Stories (1991)
Where is Here? (1992)
Black Water (1992)
Foxfire (1993)
Where Are You Going, Where Have You Been? Selected Early Stories
    (1993)
Haunted (1994)
What I Lived For (1994)
Zombie (1995)
Will You Always Love Me? (1996)
We Were the Mulvaneys (1996)
Man Crazy (1997)
My Heart Laid Bare (1998)
The Collector of Hearts (1998)
Broke Heart Blues (1999)
Blonde (2000)
Middle Age: A Romance (2001)
Faithless (2001)
I'll Take You There (2002)

NOVELS WRITTEN AS ROSAMOND SMITH

Lives of the Twins (1987)
Soul/Mate (1989)
Nemesis (1990)
Snake Eyes (1992)
Starr Bright Will Be With You Soon (1999)
The Barrens (2001)

POETRY

Women in Love and Other Poems (1968)
Anonymous Sins and Other Poems (1969)
Love and Its Derangements (1970)
Angel Fire (1973)
Dreaming America and Other Poems (1973)
The Fabulous Beasts (1975)
Women Whose Lives Are Food, Men Whose Lives Are Money (1978)
Invisible Woman: Selected Poems (1982)

The Time Traveler (1989)
Tenderness (1996)

PLAYS

Miracle Play (1974)
Three Plays (1980)
In Darkest America: Two Plays (1991)
Twelve Plays (1991)
I Stand Before You Naked (1991)
The Perfectionist and Other Plays (1995)
New Plays (1998)

NONFICTION

The Edge of Impossibility (1972)
The Hostile Sun: The Poetry of D. H. Lawrence (1973)
New Heaven, New Earth (1974)
Contraries (1981)
The Profane Art (1983)
On Boxing (1987)
(Woman) Writer (1988)
George Bellows: American Artist (1995)
Where I've Been, and Where I'm Going: Essays, Reviews, and Prose (1999)

WORKS EDITED BY

First Person Singular (1983)
The Sophisticated Cat (1992)
Telling Stories: An Anthology for Writers (1998)

FOR CHILDREN

Come Meet Muffin! (1998)

Karl Shapiro (1913–2000)

POETRY

Poems (1935)
Five Young American Poets (Second Series) (1941)
The Place of Love (1942)

Person, Place and Thing (1942)
V-Letter and Other Poems (1944)
Essay on Rime (1945)
Trial of a Poet (1947)
Poems 1940–1953 (1953)
Poems of a Jew (1958)
The Bourgeois Poet (1964)
Selected Poems (1968)
White-Haired Lover (1968)
Adult Bookstore (1976)
Collected Poems 1940–1978 (1978)
Love & War, Art & God (1984)
New & Selected Poems 1940–1986 (1987)
The Old Horsefly (1992)
The Wild Card: Selected Poems, Early & Late (1998)
Essay on Rime with Trial of a Poet (2003)

FICTION

Edsel (1971)

NONFICTION

English Prosody and Modern Poetry (1947)
A Bibliography of Modern Prosody (1948)
Beyond Criticism (1953)
American Poetry (1960)
In Defense of Ignorance (1960)
The Writer's Experience (with Ralph Ellison) (1960)
Prose Keys to Modern Poetry (1962)
Start with the Sun: Studies in Cosmic Poetry (with James E. Miller, Jr., and
     Bernice Slote) (1965)
A Prosody Handbook (with Robert Beum) (1965)
To Abolish Children and Other Essays (1968)
The Poetry Wreck: Selected Essays 1950–1970 (1975)
The Younger Son (1988)
Reports on My Death (1990)

William Goyen (1915–1983)

FICTION

The House of Breath (1950)
Ghost and Flesh (1952)
In a Farther Country (1955)
The Faces of Blood Kindred (1960)
The Fair Sister (1963)
Come, the Restorer (1974)
Selected Writings of William Goyen (1974)
The Collected Stories (1975)
Wonderful Plant (1980)
Arcadio (1983)
Had I a Hundred Mouths: New & Selected Stories 1947–1983 (1985)
Half a Look of Cain (1994)

NONFICTION

A Book of Jesus (1973)
William Goyen: Selected Letters from a Writer's Life (1995)

POETRY

Nine Poems (1976)

Marya Zaturenska (1902–1982)

POETRY

Threshold and Hearth (1934)
Cold Morning Sky (1937)
The Listening Landscape (1941)
The Golden Mirror (1944)
Selected Poems (1954)
Terraces of Light (1960)
Collected Poems (1965)
The Hidden Waterfall (1974)
New Selected Poems (2002)

NONFICTION

Christina Rossetti: A Portrait with Background (1949)
A History of American Poetry, 1900–1940 (with Horace Gregory) (1946)
The Diaries of Marya Zaturenska: 1938–1944 (edited by Mary Beth
    Hinton) (2002)

WORKS EDITED BY

Love's Cross Currents by Algernon Charles Swinburne (1964)
Collected Poems of Sara Teasdale (1966)
Selected Poems of Christina Rossetti (1970)

WORKS EDITED BY (WITH HORACE GREGORY)

The Crystal Cabinet: An Introduction to Poetry (1968)
The Mentor Book of Religious Verse (1957)
The Silver Swan: Poems of Mystery and the Imagination (1968)

Elizabeth Spencer (1921–)

FICTION

Fire in the Morning (1948)
This Crooked Way (1952)
The Voice at the Back Door (1956)
The Light in the Piazza (1960)
Knights and Dragons (1965)
No Place for an Angel (1967)
Ship Island and Other Stories (1968)
The Snare (1972)
The Stories of Elizabeth Spencer (1982)
The Salt Line (1984)
Marilee: Three Stories (1982)
Jack of Diamonds and Other Stories (1988)
The Night Travellers (1991)
On the Gulf (1991)
The Light in the Piazza and Other Italian Tales (1996)
The Southern Woman: New and Selected Fiction (2001)

NONFICTION

> *Conversations with Elizabeth Spencer* (1991)
> *Landscapes of the Heart: A Memoir* (1998)

William Jay Smith (1918–)

POETRY

> *Poems* (1947)
> *Celebration at Dark* (1950)
> *Typewriter Birds* (1954)
> *Poems 1947–1957* (1957)
> *The Tin Can and Other Poems* (1966)
> *New and Selected Poems* (1970)
> *Venice in the Fog* (1975)
> *Journey to the Dead Sea* (1979)
> *The Traveler's Tree: New & Selected Poems* (1980; 1981)
> *Plain Talk: Epigrams, Epitaphs, Satires, Nonsense, Occasional, Concrete,*
>   *and Quotidian Poems* (1988)
> *Collected Poems 1939–1989* (1990)
> *The Cyclist* (1995)
> *The World Below the Window: Poems 1937–1997* (1998)
> *The Girl in Glass* (1999)
> *The Cherokee Lottery: A Sequence of Poems* (2000)

NONFICTION

> *The* Spectra *Hoax* (1961; 2000)
> *Herrick* (Introduction) (1962)
> *The Streaks of the Tulip: Selected Criticism* (1972)
> *Army Brat: A Memoir* (1980)

PLAYS

> *The Straw Market* (1966; 1969)
> *Army Brat: A Dramatic Narrative for Three Voices* (1980)

TRANSLATIONS BY

Scirroco by Romualdo Romano (1951)

Poems of a Multimillionaire by Valery Larbaud (1955)

Selected Writings of Jules Laforgue (1956; 1957; 1972)

Two Plays by Charles Bertin: *Christopher Columbus* and *Don Juan* (1970)

Poems from Italy (1974)

Agadir by Artur Lundkvist (with Leif Sjöberg) (1979)

The Pact: My Friendship with Isak Dinesen by Thorkild Bjørnvig (with Ingvar Schousboe) (1983; 1984)

Moral Tales by Jules Laforgue (1985; 1987)

Poems from Italy (with Dana Gioia) (1985)

Wild Bouquet: Nature Poems by Harry Martinson (with Leif Sjöberg) (1985)

Collected Translations: Italian, French, Spanish, and Portuguese (1985)

An Arrow in the Wall: Selected Poetry and Prose by Andrei Voznesensky (with F. D. Reeve) (1987)

Eternal Moment: Selected Poems by Sandor Weöres (with Edwin Morgan and others) (1988)

The Madman and the Medusa by Tchicaya U Tam'Si (with Sonja Haussmann Smith) (1989)

Christopher Columbus by Charles Bertin (1992)

Songs of Childhood by Frederico García Lorca (1994)

The Forest of Childhood: Poems from Sweden (with Leif Sjöberg) (1996)

What You Have Almost Forgotten: Selected Poems by Gyula Illyés (with Charles Tomlinson, Daniel Hoffman, and others) (1999)

WORKS EDITED BY

The Golden Journey: Poems for Young People (with Louise Bogan) (1965)

Light Verse and Satires by Witter Bynner (1978)

A Green Place: Modern Poems (1982)

Brazilian Poetry 1950–1980 (with Emanuel Brasil) (1984)

Dutch Interior: Post-War Poetry of the Netherlands and Flanders (with J. S. Holmes) (1984)

Life Sentence: Selected Poems by Nina Cassian (1990)

Here is My Heart: Love Poems (1999)

WORKS FOR CHILDREN

Laughing Time (1955; 1956)
Boy Blue's Book of Beasts (1957)
Puptents and Pebbles: A Nonsense ABC (1959; 1960)
Typewriter Town (1960)
What Did I See? (1962)
Ho for a Hat! (1964; 1989)
My Little Book of Big and Little (1963)
If I Had a Boat (1966; 1967)
Mr. Smith and Other Nonsense (1968)
Around My Room and Other Poems (1969)
Laughing Time and Other Poems (1969)
Grandmother Ostrich and Other Poems (1969)
The Pirate Book by Lennart Hellsing (tr.) (1972)
The Telephone by Kornei Chukovsky (with Max Hayward) (tr.) (1977)
Laughing Time: Nonsense Poems (1980)
Birds and Beasts: Poems (1990)
Laughing Time: Collected Nonsense (1990)
Big and Little (1992)
Behind the King's Kitchen: A Roster of Rhyming Riddles (with Carol Ra)
    (1992)
The Sun Is Up: A Child's Year of Poems (with Carol Ra) (1996)
Around My Room (ill. by Eric Blegvad) (2000)

William Styron (1925–)

FICTION

Lie Down in Darkness (1951)
The Long March (1953)
Set This House on Fire (1960)
The Confessions of Nat Turner (1967)
Sophie's Choice (1979)
A Tidewater Morning: Three Tales from Youth (1993)
The Way of the Warrior (forthcoming)

NONFICTION

This Quiet Dust (1982)
Darkness Visible (1990)

DRAMA

In the Clap Shack (1972)

Index

Italic page numbers denote illustrations.

In a sense, it is not a war novel. It only deals peripherally with the war. The later books of Jim Jones, especially *The Thin Red Line,* deal head on with the war. I think *The Thin Red Line* is a very fine book. But as for *The Naked and the Dead,* I think it probably still stands up as the very best account of warfare—certainly Pacific warfare—in our literature, and I think that it is almost unique in that sense.

PHILLIPS. Is there a novel from the Vietnam conflict that you admire?

STYRON. I remember reading *Going After Cacciato* and being very impressed by it. I think Tim O'Brien is easily the premier fiction writer of the Vietnam War.

PHILLIPS. I'm glad you said fiction, because I think Michael Herr's *Dispatches* is also fine. It's nonfiction.

STYRON. Yes, that is a wonderful book. And I might add a book that I think is damned close to it: Philip Caputo's *A Rumor of War,* which is a remarkably good book. I think it's in the same class as Michael Herr's book. I reviewed it for the *New York Review of Books* when it first appeared, and I was enormously impressed by it.

PHILLIPS. Your first novel and other works have been set in territory you knew very well—your hometown or home area. Then, in your second novel, you went to Italy, which presented a radically different culture. Do you hold with that old adage that a writer should write only about what he or she knows? How well did you know Italy at that point?

STYRON. I knew Italy only as a visitor. I think that, basically, that's an irrelevant consideration. So many novels written by Anglo-Saxons and Americans were the product of a visit rather than being entrenched in the soil. I'm thinking of a book like *The Marble Faun* of Hawthorne.

PHILLIPS. A lot of James.

STYRON. A lot of James. And many, many others were the product of being sojourners rather than residents. So that never bothered me.

AUDIENCE MEMBER. Gabriel García Márquez and Carlos Fuentes have said that you and Faulkner and other Southern writers are really writers of the Caribbean—that you reach into Latin America, and that you share something with those writers. Could you comment on that?

STYRON. That is a compliment. I happen to know both of those writers very well personally. And I'm flattered in a sense. I think that there is possibly something to it. To some degree, Southern writers do—even though they are more often than not Presbyterians or Methodists—share a romantic bent. And I think there is a kind of romanticism in Southern writing which corresponds to that of the Latin American boom period . . . people like the two you mentioned and others, like Vargas Llosa of Peru. But I'm going to leave that to the critics to deal with. I'm not really capable of making a good judgment about that.

AUDIENCE MEMBER. What contemporary writers do you like to read? Today at the university, you were talking about the fact that you really care about novels of ideas, about some of the contemporary literature you were reading feeling like something you've read before. And I'm really wondering who in this generation you've come to admire, whose work is interesting?

STYRON. That's a question I usually try to dodge because, you know, you have to start making lists and leaving out favorites and . . .

AUDIENCE MEMBER. I know, just a few.

STYRON. Well, I'll just say one. I was recently on a committee of the American Academy of Arts and Letters to choose a recipient of the William Dean Howells Medal. It's a prestigious medal awarded every five years for the best book during the five years. And I was quite taken by a very flawed but amazingly rich book—Don DeLillo's *Underworld,* which I think is an extraordinary work. It's a kind of fiction that doesn't ordinarily appeal to me, but he is so gifted, and he is so torrential and amazing in his insights and humor, that . . . just let me say Don DeLillo.

AUDIENCE MEMBER. Willie Morris mentions you and your work in his book *North Toward Home.* Could you tell us something about your friendship with him?

STYRON. Willie Morris and I became close friends in the mid-1960s, when he was editor in chief at an amazingly young age—like thirty-one or thirty-two—of *Harper's* magazine. He had read *Lie Down in Darkness* and liked it a lot, and he asked me to write an essay for the 1965 *Harper's,* which commemorated the end of the Civil War. I wrote an essay on Nat Turner, and Willie accepted it. We became close friends after that. We went through the sixties wars—you know, the whole 1968, '69, '70 thing, the incredibly turbulent time—together. We became fast friends. He died just recently, and I mourn his passing severely.

AUDIENCE MEMBER. Could you say a few words about the character Stingo, particularly about his voice?

STYRON. As a matter of fact, it touches me that all of the letters that Willie Morris wrote to me would say, "Dear Stingo." This is an indication of the close identification that I, perforce, have with that fictional character. He is partly me, but it has to be understood that the events that took place in his life were not by any means the events that took place in my own. Some of them were, but most of them were not. They were dreamed up. But I think that *Sophie's Choice* works as a result of there being a consistent voice—the voice of a young man from the sticks who doesn't know anything, and suddenly, over the course of the summer, learns the nature of evil and the nature, in fact, of the mystery of human existence. I think that Stingo and I are sort of intertwined.

AUDIENCE MEMBER. Thank you very much for your courage to write such a beautiful and personal book on your experience with depression. Your book, and your coming out, have not only encouraged other people who have that illness to get help, but have also made an important stab against the stigma of mental illness, which destroys just as much as the disease does itself. I wonder, how has that experience of depression influenced your writing?

STYRON. Thank you for saying that. I wrote *Darkness Visible* only as an exercise in self-discovery. As I mentioned this afternoon to the audience of students, I said to myself as I sank down into this terrible pit, that if I survived I would write about it. Because it was—I don't mean to stretch the parallel too tightly—the worst experience one can imagine, next to going into combat. It is totally destroying. The mind, spirit, and body are brought close to annihilation. It is such a terrifying experience that I felt an obligation as a writer someday to write about it, so that people who had a blasé attitude toward it—who, like so many people, tend to think it was a character defect, a behavioral blot—would really understand that the person who is suffering from severe depression is suffering the agony of the damned. And I think the book has succeeded in making a lot of people understand that it is just that. And in addition to which— hallelujah—it is an illness from which most people can recover.

PHILLIPS. What makes a man of your sensibilities join the Marine Corps?

STYRON. The same thing that leads me to suicidal instincts, I think . . . a propensity towards self-destruction. I regretted it the moment I landed on Saipan.

AUDIENCE MEMBER. I read recently that you formed an informal support group with such people as Art Buchwald. Could you talk about that?

STYRON. Well, yes, there are three of us, we are close friends, and by coincidence have suffered, each of us, a horrifying depression, within a few months of each other. This is Mike Wallace, Art Buchwald, and my-self. We happen to be neighbors in the summer on Martha's Vineyard, where we all own houses. We were all three Pacific veterans. And so someone has rather rudely called us the Blues Brothers. But we have, I think all of us, dedicated part of our lives to doing something about de-pression, and talking about it and trying to spread the gospel about the need to understand it, and to help alleviate the suffering of each of the victims.

DATE DUE